# THE SOCIOLOGY OF TASTE

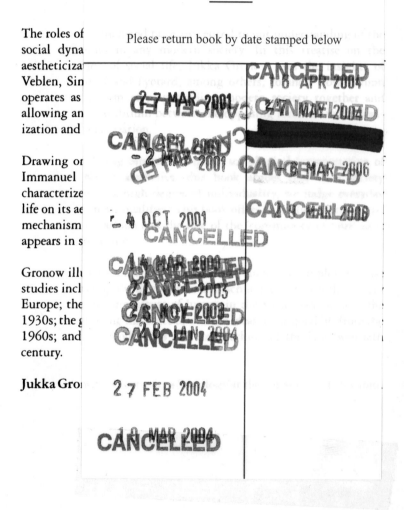

The roles of
social dyna
aestheticiza
Veblen, Sim
operates as
allowing an
ization and

Drawing or
Immanuel
characterize
life on its ae
mechanism
appears in s

Gronow illu
studies incl
Europe; the
1930s; the g
1960s; and
century.

**Jukka Gro**

# THE SOCIOLOGY OF TASTE

*Jukka Gronow*

London and New York

First published 1997
by Routledge
11 New Fetter Lane, London EC4P 4EE

Simultaneously published in the USA and Canada
by Routledge
29 West 35th Street, New York, NY 10001

Reprinted 2001

*Routledge is an imprint of the Taylor & Francis Group*

© 1997 Jukka Gronow

Typeset in Garamond by Routledge
Printed and bound in Great Britain by
T.J.I. Digital, Padstow, Cornwall

*British Library Cataloguing in Publication Data*
A catalogue record for this book is available from the
British Library

*Library of Congress Cataloguing in Publication Data*
Gronow, Jukka.
The sociology of taste / Jukka Gronow.
Includes bibliographical references and index.
1. Aesthetics–Social aspects. 2. Popular culture.
3. Fashion. 4. Fads. I. Title.
HM299. G75 1997            96–25692
306–dc20        CIP

ISBN    0–415–13294–0 (hbk)
ISBN    0–415–13295–9 (pbk)

One has no taste if one has a one-sided taste. True taste is universal, extending to beauties of every kind, but expecting from none no more satisfaction and enchantment than it can, according to its kind, provide.

G. E. Lessing, *Hamburg Dramaturgy*

In sociological studies fashion plays the role which has been allotted to *Drosophila*, the fruit fly, in the science of genetics. Here at a glance we can perceive phenomena so mobile in their response to varying stimuli, so rapid in their mutation, that the deceptive force of inertia, which overlays and obscures most other manifestations of human activity, is reduced to a minimum.

Quentin Bell, *On Human Finery*

# CONTENTS

# CONTENTS

# PREFACE

This book is a treatise on taste. Unlike many other publications on the sociology of taste, however, it is not mainly concerned with the social determination of taste or with the differences in tastes in various groups and classes of society. Its object is the role of taste – or the aesthetic reflection – in society at large and in modern society in particular. In other words, this is a book on aesthetic sociology and not on sociological aesthetics.

In the classical humanistic tradition of philosophical aesthetics there was a strong parallel between the physiological sense of taste and aesthetic taste, or taste as judgment power, between 'gastronomy and aesthetics. The physiological sense of taste acted as the model for the judgment power. Both were regarded as equally self-evident and universal. The sense of taste, however, gradually lost its privileged position in aesthetic discourse. In Kant's thinking, the 'near' senses, taste and smell, were treated with suspicion because they were thought to be capable of serving only lower sensual pleasures, whereas hearing and sight, in particular, were held up as the senses capable of mediating pure, and therefore more noble, aesthetic pleasures. A similar parallel can be drawn between the discourse of need and luxury, on the one hand, and the discourse of nutrition science, on the other hand. Both operated with a seemingly clear and self-evident conception based on universal human needs, and morally condemned as unnecessary luxury all such acts of consumption that exceeded those needs. One can easily recognize a trend of social and cultural critique of modern patterns of consumption continuing both of these parallels up until the present day. Therefore, this book includes a modest history of aesthetic ideas, as well as conceptions of nutrition and gastronomy. Also, many of the examples and case studies presented deal with the consumption of food.

Instead of arguing for or defending a universal human sense of beauty it has been almost a commonplace in sociology to presume that taste is socially determined. Different socio-economic groups or classes have different tastes. Consequently, in society taste is an empirical category. Both Terry Eagleton and Pierre Bourdieu, whose ideas and theories are discussed in the second chapter, criticized Kantian aesthetics because, in their understanding, it presented the taste of the ruling class as the only universally valid or legitimate taste. Pierre Bourdieu's sociological critique of 'pure' aesthetics is especially interesting since it identified the mechanism of social emulation which constantly reproduces these standards of good taste. In doing so Bourdieu also joined – in a very eloborate way – the long tradition of sociological critics of modern consumer society who have explained the dynamics of consumption and the eagerness of modern consumers to exceed their previous or traditional patterns of consumption by their eagerness to imitate social superiors. Modern consumers are, to use the phrase coined by Vance Packard, 'status seekers'. In his classical study *Theory of the Leisure Class* (1961 [1899]) Thorsten Veblen, spoke about 'conspicuous consumption'. In sociological tradition fashions have often until recently been understood to be class fashions and the dynamics of novelty inherent in fashion explained also as the result of this social mechanism of emulation: the lower classes imitate the models of the higher echelons of society. This has also been supposed to be the main reason why people today are willing to consume and buy more, and always the newest and latest things. However, as is argued in the second and third chapters, as an explanation for the dynamics of modern consumption there is serious doubt about this. There are strong empirical and theoretical arguments in favour of another theoretical model of fashion and consumption – some of which are discussed in this study.

It can, however, be shown that there was a historical stage of mass production and marketing which produced mainly kitsch, cheap imitations of finer models that carried easily recognizable signs of culture which could be identified as part of the lifestyle of 'high society' or the social nobility. The presumed 'distortion of human taste' caused by kitsch and the gradual democratization of consumption was, at the turn of the present century, the main target both of the various reform movements of industrial design and of early sociological critics. The consumption patterns in the former Soviet Union, and Soviet kitsch, were good examples of another 'undeveloped' culture of consumption which was, moreover, regulated by the state.

In Stalin's time, however, something that could be called 'democratic luxury' was created. A discussion of the role played by consumers in the transition processes of the former socialist states ends the third chapter of this book.

According to the famous antinomy of taste formulated by Immanuel Kant in his *Critique of Judgment*, taste, or the judgment power, is both totally private and universal, both individual and social, subjective and objective. One of the main ideas in Georg Simmel's sociological thinking was to show how a sociological solution was to be found to this theoretically and conceptually unsolvable antinomy. This antinomy is solved daily in everyday life in various social formations which, however, only provisionally and tentatively overcome the duality or opposition between the individual and the social, between the particular and the general. This duality was, in Simmel's opinion, the greatest problem facing modern human beings.

As is argued in the fourth chapter, the modern fashion pattern is one of the main and, at the same time, the most typical social formation used to cope with this antinomy. In fashion, the antinomy is overcome on a daily basis: fashion is based on private and subjective preferences of individual taste and yet it forms a socially binding standard of conduct. As Simmel said, fashion does not have to decide whether to be or not to be; it both is and is not. It is an ethereal social formation, or, as one could say following – somewhat freely – Lyotard's suggestion, only the 'cloud of a community'.

In a modern abundant consumers' society, the extension of fashion has greatly increased. As Simmel has taught us, it is not only operative in the fields of clothing and decoration. Nowadays, fashion operates equally in various commercial (from cars to cultural products) and non-commercial (from science to first names) fields of social activity. To claim that fashion can be found everywhere would obviously be trite. There are interesting and important criteria for its existence, analysed by Herbert Blumer among others, that can be applied and identified in different social settings.

One of the main theses of this book is that one cannot understand the modern consumer society and the meaning of consumption in a modern society if the social mechanism of fashion, a self-dynamic social process, is not properly understood and analysed. The fourth chapter includes two empirical or historical excursions and case studies about the role of fashion in different fields of society. The first case concerns the self-understanding of fashion designers about their role in the fashion industry. The second applies the fashion approach to the recent developments in our food culture.

Simmel's 'formal sociology' was also strongly indebted to Immanuel Kant in another way. By analysing and paying attention to the pure forms of sociation, he identified an inherent aesthetic dimension in all social interaction. The fifth chapter of this book is an attempt to develop further this idea of Simmel's. Following Simmel, one could claim that social forms can be beautiful. Such forms he often called the play forms of sociation. All social activities and games, art included, that were played only for their own sake, for the sake of the pleasure received from the very act of taking part, were typically aesthetic by their nature. Fashion was to Simmel such a typical play form of sociation which was not instrumental in achieving any other ends. But, in principle, we can, following Simmel, recognize an aesthetic dimension in the more 'serious' social formations, like economic or political competition, too. Friedrich Schiller's famous programme of aesthetic education is, in fact, realized daily by ordinary people in the most frivolous forms of social interaction. It was the main task of Simmel's sociology to understand the nature and importance of such aesthetic forms in society: therefore, his sociology was aesthetic sociology.

The book ends with a discussion about the relevance and different possible interpretations of the thesis of the aestheticization of everyday life. The problem and possibility of understanding post-traditional, reflexive communities as typically aesthetic communities is also discussed. With a certain caution, one could claim that our social world is becoming aestheticized, and potentially more beautiful, insofar as the richness in the forms of social interaction in which individuals can choose to take part is increasing.

# ACKNOWLEDGEMENTS

This study was inspired by the intercourse in two important scientific seminars. In the 1980s, on the initiative of Kaj Ilmonen, Daniel Miller, Per Otnäs, and Pekka Sulkunen, among others, a series of international seminars on consumption was started. These seminars, the participants of which were mainly Scandinavian and British, were characterized by an informal and friendly atmosphere and offered an excellent opportunity both to learn what was going on in the minds of other scholars interested in similar problems and to present one's own views to a critical audience. Colin Campbell, who took part in the seminars from the beginning, presented the main ideas of his, then, new book, *The Romantic Ethic and the Spirit of Consumerism*. Anyone familiar with Campbell's study will certainly recognize to what extent my own thinking was inspired and influenced by it.

From the beginning of the 1990s I have conducted post-graduate seminars on the sociology of consumption at the Department of Sociology, University of Helsinki. Among the many personal friends and colleagues, who also took an active part in the seminars, are Pasi Falk, Kaj Ilmonen, Riitta Jallinoja, Johanna Mäkelä, Arto Noro, Keijo Rahkonen, and Aino Sinnemäki. Without the enthusiasm and the contributions of them and the students, this book would certainly never have been written or received the form it has today. I owe them all my deepest gratitude.

This study was also inspired by reading Georg Simmel's sociology. David Frisby, the living encyclopedia on Simmel's work, was kind enough to share his immense knowledge with me and gave precious hints about Simmel's publications previously unknown to me. Arto Noro's insightful reading of Simmel's works based on a long-lasting interest has also been a helpful guide to me in my efforts. I am also grateful to Alan Warde who read the manuscript and offered invaluable advice of an improving nature.

Aino Sinnemäki, both as my research assistant and as an experienced editor of scientific texts, has been of great help at various stages of this work.

Earlier versions of some sections of the chapters in this book have been published elsewhere.

Part of the Introduction is based on the article 'Need, Taste, and Pleasure: Understanding Modern Consumption', published in Fürst, E. *et al.* (eds) *Palatable Worlds*, Oslo: Solum: 33–52. It is reprinted with the permission of *Solum Förlag AS*, Oslo.

An earlier version of the section 'What is Good Taste?' in Chapter 2 was published as an article with the same title in *Social Science Information* 1993 (36): 279–301 and is reprinted with the permission of Sage Publications, London.

The chapter 'Taste and Fashion' is, with minor alterations, reprinted from Jukka Gronow, 'Taste and Fashion: The Social Function of Fashion and Style', *Acta Sociologica* 1993 (36): 89–100, by permission of Scandinavian University Press, Oslo, Norway.

The section 'Food Fashions and Social Order' in Chapter 4 is a slightly modified translation of my article 'Moden des Speisens und "Geschmack an der Gesundheit" ', originally published in German in *Österreichische Zeitschrift der Soziologie* 1993 (18): 4–18 and is reprinted with the permission of Österreichische Gesellschaft für Soziologie.

# 1

# INTRODUCTION

## Need, taste and pleasure – or understanding modern consumption

### The parallel between philosophy and gastronomy

In the following discussion, three aspects of our relationship to consumption are going to be analysed. They can be compressed into three concepts: need, taste and pleasure. Different ways of talking about consumption are centred around these concepts. They are unavoidably present in the different attempts to analyse and explain the development of the modern food culture and its various features. As will be shown in more detail later on, there are major conceptual problems involved with each of these approaches which are particularly evident in the ways we understand food and eating. There is a strong parallel between the development of the discourses of need and taste, on the one hand, and gastronomy and nutrition science, on the other.

The two concepts, need and taste, in their pure and classical form can be identified in the philosophical discussion during the latter part of the eighteenth century. The two discourses on food were also differentiated in seventeenth-century Europe. Before then, all aspects of food, its effects on health, its taste and the pleasures connected with it, were still discussed inseparably in various cookbooks and dietary recommendations (see Falk 1990). Whereas need and taste constitute two distinct and antithetical discourses on food, pleasure cannot be separated from taste (taste is a source of pleasure) nor taste from pleasure (tastes are either pleasant or unpleasant). However, the more reflexive the concept of taste and the more refined the sense of taste, the more it was separated from immediate sensual pleasure. On the other hand, in modern discussions the concept of pleasure has also become more diffuse and less sensual.

The discourse of need can first be identified in discussions about necessary needs versus luxury in moral philosophy preceding classical political economy (see Springborg 1981). The discourse on taste can be identified in the tradition of the aesthetics of taste, or the so-called moral sense theories (see Caygill 1989). Hedonism is naturally also an old theme in problematizing what constitutes a virtuous and decent life, but in modern discussions it has gained new, broader meanings. Modern consumption is often thought to be caused by the desire for pleasure. The modern consumer is essentially a hedonist; and hedonism is also functional in a modern economic system. An action oriented to the principle of hedonistic pleasure is often thought to emerge as a result of a drastic transformation of cultural values (cf. Bell 1976), or with the birth of a new personality type (the narcissistic personality; cf. Lasch 1978). It is accompanied by historical changes that often are thought to be caused by the emergence of some new social group or class (e.g. the new middle class; cf. Bourdieu 1984).

The new ethics of pleasure or 'fun ethics' is often contrasted with the earlier dominant ethic of work; hedonism is contrasted with asceticism. The older culture of character, which stressed moral qualities, has been replaced by a culture of personality which emphasizes being liked and admired (see Sussman 1984: xxii). The older culture of work and rationality is also often understood to be threatened by this new ethic of consumption which, on the other hand, is thought to be essential in creating predictable and expanding consumer demand. Such a demand 'required the nurture of qualities like wastefulness, self-indulgence, and artificial obsolescence, which directly negated or undermined the values of efficiency and the work ethic on which the system was based' (Marchand 1985: 158). This 'paradox' of modernity, the contrast between efficiency and pleasure, can also be interpreted as not being real. As stated by Rosalind Williams (1982: 66), these different aspects of modern culture in fact complement each other: 'The seemingly contrary activities of hard-headed accounting and dreamy eyed fantasizing merged as business appealed to consumers by inviting them into a fabulous world of pleasure, comfort, and amusement.'

As has already been claimed, there is a close parallel between the aesthetic of taste and gastronomy, on the one hand, and between the need discourse and modern nutrition science, on the other hand. The question of consumer hedonism is, however, more problematic. It can mostly be identified in various critiques of modern culture. The

2

former parallels are not only historical and contingent. There is a stronger conceptual relation between them. Consequently, by analysing the argumentative logic of gastronomy and nutrition science, respectively, it is possible to shed light on the parallel logic of argumentation in social sciences, and vice versa. The taste of food offered the paradigmatic example of the aesthetics of taste in the seventeenth and eighteenth centuries (see e.g. Schümmer 1955). The ideas about the physiological sense of taste were crucial to the development of ideas about the sense of taste as the power of judgment (*Urteilskraft*) until Immanuel Kant. The antinomy concerning the simultaneous self-evident and private nature of taste was shared both by the concept of taste in the 'narrow' sense and by the concept of taste as *Urteilskraft* (see Kant 1980 [1798]: 349–78). In a similar way, the seemingly natural and self-evidential nature of the need for food made it an exemplary model for any argumentation following the logic of needs.

One can still today clearly recognize a discourse of needs, emphasizing the beneficial or detrimental effects of eating on health, in food guides and dietary recommendations based on the standards of modern nutrition science. Among the specialists, at least, there similarly still exists a gastronomic discourse which classifies and evaluates food and foodstuffs according to their taste and tastefulness (cookery books, books on etiquette, gastronomic guide books and magazines). Taste is also scientifically analysed in sensory evaluation studies. These two discourses are not only separate but antithetical to each other as evidenced by the difficulty in taking any considerations of the taste of food into account in present-day nutritional recommendations and health food guides. In earlier recommendations, 'elaborate methods of food preparation and dazzling combinations of ingredients were anathema to those who wanted to develop easy recipes whose nutritional content could be calculated' (Levenstein 1988: 83). The difficulty did not, however, result only from inadequate methods of measurement. In the latest edition of the official *Recommended Dietary Allowances* (1989: 13) the authors, after a lengthy discussion of all the necessary nutrients, vitamins and minerals, suddenly seem to remember that humans do not simply ingest dietary allowances but that they eat food: 'However, RDAs should be provided from a selection of foods that are acceptable and palatable to ensure competition.'

· In both the gastronomic and sociological discourses on need and taste a problem emerges: they produce a certain surplus – or luxury –

an action orientation that cannot be reduced either to the principle of good taste or the principle of need satisfaction. Such an argument also leads to postulating a norm or standard of right or decent conduct, from which any deviation is either pathologized or labelled indecent. This deviation from the norm – or surplus – is often thought to be in need of an explanation in terms of cultural factors or social interaction. Any consumer or eater who exceeds the standards of nutrition determined by the 'natural need' of food is thought to be indecently seduced by the world of goods or to be stimulated by social competition. This superfluous part or 'luxury' consumption (or eating) is then thought to be somehow artificial and even unnatural.

In the discussions concerning the modern hedonistic consumer the whole set-up is turned upside down. The concept of hedonism is to explain the formation of this surplus part of consumption, which is not an exception any more but the main object of concern. Insofar as the analyses have been more ambitious and are not simply satisfied by naming or recognizing some new cultural features, some such social mechanisms are often postulated which are supposed to nurture a hedonistic orientation of action. Hedonism – according to this logic– is something which is in need of explanation contrary to any 'natural' or need-oriented behaviour. Hedonism can also be considered a social problem as a pathology. The different characterizations of this new hedonism, however, are often rather vague: either the desire for pleasure is meant to explain any irrational form of action or its explanatory power is lost in tautology: modern hedonism becomes identical to anything that is demanded by modern consumption.

## The need for food and nutrition science

In a recent article, Mike Featherstone (1990, see also Featherstone 1991) identified three different approaches to the study of consumer culture. First, consumption can be understood in terms of an expanding capitalist commodity production: consumption is functional to the demands of economy. The second approach is mainly interested in the different ways in which people use goods in order to create social bonds or distinctions. The third perspective is concerned with the emotional pleasures of consumption, with the dreams and desires associated with the world of goods. Alan Warde (1991), in his turn, divided the different approaches to the sociology of consumption into three classes according to the functions or meanings attached to consumption which, in their turn are determined by values guiding them. Warde's first two alternatives, use-value and exchange-value, are familiar from political economy, but the third class of identity-value is more original and interesting. It is reminiscent of the second perspective mentioned by Featherstone. The question of the identity-value or socio-symbolic value of goods is actualized whenever people engage in consumption with a view to expressing their social identity (cf. also Miller's (1987: 114) emphasis on the recontextualization, as well as the appropriation, of goods taking place during any act of consumption).

Discussing the social theories of Anthony Giddens, Ulrich Beck and Zygmunt Bauman, Alan Warde identified a common theme in these, in many other respects disparate, conceptions:

> One feature common to the social theories of Ulrich Beck, Anthony Giddens and Zygmunt Bauman is the notion that, today, people define themselves through the messages they transmit to others through the goods and practices that they process and display. They manipulate or manage appearances and thereby create and sustain 'self-identity'. In a world where there is an increasing number of commodities available to act as props in this process, identity becomes more than ever a matter of the personal selection of self-image. Increasingly, individuals are forced to choose their identities.
>
> (Warde 1994: 878)

It is the use of goods to express one's social identity and to distinguish oneself from others, in a world in which traditional social bonds and class boundaries are weakening, which has been the proper field of sociological consumption studies. Consequently, it has been the role of sociology to complement the often one-sided picture of consumption presented by economics. 'Status seekers' – to use an expression made popular by Vance Packard (1960) – brought an element of irrationality – or another type of rationality – into the economists' view of *homo economicus*.

In his tract on social inequality, Jean-Jacques Rousseau separated two forms of self-love: genuine self-love and selfishness. It is the second form of self-love that leads to the emergence and development of artificial needs (see Springborg 1981: 35–41). A person is able to measure and control those needs which stem from genuine self-love; selfishness is caused by social interaction. Social emulation leads to a state of endless insatiability. (I compare myself with you; you with me; and so on *ad infinitum*.) The development and maintenance of

5

artificial needs is thus for Rousseau intimately tied up with social interaction, in general, and with the increase in the division of labour and commerce, in particular; it is inseparable from private property as well. Rousseau, contrary to most other Enlightenment philosophers, was a critic of civilization (see Carlsen *et al.* 1980 and Schmidt 1987).

Making a difference between natural and artificial needs is typical of sociological discussions operating with the concept of need and analysing modern consumption. Often a similar conception of social comparison and emulation, which was first recognized by Rousseau, figures in the background of such analyses. Certain items of consumption (or foodstuffs) have a high social status or value because their consumption is restricted to the higher echelons of society. The lower classes are tempted to buy and eat these foodstuffs or prepare meals from them – even though they actually cannot afford to, or even if they are detrimental to their health – because of this higher social value or status associated with them. They represent a lifestyle which is seen as worth imitating. Such explanations of the irrational elements of consumption seem to have been extremely common in the United States at the turn of the century, equally among advertising men and cultural critics, but they certainly gained currency in Europe, too. Thorsten Veblen's (1961) study of conspicuous consumption is often mentioned as the classical example. Both Featherstone and Warde mention Pierre Bourdieu's *Distinction* (1984) as a recent and sophisticated version of such an approach.[1]

In England, during the eighteenth century, the discussion about luxury, about superfluous consumption which exceeded necessities, was the most common theme in analysing the causes of new social problems. The detrimental effects of luxury were not being recognized for the first time, but were then thought especially likely to corrupt the common people. Previously, luxury had posed a threat to gentlefolk, whose peace of mind was disturbed by insatiable needs. Even then, no one seriously claimed that the lower estates were actually indulging in pleasures. The problem with artificial needs was rather that once stimulated they could never be satisfied. Once liberated from the constraints of tradition, it was thought, there would be no limits to man's needs.

There is a more specific parallel to this general discussion concerning luxury. In the middle of the eighteenth century a new interest in the relation between food, eating and health emerged in England. A new dietetic regimen was born (see Turner 1982; Aronson 1984; see also Falk and Gronow 1985). It still followed the principles of classical humoral medicine, but at the same time it invented a new disease, the English Malady, which was caused by gluttony and luxury. This new malady threatened all the members of the middle class, and the professional man in particular. The best-known representative and promoter of these new dietetics was a physician named George Cheyne (1991 [1733]). Many diseases of both the body and the soul (from gout to melancholy), and the accompanying social problems, were thought to be caused by overeating and obesity.

According to Cheyne, major social changes had been taking place in Britain which stimulated gluttony. Increasing foreign trade and the import of colonial goods were among the most important ones. New strange and exotic foodstuffs and seasoned food – hot spices – were seducing Englishmen towards overeating. In Cheyne's dietary recommendations, the emergence of new – and artificial – needs was, thus, rather concretely identified with increasing international and colonial trade and commerce, which was thought to seduce Englishmen to loosen the constraints of their behaviour and promote a lack of self-discipline. More generally, Dr Cheyne evidently shared Rousseau's ideas about the corrupting influence of social interaction, exchange and commerce, warning that once the traditional and limited structure of needs had been overstepped there was no return to it – at least not without a new kind of a discipline of the body.[2]

Contrary to older dietetics, the New Nutrition, born at the turn of the present century, was based on the ideas of scientific chemistry. Its practical recommendations were, however, inspired by the *Arbeiterfrage* or by the hope of conclusively solving the problem posed by the iron law of wages: if real wages could not permanently rise, a belief shared by many experts, the only way to improve the lot of the wage worker was to teach him to spend his money more economically. As a solution to this problem W. O. Atwater, the director of Human Nutrition Studies of the Office of Experiment Stations in the US, introduced the concepts of the *physiological economy* and the *money economy* of food. Physiological economy aimed at determining the minimum needs of nutrition and energy for different social groups, divided according to the amount of energy expended in different foodstuffs, taking into account the economic resources of different groups of people. If only workers could be persuaded to substitute cheaper food, with equal nutritional value to that of more expensive food, they could save money and still keep their 'labour machines' running. The money saved could then be used for better housing and clothing, and the standards of living improved without any need for higher wages (see Aronson 1982: 52–3).

The major issue in Atwater's, and many contemporary nutrition-ists', recommendations was the consumption of meat (see also Hirdman 1983). Natural science had learned to analyse and separate proteins, fats and carbohydrates from each other. The need for protein was estimated relatively highly compared to modern standards. Meat was seen to be the main source of protein in workers' diets and it was rather expensive. If only workers would learn to buy and eat cheaper cuts of meat (say meat soup cooked with bones and offal), which included as much or more protein than finer cuts (steaks etc.), they could radically cut down on their food expenses. In their hopes for dietary reforms the nutritionists were disappointed time and time again; the American worker was not particularly receptive to the arguments of the new science – because of the bad example set by 'the overfed middle-class and the beautiful people', as Edward Atkinson, among others, had to admit (see Levenstein 1988: 201–2).

Although the New Nutrition understood the need for nutrients to be natural, and in this respect unproblematic and universal, a new problem emerged. Individual people could no longer know or recognize their 'natural needs'. These could only be recognized with the help of experimental science, and with the help of new kinds of specialists, the nutritionists. The classification of different food-stuffs, and the analysis of their usefulness or uselessness to the human body, no longer followed the properties which could be recognized by taste or sight (e.g. red or white meat, raw or cooked, fresh or spoilt food, etc.). This marked a decisive rupture with the older tradition of dietetics. False or wrong needs could now be explained as resulting from ignorance. They could be 'cured' only with the help of the right kind of instruction. The question of false or genuine needs, thus, could only be solved by scientific expertise. But who, really, was in possession of the right kind of knowledge? Experts' opinions varied and changed from time to time, and new false or superfluous needs were continuously discovered. (The dispute over the right amount of protein is a good, early example of the problem.)

## Good taste, gastronomy and social distinctions

Nutrition science has been active in creating a modern food consumer, who is able to recognize his or her needs, and to satisfy them rationally within the limits of his economic resources. Ideal rational consumers are also able to recognize their false or artificial needs, and to interpret unerringly the needs of their bodies. They are equally able to avoid the temptation of gluttony. Modern gastronomy has been equally active in disciplining and controlling the bodily needs of the modern individual. It can be claimed that gastronomy has civilized the modern consumer's taste by introducing new distinctions and classifications of food and drink which, gradually, have been conducive to restraining the human passion for food and eating. Instead of classifying different foodstuffs or meals according to their nutritional components, gastronomy introduced another and even more finely divided system of classifications based on the taste of food. This process of the refinement of taste is often thought to have achieved its peak in the French cuisine of the eighteenth and nineteenth centuries. (See Revel 1979 and Mennell 1985; for the French struggle over European culinary hegemony with the Mediterranean-Arabic cuisine during the Renaissance, see Peterson 1994.)

The old saying that one cannot dispute over matters of taste (*De gustibus disputandum non est!*) did not originally refer to the fact that taste is a private matter for every individual. Instead, it was taken to mean that taste – or good taste – was somehow self-evident and beyond dispute. One could not legitimately have differing opinions about it. Taste was thought to be based on one's sense of taste alone. What felt or tasted good was both good and beautiful. In the same way that we do not usually make mistakes in our judgments of the taste of food and drink, we are equally unerring in our judgments of taste in general. As Edmund Burke (1987 [1757]) saw it, if the possibility of a mistake is ruled out, only a fool could fail to distinguish between the beautiful and the ugly, as well as the right and the wrong. They were as self-evident as the tastes of sugar and salt. What is of equal importance, judgments of taste cannot be reflected upon rationally and one cannot legitimately formulate any maxims or rules concerning them. As the tradition taught, a man simply possesses a sense of good taste expressed in his conduct and choices. Good taste is also an expression of decency. A virtuous man shows good taste in his behaviour and his outward appearance. Good taste in dressing or eating, thus, not only indicates one's sense of beauty, but has strong moral connotations as well (see Schümmer 1955 and Grean 1965; see also Campbell 1987).

· Taste was an ideal means for making social distinctions. Any parvenu who tried to act as a gentleman could always be put in his proper place by letting him know – through small gestures – that even though he thinks he is acquainted with the right etiquette, he still does not master the requirements of good taste. Gastronomic literature – cookery books, guides and books on etiquette, which had been gradually diverging into a literary genre of their own – often operated with such an unproblematic concept of good taste. It also offers a good example of the theoretical paradox of which at least some of its leading representatives were conscious. This paradox or antinomy led gradually, during the eighteenth century, to the dissolution of the whole tradition of the aesthetics of taste – or common sense theory (see Hooker 1934; Caygill 1989). Educators and instructors were posed with a practical problem: if a person is the best judge of his or her taste, it is both useless and impossible to teach anyone the standards of good taste. On what grounds could any particular scale of taste be preferred to another, and how could it alone demand the status of legitimate or good taste that, somehow, is exemplary and binding by its nature? Gastronomers tried to solve this puzzle by claiming that not everyone is a connoisseur. A born connoisseur is not in need of any rules of conduct, but food grammars are needed for those who do not possess a natural mastery of good taste.[3]

## Good taste and the problem of the aesthetics of taste

Taste and legitimate or good taste are the basic concepts of Pierre Bourdieu's social theory of distinctions (see Bourdieu 1984: 56). By writing that 'taste is the basis of all that one has – people and things – and all that one is for others, whereby one classifies oneself and is classified by others', Bourdieu (ibid.) could be echoing the classical tradition. Furthermore, both food preferences and table manners are important indicators of lifestyles and class tastes in his study (ibid.:77).

To Bourdieu, taste is always a disposition forming part of the habitus of any person. As a matter of fact, Bourdieu criticized the 'pure' aesthetics of the beautiful and the sublime, for which, in his opinion, Immanuel Kant is mainly to be blamed. In so doing he actually used the argument of the old aesthetics of taste, or moral sense theory, to which, however, he gives a specific sociological interpreta-tion. His main critical argument against Kant's pure aesthetics is that it conceals its class origins and interests behind its seemingly objective and disinterested façade. In this respect, he shared Nietzsche's anti-

10

Kantian position (Rahkonen 1995). Bourdieu does not explicitly refer to the classical discussion about good taste which flourished in Europe in the seventeenth and eighteenth centuries.

The intellectual tradition of the aesthetics of taste came to an end or to a final fulfilment in Immanuel Kant's *Critique of Judgment* (see Caygill 1989; see also Schümmer 1955). In his third critique Kant formulated the famous antinomy of taste which the tradition had not been able to solve and to which no possible conceptual solution could be found: the feeling of beauty requires that it be shared universally, but how could something that was exclusively based on the subjective feeling of pleasure be universally valid, too (Kant 1987: §31)? In the tradition of the moral sense theory there were various attempts to solve this dilemma. Good taste was understood either to be an empirical category, the standards of which were shared by the majority, if not all, of the members of a society and identifiable solely through empirical studies; or it was to be the taste of a specific social group, 'high society', in particular (see Hooker 1934). However, these solutions were not theoretically satisfying and they were criticized by Kant, in whose opinion, the empirical generality and validity of a taste had nothing to do with the universal validity expected from a genuine judgment of taste.

Bourdieu adopted one possible empiricist solution to the antinomy of taste by claiming that the taste of the ruling class is always the legitimate taste of a society. But in his opinion this legitimate taste is not genuine good taste: in fact, there could not possibly be any genuine good taste. Legitimate taste pretends to be the universally valid and disinterested good taste, whereas in reality it is nothing more than the taste of one particular class, the ruling class.[4]

As mentioned in the previous section, the old saying that it is useless to dispute over matters of taste was not originally understood to refer to the private nature of judgments of taste. The meaning was rather the opposite. Because taste was something self-evident and shared by all, it was both futile and unnecessary to argue about it. On the other hand, within this tradition of thought, taste was always understood to be a reflection of genuinely individual preferences alone: something was tasteful and good because it really felt good (see e.g. Burke 1987). More importantly, matters of taste were beyond dispute because there could not in principle be any general rules governing them. If they were to be disputed, there would have to be presuppositions that there were some general standards which could be criticized, questioned or defended (cf. Kant 1987: §18).

11

According to the understanding of representatives of the moral sense theory, taste was based on a sense or feeling about the goodness or badness of objects or forms of conduct. This could not be reflected upon conceptually. It was, in principle, impossible to formulate any general maxims of good taste.[5]

As Gadamer (1975: 33) pointed out, taste was basically a *Bildungsbegriff*, and as such an ideal of education and emancipation. In this tradition of thought, good taste was increasingly understood not to be predetermined by the privilege of birth or social origins. It was something that could be adopted by learning, regardless of one's social standing. Anyone who showed good taste in their choices and conduct was a gentleman (or gentlewoman). Good taste, thus, was both an indicator of belonging to 'good society', and the main criterion of entry into it.

Sole reliance on one's sense or 'instinct' of good and bad, tasteful and tasteless, precluded distinction between beauty, goodness and virtue: 'sense of beauty' and 'sense of right and wrong' were inseparable. Taste was essentially both an aesthetic and a moral category; in other words, these senses could not be separated from each other. Thus, decent conduct, dress and decorum were all indicators of an individual's moral and aesthetic value, or good taste. What was tasteful was both decent and virtuous, too (see Grean 1965). In this sense, too, Bourdieu shared the basic postulates of this tradition. As has already been pointed out, both food preferences and table manners are important indicators of lifestyles and class tastes in Bourdieu's study because all such choices (like dressing, eating, furnishing one's home, etc.) fall largely outside the formal schooling and education system. They are made on the basis of pure taste dispositions rather than following any explicit rules and norms of conduct.

Whereas the criterion of good taste gradually disappeared from the aesthetics of fine arts during the eighteenth century, it retained its role in the aesthetics of everyday life and popular culture, in the aesthetics of the 'lower' arts. In gastronomy, in particular, it has played a prominent role to date.

# 2

# PHILOSOPHICAL AESTHETICS AND THE REFINEMENT OF TASTE

## SOCIOLOGICAL AESTHETICS OR AESTHETIC SOCIOLOGY

### Custom, public opinion and social cohesion

In the classical European humanistic tradition fashion was always thought to be antithetical to good taste. A person blindly following the whims of fashion was without style, whereas a man of style – or a gentleman – was using his own power of judgment. Immanuel Kant shared this conception with many of his contemporaries. Georg Simmel's famous essay on fashion can best be understood as a somewhat ironic commentary on Kant's idea of a *sensus communis*: the community of fashion is the real, even though ephemeral, community of universal taste.

Terry Eagleton, in his ideological-critical history of European aesthetic thought, came to a conclusion reminiscent of Bourdieu's and Veblen's sociological positions. To Eagleton (1990: 96) as well as to Bourdieu, Kant's 'sensus communis is ideology purified, universalized and rendered reflective, ideology raised to the second power...'. His evaluation of Schiller's teaching is even more critical: 'Schiller's aesthetic is in this sense Gramsci's hegemony' (1990: 106). Bourdieu expressed the same idea by claiming that the good or legitimate taste conceals its real class origins behind its seeming objectivity and disinterestedness. The tradition of European aesthetic thought exemplified and culminated in Kant's and Schiller's writings presents a hegemonic bourgeois project which, in Hegelian terms, tries to come to terms with the dilemma of the 'bad' particularity of the individual living in the civil society and the 'bad' – because abstract and coercive – universality of the laws of the state, by imposing and postulating a

13

third sphere of social relations in between the individual and the state, determined by sentiments or taste, that of spontaneous habits:

> Custom, piety, intuition and opinion must now cohere an otherwise abstract, atomized social order. Moreover, once absolutist power has been overturned, each subject must function as its own seat of self-government. . . . Like the work of art as defined by the discourse of aesthetics, the bourgeois subject is autonomous and self-determining, acknowledges no merely extrinsic law but instead, in some mysterious fashion, gives the law to itself. In doing so, the law becomes the form which shapes into harmonious unity the turbulent content of the subject's appetites and inclination.
>
> (Eagleton 1990: 23)

As Eagleton admits,

> the aesthetic is from the very beginning a contradictory, double edged concept [cf. also Luhmann's (1981: 60) parallel critique of Simmel's formal sociology – J. G.]. On the one hand, it figures as a genuinely emancipatory force – as a community of subjects now linked by sensuous impulse and fellow-feeling rather than by heteronomous law, each safeguarded in its unique particularity while bound at the same time into social harmony. . . . On the other hand, the aesthetic signifies what Max Horkheimer has called a kind of 'internalised repression', inserting social power more deeply into the very bodies of those it subjugates, and so operating as a supremely effective mode of political hegemony.
>
> (ibid.: 28)

It is this hegemonic side of the 'aesthetic' that mainly interested Eagleton in his history of the European classical aesthetic thought. To him

> Kant's selfless aesthetic judge, absolved from all sensual motivation, is among other things, a spiritualized version of the abstract, serialized subject of the market place, who cancels the concrete differences between himself and others as thoroughly as does the levelling, homogenizing commodity. . . . Culture is thus part of the problem to which it offers itself as a solution.
>
> (ibid.: 97–8)

Eagleton even presented as an empirical, historical fact that the

14

solution offered to the middle class by the adoption of a common culture 'depends on an activity for which, as Karl Marx wryly commanded, the middle class has exceedingly little time'. *Summa summarum*: the sought after aesthetic harmony is hardly anywhere to be found! It is only an ideological illusion (Eagleton 1990: 99).

Thus, to Eagleton, Hegel's approach to the social mediation between the bourgeois individual and the state through the 'complex [and conceptual – J. G.] mediations of family, class, corporations, and the like' is more promising an approach than the 'abstract immediacy' and the resulting 'aestheticized morality' offered by Kant's and Schiller's aesthetic projects. He recommends us to adopt 'a properly dialectic form of reason, and so to break with aestheticization in the sense of mere intuitive immediacy' (Eagleton 1990: 147).

One of the very starting points of Terry Eagleton's critical interpretation of the aesthetic tradition was Rousseau's famous dictum about the social and moral importance of 'the habits of the heart' (cf. Bellah *et al*.1986) in his *Social Contract* (1994). As also explicitly cited by Eagleton, Rousseau wrote in it about a law

> which is not graven in marble or bronze, but in citizens' hearts; in it lies the true constitution of the state; its strength augments day by day; when other laws decay or become extinct it revives or replaces them, it maintains in the nation the spirit of its constitution, and imperceptibly changes the force of authority into the force of habit. I refer to moral standards, to custom, and above all to public opinion: a part of law that is unknown to our political theorists, although success in every part depends on it.
> (Rousseau 1994: 89–90, cited in Eagleton 1990: 18–19)

As Eagleton reminded us, according to Rousseau's conception the citizen can surrender his 'bad' particularization only by identifying through 'the general will' with the good of the whole: 'he retains his unique individuality, but now in the form of a disinterested commitment to a common well-being' (Eagleton 1990: 25). It is this 'bad' and too hasty fusion of the general and the particular – at the cost of the particular individuality with its unique interests and sensitivities – which is time and time again repeated in the following aesthetic tradition from Edmund Burke and David Hume to Kant and Schiller.

As Arto Noro (1993: 58) has pointed out, not even Lenin could offer any other recipe for the organizing principle of the future stateless communist society than these very same 'habits of the heart' which would be adopted automatically and without any outer coercion – purely out of the force of habit – by every common worker: as Lenin wrote in his *The State and Revolution*, at the highest communist stage of social development the state can totally wither away as soon as men learn to follow the basic and similar rules of decent social life 'out of pure habit':

> freed from capitalist slavery, from the untold horrors, savagery, absurdities and infamies of capitalist exploitation, people will gradually *become accustomed* to observing the elementary rules of social intercourse that have been known for centuries and repeated for thousands of years in all copy-book maxims. They will become accustomed to observing them without force.... Only habit can ... have such an effect.
>
> (Lenin 1980: 467)

Neither does Gramsci's famous concept of hegemony offer much more. As Gramsci understood hegemony, it is a stage of consensus (i.e. of common habits and public opinion – J. G.) plus cultural leadership of the intellectuals (see Gramsci 1975: 235). In fact, Gramsci only reminded us that there is a cultural and social dimension to every society which cannot be reduced to the laws of the state or the functioning of the economic order.

In criticizing classical aesthetic thought Eagleton certainly is right in emphasizing the strong and active utopian element which aimed – through *Bildung*, *Kunst* and *Kultur* – at reconciling the contradictions of the bourgeois social order. But his total dismissal of the importance of these 'customs', 'habits' and common sensitivities, often adopted by the actors through unreflective imitation, as Edmund Burke knew, is defensible only from his perspective of a totally transparent and rational social order. In such an order people's social conduct would be regulated only by moral laws, the source and validity of which are directly accessible to the reasoning of all the members alike.

It certainly is an historical and empirical question, though by no means an easy one to solve by any empirical study, how much the 'middle classes' of Marx's day had any time to spare for cultural activities or the admiration of works of art. To judge from contemporaries' reports they certainly did – more or less regularly – visit the opera, or at least a cabaret or a popular concert hall. But what is more important, they quite evidently did enjoy aesthetic artefacts in their everyday lives, i.e. admired and promoted fashion. What is even more important, their daily life, in a similar way to ours, was full of social interaction which was not only instrumental and regulated by the purposive activity of realizing their interests – businessmen met at public houses and cafés, or played cards, and their spouses organized dinners, salons and balls. In other words, their daily conduct was not only oriented towards obtaining a profit; it was also governed by a 'useless' etiquette and numerous 'irrational' habits and customs.

It is an open question whether such 'useless' cultural artefacts and idle social forms have become exceedingly important in modern culture and whether we can really, in this sense, speak of the aestheticization of the social world in modern times. The main thing is to note and acknowledge the great social and cultural importance of such play forms of sociation at all times. In a sense, one could claim that it has only become possible in the modern, differentiated society, where such forms have become less ritualized, to distinguish and recognize their independent role and to understand their full importance. In this respect, it was the great merit of the philosophical aesthetics to be the first school of thought to try to come to grips with these phenomena. In an important sense, sociology is the legal and sole inheritor of this interest or orientation in the present day intellectual world.

In this treatise it is suggested that instead of 'simply' empirically identifying the carriers and promoters of 'good' or legitimate taste or the role of taste in status competition, and instead of studying the empirical generality of a taste or an 'opinion' in a society – an approach already proposed by David Hume – we should, following the example set by Georg Simmel, direct our attention to the various aesthetic forms of sociation, 'communities of taste', and to try to understand their role in society. Fashion is such a social formation *par excellence*.

To Simmel (1981), fashion was a social formation always combining two opposite forces. The charm of novelty offered by fashion is a purely aesthetic pleasure. Fashion is a play form of sociation. Studying fashion offers an excellent opportunity of understanding this important dimension of modern life. This can also help us better to understand the role of aesthetic pleasures in our everyday life in general. These 'frivolous' elements and 'ephemeral' forms of social life can neither be reduced nor submitted to a rational morality or objective economic interests. However, no social formation could survive without them.

# WHAT IS GOOD TASTE?

## The refinement of taste in France

In his inspiring study, *All Manners of Food*, Stephen Mennell (1985; see also Mennell 1987) identified the social mechanism which led to the development of royal or haute cuisine in France and to its rapid and continuous revival. He was especially interested in an issue which has been widely discussed by gastronomes: why did French cuisine achieve such a prominent role in Europe during the seventeenth and eighteenth centuries, a position it has been able to retain to some extent up to the present day (cf. Revel 1979; Wheaton 1985)? Mennell's interpretation relies to a great extent on the theory of civilization developed by Norbert Elias (1978, 1983). The same process which marked the gradual development of increasing individual self-control at the beginning of modern times also manifested itself in the gradual restraint of appetite and refinement of table manners. Ostentation with regard to food and drink was increasingly regarded as a sign of bad manners and was not considered to be in accordance with the demands of etiquette.

Mennell was mainly interested in the differences in the development of food culture in France and Britain and in their gradual process of differentiation during the seventeenth and eighteenth centuries.[1] Why did France – more obviously and earlier than any other part of Europe – give birth to a particular 'high' culture of food and why was its development and its renewal more rapid during those centuries? Haute cuisine or 'royal cuisine' was developed in France, a cuisine which was clearly different from bourgeois or peasant cuisine. It was characterized by extremely refined meals and dishes and by a very complicated order or hierarchy of tastes. The process of change was much slower and less noticeable in England during the same period. More markedly medieval habits prevailed and tastes preserved their ancient flavour even among the higher orders of society.

Following Norbert Elias' interpretation, Stephen Mennell identified the mechanism of the renewal and refinement of food culture with the peculiar process of rationalization of a court society:

> The revenues, political power and social function of the old *noblesse d'épée* were gradually declining, while those of the bourgeoisie and of the essentially bourgeois *noblesse de robe* were increasing. Parts of the old nobility acquired positions at court and became highly dependent on royal favour. They became in

effect specialists in the art of consumption, entrapped in a system of fine distinctions, status battles and competitive expenditure from which they could not escape because their whole identity depended upon it.

(Mennell 1987: 389–90)

The lifestyle of the court nobility was thus not only an indicator of its social position but rather determined it. A court nobleman was continuously obliged to set himself apart from his equals and to emphasize the superiority of his lifestyle to members of other social groups and estates, especially the rural aristocracy and the prosperous bourgeoisie of the towns. Lifestyle and etiquette became arenas of social competition and emulation (see also Luhmann 1980:128–9). The pleasures associated with taste and food also became important elements or stakes in this game of social competition. Complex small but expensive dishes, a complicated hierarchy of tastes and even the ability to discuss and argue about taste, cuisine and cooking methods made it possible to make more and more refined distinctions and to establish an elaborately differentiated system. Only an expert on etiquette and a real gourmet could always infallibly decide what was good or bad, what was valuable and what was valueless. A gentleman's choice was an expression of good taste and he could always 'smell' people with bad taste. Pretenders or would-be gentlemen were easy to detect. Mennell characterized court nobility as a group of virtuoso consumers and even referred to Veblen's concept of conspicuous consumption (see Veblen 1961). The main purpose of a nobleman was the maintenance and accentuation of his own social prestige.

In England, according to Mennell's testimony, the process of the refinement of taste was much slower during the same period. The impetus for the continuous renewal and refinement of 'the manners of food' was weaker. The wings of royal power had already been clipped during the seventeenth century, and consequently the royal court and court nobility never played such influential roles as their French counterparts. Relations between the various groups of nobility and between nobility and the higher bourgeoisie remained more open and their boundaries more flexible. For part of the eighteenth century the influence of French cooking was noticeable in England, but it was never able to displace traditional English country cooking on the tables of noble houses. The English bourgeoisie was much more inclined to economize than to indulge in extravagance in eating.

Even in Britain, obesity and gluttony gradually fell 'out of fashion'

19

and ostentation in matters of food and drink was regarded as bad taste. It would be tempting to claim that emerging nutritional science and various dietetic regimens, in England at least, played to some extent a similar role to that of gastronomy in France (see Falk and Gronow 1985; see also Turner 1982 and Aronson 1982, 1984). Such regimens were certainly not unknown in France either. Dietetics aimed at restraining people's appetites, not by developing a system of tastes but by emphasizing the different nutritional values of foodstuffs and by classifying them accordingly. Even though these recommendations about diet were presented in the spirit of humoral medicine, they dealt with the problems of overeating in a new way. Many diseases – both physical and social ones – were found to be caused by unhealthy eating habits.

Elias' and Mennell's analyses of the rationality of court society were restricted to a specific historical constellation in European societies. In general, such explanations are common enough. The aping of one's superiors and the almost compulsory impetus to distinguish oneself from one's equals and inferiors are offered in different theoretical traditions as valid explanations of changing lifestyles, fashions and tastes and even consumption patterns in general. The best known and classical examples in sociology were presented by Georg Simmel (1981) and Thorsten Veblen (1961) (for a more specific analysis of food culture see Simmel 1910). In this respect, Bourdieu's *Distinction* (1984) further develops many of the ideas presented by Simmel, Veblen and Elias. In the following section Bourdieu's study is mainly discussed as a prominent example of a certain type of theoretical analysis which, because of the sophisticated level of argument, is more revealing of the general theoretical problems connected with this kind of approach. A short presentation inevitably fails to do justice to the complexity of Bourdieu's analyses and the richness of his ethnographic observations concerning modern French culture.

## Distinction and class tastes

It is interesting to compare the general results of Bourdieu's study of modern France with Mennell's historical research on England and France in the seventeenth and eighteenth centuries. There are many similarities between the aesthetic dispositions found in Bourdieu's present-day France and the court society of the *ancien régime* analysed by Mennell. The modern working class keeps up the traditions of the medieval common people: its members drink and eat without regret and live only for the present. Their taste pleasures are simple and sensual. The lifestyle of the modern ruling class or bourgeoisie resembles that of Mennell's court nobility: knowledge of etiquette is self-evident and its members are sovereign in their mastery of good manners. All the sensual and corporeal aspects of eating are concealed behind the strict formality of table manners. Pleasure is anticipated and constrained rather than satisfied. The modern French petit bourgeois is a typical parvenu, a country squire or a nouveau riche who longs for rules and guidance in etiquette, for gastronomic guide books, in order to be able to live *à la mode* but never really succeeding in his efforts. He only reveals his real social origins by the insecurity of his conduct and by following the rules of etiquette all too rigorously. The main problem is not the thickness of the wallet, but rather the fact that it takes more than that to make a gentleman.

It is certainly not surprising to find such a close correlation between these two descriptions or analyses. To support Bourdieu's argument one does not have to postulate any long tradition of French culture which is still evident despite the somewhat clandestine structures of its present-day counterpart. It would be completely possible to argue that, in any 'class society', a similar system of lifestyles and class tastes would emerge and a similar mechanism of distinctions would be in operation. In such a society the different classes have different positions according to their respective economic and cultural capital and the boundaries separating the classes are relatively open but hierarchically ordered.

What makes this kind of an analysis problematic, however, is the fact that it is in the nature of a society which is understood to be functioning through social competition and emulation, to become rather static. The classification of tastes tends to become more and more refined and subtle. As Claude Fischler (1990: 170) has pointed out, in such a social order manners and mores are continuously descending down the social ladder, but the hierarchical structure of tastes and their criteria are never really challenged by social competitors. In another context altogether – in discussing the problem of the emergence of the modern consumer and the logic of modern consumption – Colin Campbell (1987) claimed that the kind of aristocratic aesthetics of a ruling class, of which Bourdieu's bourgeoisie is a good example, and which the other classes are eager to imitate, necessarily leads to conforming and static lifestyles. The continuous refinement of an order of classification does not lead to the questioning of the prevalent cultural code but rather to endless variations within it.

21

## The hedonism of the new classes and the emergence of the ideal consumer

What makes Bourdieu's analysis more interesting and exceptional is the fact that his analysis of lifestyles and tastes is not restricted to the characterization of these three hierarchically ordered classes. Competition between the different groups within these classes is of special interest, too. Bourdieu is mainly interested in analysing the social groups which can be considered new in some respect and show an upward trajectory in social space. In particular, the new ruling class or the new bourgeoisie is presented as the vanguard of all aesthetic and ethical renewal in society. Its disposition even satisfies the demands of economic development. By eagerly adopting this disposition, the members of the new middle class help both to legitimate and to spread it through society. Its members are ideal consumers. They cherish the hedonistic ethic of consumption which is based on loan taking and waste. In all essentials, this new class is the direct opposite of the classical bourgeoisie which was an ascetic saver willing to sacrifice the present for the future (see Bourdieu 1984: 310).

The new petite bourgeoisie acts for Bourdieu (ibid.: 365) 'as a transmission belt and pull into the race for consumption and competition those whom it means to distinguish itself from'. In so doing it legitimates both itself and the taste and the lifestyle of the ethical avant-garde. This new ethic, put forward as a model by the avant-garde of the bourgeoisie, is essentially an ethic of hedonism: 'the new ethical avant-garde urges a morality of pleasure as duty... pleasure is not only permitted but demanded, on ethical as much as on scientific grounds' (ibid.: 367).

This new ethic of hedonism is also functional to the economic system by judging people as much by their capacity to consume and by their lifestyles as by their capacity to produce (ibid.: 311). The members of the new petite bourgeoisie are 'perfect consumers whom the economic theory has always dreamed of' (ibid.: 371). Bourdieu also claims that

> the new petite bourgeoisie is predisposed to play a vanguard role in the struggles over everything concerned with the art of living, in particular, domestic life and consumption, relations between sexes and the generations, the reproduction of the family and its values. It is opposed on almost every point to the repressive morality of the declining petite bourgeoisie...
>
> (ibid.: 366–7)

In Bourdieu's opinion the new petit bourgeois is not an ideal consumer simply because of her or his willingness to consume and to consume the latest thing. The main 'merit' of the new ethic is that it produces isolated consumers whose demands are not constrained any more by any traditional moral order. On the other hand, it could be claimed that the willingness to consume the latest thing already presupposes that there are no traditional constraints on behaviour. As emphasized by Featherstone (1991: 91), Bourdieu's new petite bourgeoisie does not adopt a lifestyle unreflectively, through tradition or habit. These 'new heroes of consumer culture' make style a life project: the new petite bourgeoisie is not promoting a particular style but rather catering for an interest in style itself.

Bourdieu's analysis of the lifestyles and ethos of this new middle class and the new bourgeoisie are the most interesting parts of his extensive study. He makes the new middle class representative of almost everything that is 'modern' in the modern society. The ethic of the new middle class is the ethic of fun (Bourdieu 1984: 364; see also Sulkunen 1992: 152–3). It is opposed to the old middle-class morality of duty:

> the old morality of duty, based on the opposition between pleasure and good, induces a generalized suspicion of the charming and attractive, a fear of pleasure and a relation to the body made up of 'reserve', 'modesty' and 'restraint', and associates every satisfaction of the forbidden impulses with guilt . . .
>
> (Bourdieu 1984: 367)

It succeeds in concealing its moralizing tone behind a pseudo-scientific analysis of everyday practices. It is the main consumer of all kinds of therapeutic service which provide 'scientific' solutions to moral questions:

> Guided by their anti-institutional temperament and the concern to escape everything redolent of competitions, hierarchies of knowledge, theoretical abstractions or technical competences, these new intellectuals are inventing an art of living which provides them with the gratifications and prestige of the intellectual at the least cost: in the name of the fight against 'taboos' and the liquidation of 'complexes' they adopt the most external and most easily borrowed aspects of the intellectual

lifestyle, liberated manners, cosmetic or sartorial outrages, emancipated poses and postures . . .

(ibid.: 370–1)

Bourdieu does not only characterize the main features of this new aspiring taste. He also reduces the ethos and lifestyle of the different classes to their respective social positions. In particular, the social positions occupied by the new classes are of a totally new kind. They fall outside all formal hierarchies. No formal entry qualifications are required, no reports or certificates asked for. The new professionals have created their professions by themselves from the very beginning. Furthermore, they are selling mainly 'symbolic goods or services' and are working in a 'substitution' industry which sells words instead of goods (see Bourdieu 1984: 365). By explaining the new ethic in terms of social positions which can be identified by certain objective criteria, Bourdieu draws historically and socially close narrow boundaries around the possible representatives of the ethics of fun. To him, the core of the new petite bourgeoisie is comprised mainly of various cultural intermediaries and new craftspeople (ibid.: 300). He makes it seem as if the hedonistic consumer was born in France only yesterday in the guise of these new professionals. In this respect, his diagnosis resembles the analyses of many cultural critics who were anxious to prophesy the victory of the new hedonist over the old ascetic (cf. Bell 1976). Bourdieu's hedonistic consumer, who is functional to the capitalist economy, first emerged in late capitalism.

It is not very surprising that Bourdieu recognized hedonism as one of the main characteristics of the culture of the new middle class. That the previous ethics of work and asceticism has been displaced by hedonism is a common theme in various critiques of everyday life in post-industrial society, from Daniel Bell to Christopher Lasch. To Bourdieu, however, this fun ethic is essentially part of a game of distinctions. Through adopting a new lifestyle based on hedonism, this new class can distinguish itself from its social competitors, and by putting itself in direct ethical – and aesthetic – opposition to the ruling class it can challenge prevalent legitimate taste. For the new middle class – or rather the new bourgeoisie, whose ethical and aesthetic standards the new middle class only helps to universalize – this game of distinctions functions in a particular way. Its members do not try to ascend along the same scale or hierarchy of values as their predecessors; on the contrary, their dispositions and preferences tend to deny the importance and relevance of the old order. In disregarding the tastes and lifestyles of their superiors, they tend to establish a completely new hierarchy of tastes demanding the status of legitimate or good taste. Thus they are challengers of the old culture, not social climbers trying to ascend its ladders.

Strictly speaking, any analysis of the social mechanism of distinction and competition alone will show that there always are, in principle, two ways of social ascent open to any group in a society: strict adherence to the rules of the game, or the creation of new rules. In addition Bourdieu seems to assume that new taste which aspires to become the new legitimate or good taste always has to take a totally different or opposite form from the old one. In order to qualify as legitimate taste, it must also be presented as falling outside all classifications and hierarchies (see Bourdieu 1984: 370). Seemingly, denying the relevance of all classifications only conceals the fact that, in reality, the new taste represents just another competing system of classifications and distinctions.

Such a system of competing tastes, as presented by Bourdieu, would, however, seem to be rather ill-suited to characterize the rapidly changing tastes and styles of a modern fashion cycle. These tastes always present themselves as new and different from the old ones but they do not by any means have to challenge the previous taste and style in such a drastic way (however, cf. Bourdieu 1986). The old fashion of yesterday is simply forgotten today.

In the 'classic' class society systematically analysed by Mennell, the situation was different. The gastronomic literature of the eighteenth century analysed by Mennell (1985: 69–101) – cookery books like Massialot's *Le Cuisinier roïal et bourgeois* (1691), Vincent Chapell's *The Modern Cook* (1733), Marin's *Les Dons de Comus* (1739), Menon's *La Cuisinière bourgeois* (1746), Eliza Smith's *The Complete Housewife* (1727), Hannah Glasse's *The Art of Cookery Made Plain and Easy* (1747) and John Farley's *London Art of Cookery* (1783) – offers excellent examples of Bourdieu's two possible processes of taste formation. The cookery books and gastronomic treatises were mainly directed at members of the ascending and increasingly prosperous bourgeoisie and the members of lower nobility who aspired to live *à la mode*. By presenting well-chosen examples describing the menus of famous dinners and banquets they taught their readers what was in accordance with good – or latest – taste. As pointed out by Mennell, the bourgeoisie still did not have the resources to eat on such a lavish scale and they were therefore under more pressure to choose. The demand for gastronomic guidance and, consequently, the demand for cookery books, was therefore also more urgent among them (see Mennell 1987: 391). At the same time, it was continuously emphasized that it was always better to live according to the demands of one's own social position rather than to ape and imitate the manners of one's superiors, even if one could afford it. It was bad taste to try to imitate good taste, if, in reality, one did not have good taste. At the same time, there gradually appeared new arguments demanding the return to more simple and natural table manners and ways of eating. Excessive refinement and cultivation of taste, examples of which could all too easily be recognized in certain social classes, were in fact wholly artificial and consequently expressions of bad taste. (This accusation of artificiality and excessive refinement could more often be read in English than Continental cookery books.)

One can thus easily identify in the gastronomic field many examples of the oppositions typical of cultural production in Bourdieu's sense (see Bourdieu 1983). The avant-garde – or practically every new generation of cookery book authors – was inclined to present its ideas as totally antithetical to the ideas of its predecessors, the 'consecrated avant-garde', even if the new recipes often were direct plagiarisms of earlier works. Once the art of cookery became public and retreated from the private kitchens of the nobility and entered the open Parnassus, it tended to direct its 'good message' to as broad an audience as possible. In a sense, it was a commercial art form from the very beginning. But still it certainly is possible to identify those 'artists' who aimed their products only at genuine connoisseurs or a strictly restricted audience. Even in this field of cultural production it would, thus, be interesting to analyse in more detail the emergence and the functioning of the opposition between these sub-fields of restricted production (art for art's sake) and large-scale production (commercial or popular art) (see Bourdieu 1983: 333).

It should, however, be kept in mind that even though it is always in principle possible to identify different mechanisms of legitimating and questioning the ideals of good or legitimate taste, the boundaries between them are flexible. There are no fixed lines separating refinement, variation and innovation. The very development of nouvelle cuisine as a challenger to haute cuisine is an excellent example. While it presents its own naturalness as an alternative to the artificiality of the old cuisine, nouvelle cuisine still operates to a great extent within the same scale of tastes. Even though it is more concerned about the selection of raw materials and despite its minimalistic ideals in matters of taste and decoration, it still hardly questions the prevailing scale of good taste.

The adoption of the French haute cuisine by the nouveau riche on both sides of the Atlantic during the latter part of the last century has been cited by many studies as an excellent case proving the importance of social competition in the development of taste in culinary culture (see e.g. Levenstein 1988: 14). It is, however, rather doubtful if the process that began at the end of the eighteenth century, and regulated the renewal of food culture in Europe and North America, can be attributed to the further and gradual diffusion of the table manners of the former court nobility at Versailles, or to any similar process of competition and emulation. The emergence of a new commodity market, which included food products and services, and of which the establishment of the modern restaurant is a good example (see Mennell 1985: 135–43), would seem to demand another kind of theoretical approach. Rosalind Williams has pointed out that even though the French were nearly as preeminent in the nineteenth century in pioneering a new style of mass consumption as they had been in developing the courtly model of the earlier century, the new democratized luxury was quite different in character from the upper-class paradigm (see Williams 1982: 11). Even within food culture, the tempo of change in fashion and style has increased enormously since the French Revolution (see Mennell 1985: 161). Novelties were demanded at food markets, too. It was Escoffier, one of the creators of modern French restaurant cooking, who, with some reluctance, had to admit in 1903 that 'novelty is the universal cry – novelty by hook or crook! It is an exceedingly common mania among people of inordinate wealth to expect incessantly new or so-called new dishes' (cited in Mennell 1985: 161). It would seem to be this 'chronic' demand for novelty which is typical of modern consumption patterns alone (cf. McKendrick et al. 1982 and Campbell 1987).

Applied to the case of French cuisine, one could claim that the cuisine which, after the revolution, was being imitated by the rich, was already shaped by the new market forces, and it shared more of the properties of a mass fashion (cf. Horowitz 1975a) and mass consumption than the model which was originated at the court. Even though its etiquette and recipes were partly borrowed from the court, it was already produced for the market. The fashion mechanism of the late nineteenth century, which still openly copied many of its models from the high society – and produced mainly kitsch – was rather an intermediary form before the development of a full-fledged democratized mass fashion. The methods used in early modern advertising provide an interesting example of this fact: the prominent figures (earls, counts, princesses, etc.) recruited to guarantee the goodness of numerous products in advertisements, were little known before advertising made them so (see Richards 1990: 84). One can, thus, agree with Rosalind Williams (1982: 57) that the 'heliocentric world of consumption' had already started to be replaced by 'a vast, centreless universe'.

## From the social hierarchy of tastes to mass fashion

In the above discussion, it has been argued that the understanding of modern consumption as a game of distinctions and distinction strategies is often associated with a conception according to which lifestyles and tastes are hierarchically ordered and determined by the social position of their representatives; the lifestyles of the members of a social class are more or less homogeneous. Tastes are class tastes. The legitimate taste of a society is identified with the taste of its ruling class. In a society conceptualized along these lines, social classes are waging a continuous struggle, in which social esteem is at stake, over the determination of the good or legitimate taste. Fashions are class fashions almost always originating in the higher echelons of society.

This view was aptly summarized by Quentin Bell's classical study *On Human Finery*:

> in any stratified society you are almost certain to have a classification of dress, the upper ranks being, of course, more sumptuous than the *hoi polloi*. In both cases you have a situation in which it is possible for the lower strata to compete with the higher strata, to challenge the situation of its social superiors by adopting that form of dress which in principle was reserved for its betters, and in this situation you 'fashion', in the sense of incessant fluctuations, perpetually striving after improvement.
> (Bell 1992 [1947]:113)

As far as modern mass consumption is concerned such a theoretical perspective is, however, problematic. The pattern of social emulation leads to a process of the continuous refinement of taste and to the development of more subtle classifications rather than to the emergence of radically new tastes, fashions and styles. Such an 'aristocratic' society would tend to be rather static and its consumption patterns more conformist than creative and dynamic. In such a theoretical scheme, the modern hedonistic consumer is understood to be a relatively new historical phenomenon with a narrow social basis: the new hedonist is a member of the new middle class. Similarly, the new taste must always be understood to be totally opposed to the old, demanding hegemonic position in culture, whereas a fashion, as understood by Georg Simmel, for instance, only has to claim that it is something new and different from the old. The analyses that understand consumption mainly in terms of a 'social identity model' (cf. Warde 1991) often fail to allow for the main characteristic of modern consumption: the continuous demand for novelty and the resulting dynamics of consumption and production expressed in rapid stylistic innovations. This aspect of fashion was particularly emphasized by Lipovetsky:

> What caused the rule of lavish expense to turn into an excess of precious elegance? Always the same question: why the move beyond sumptuosity itself to the escalation of change and extravagance? In opposition to the prevailing theories, it is necessary to reassert that class rivalries are not the principle underlying the incessant variations of fashion.
>
> (Lipovetsky 1994: 45–6)

There is another approach in understanding modern consumption and the social significance of taste which would seem to be more promising and in the preliminary formulation of which Georg Simmel's and Colin Campbell's contributions, among others, have proved to be fruitful; that is, to analyse the dynamics of consumption and the social institution of fashion together with the processes of taste without postulating any hierarchically ordered lifestyles and tastes. As Herbert Blumer (1969) suggested, the secret of fashion consists of the formation of a collective taste – or as Immanuel Kant (1987: §20) would have it: a *'sensus communis'*. Such a consensus, or the 'Republic of the United Tastes' (cf. Lyotard 1988: 38), can never be actualized. Like fashion, it is rather allusive and elusive, combining both life and death. Fashion does not have to decide 'whether to be or not to be' (Simmel 1986: 47). It both is and is not!

It cannot be denied that in creating his own identity a modern individual also makes more or less free and rational use of the language of the signs of goods in order to stand out from others (cf. McCracken 1988; cf. also Goffman 1951). After all, making differences is what fashion is all about. It would also seem to be quite reasonable to claim that an important change took place in consumption patterns in the

1960s when a new post-war generation of young consumers – the 'new hedonistic middle class' – with its 'unpredictable, instant, impossible demands' entered the consumer market. As Wark (1991: 64) has put it: 'It was, in effect, a demand for production of difference on an expanded scale.' What can be seriously questioned, however, is whether this 'generation' or 'class' was the first hedonistic generation of consumers. It can also be argued that the mechanism of social differentiation adopted by this 'new class' operated within the pattern of an 'anti-hierarchical' mass fashion from the very beginning.

There was, however, in European history a historical stage between court society with its social competition between estates on the one hand, and the society of a fully fledged mass consumption with its developed fashion pattern, on the other, in which consumption goods were often provided with status symbols copied from the lifestyles of supposedly more prestigious figures. These commodities can best be characterized as kitsch.

# 3

# LUXURY, KITSCH AND FASHION

## KITSCH, FASHION AND THE CORRUPTION OF TASTE

### How social interaction is apt to corrupt taste

The discussion on luxury or unnecessary consumption – consumption that goes beyond necessities – was particularly widespread in eighteenth-century England in analyses of social problems and efforts to understand their origins. The writer Smollet was one of the last and best-known representatives of this tradition (see Sekora 1977). The corrupting influence of luxury was enough to explain almost any social problem from highway robbery to work-shyness to mob violence. This was certainly not the first time that the corrupting influence of luxury was recognized. On the contrary, the idea dates back to the old traditions of Roman and Christian moral philosophy. But whereas it was earlier thought to concern only gentlefolk, whose peace of mind might be disturbed by unsatisfied needs, it was now increasingly seen to corrupt common people. It is unlikely that many people thought that the common people were rolling in luxury – rather, their behaviour had become improper in the sense of what were the proprieties of a particular social class or estate. The problem, therefore, was the fear that once liberated from their traditional restrictions, their needs could no longer be satisfied at all: once people got what they wanted, they would never cease to want more.

The distinction between genuine and artificial needs has been typical of many sociological and culturo-critical explanations of modern consumption that operate with the concept of need. (Vance Packard, John Kenneth Galbraith and Herbert Marcuse are good examples.) It often happens that a mechanism of social comparison

31

and competition, similar to the one first identifiable in Rousseau, figures in the background of these contemporary diagnoses. As has been discussed earlier, a good example of moralizing by means of consumption is provided by the discussion on nutritional science which took place at the turn of the century. The concern over the corrupting influence of 'misplaced social pride' on taste and its harmful consequences to national health appears to have been widespread among the early nutritional scientists (see e.g. Levenstein 1988: 99). According to them, certain foodstuffs and dishes have a high value as social symbols, although their nutritional value – particularly in proportion to their price – may be low. What was worrisome was that American workers tended to buy these foodstuffs (such as steaks, for example) even when they could not really afford them, just because the upper classes ate them. These foods, therefore, represented a taste and lifestyle that was worth imitating. Such status competition was apt to corrupt the taste of ordinary people. Nutritional advice about how to choose foodstuffs in each income group in order to ensure a healthy diet remained ineffective for this reason. Edward Atkinson summed up the ideas of many of his colleagues by saying that the only way to change the Americans' eating habits was through the stomach of the upper classes (see Levenstein 1988: 47).

Such ideas concerning the fundamental irrationality of consumers' behaviour – in the sense of ordinary economical rationality – seem to have been fairly widespread, particularly in the United States both at the turn of the century and again in the 1950s (see Riukulehto 1995). But they clearly also found a response in Europe. In the United States, Veblen's work *The Theory of the Leisure Class* (1961 [1899]) was a classic in this discussion. After the Second World War, Vance Packard (1960) became known for his term 'status seekers', from his work with the same title. In his work *All Consuming Images* (1988), Stuart Ewen has collected an impressive set of examples, which shows how this angle was shared by both the cultural critics and the marketing and advertising people of the time. Both groups shared the conviction that – as *Fortune* magazine put it in the 1950s – a substantial part of the American population now had the real possibility to choose an entire lifestyle relatively freely. According to the magazine, the status symbol school of sociology describes just this situation by showing how (1) people express their personalities through symbols (mannerisms, dress, ornaments, property) rather than through words, and how (2) most people are increasingly worried about what other people think of them and their social status. Because of this, people tend to buy objects that symbolize their effort to climb up the social scale (see Ewen 1988: 123).

According to Goffman's (1951) classical thesis – still widely referred to among consumer research literature – goods may be said to take the properties of status symbols if the purchase of them is indicative of membership in a particular status group. These status symbols are efficacious only insofar as there are restrictive mechanisms limiting their 'fraudulent' use (see also Fisher 1986). By fraudulent Goffman meant that members of a society can no longer be certain that ownership of these symbols deserves a certain level of status (see also Dawson and Cavell 1986). (A good deal of the Veblenian critique of 'conspicuous consumption', very widely spread among intellectuals during the 'Gilded Age' in the USA, is actually directed against such a fraudulent use of status symbols.)

In Goffman's analyses of status symbols there are different mechanisms that can limit the inappropriate use of such objects. The most obvious one is their money price, but there are several others, ranging from time, social skills, and ability to family history. The sumptuary laws of the mercantile state were an obvious example of such restrictions.

The theory of class fashion, generally adopted by sociologists from Georg Simmel and Norbert Elias to Vance Packard and Pierre Bourdieu, starts from the presumption that goods are primarily appropriated as status symbols. In addition, it also presumes that their 'fraudulent' use is the normal case: if the restrictions limiting the appropriation of status symbols are too strict, they could not possibly 'trickle down' the social ladder. As has already been pointed out, the most refined version of such a theory is offered by Bourdieu (1984). In his opinion, the dynamics of cultural change and fashion can best be explained by the eternal flow of status symbols – and tastes – along the social ladder. Once the 'refined taste' has been adopted by the lower echelons of society (in Bourdieu's case, the new middle class, in particular), the ruling class must invest its financial or cultural capital in new signs of distinction. Ewen, who himself adopted the ideas of the social status school rather uncritically, even went so far as to claim that all sectors of consumer goods manufacturers began to furnish their products with easily recognizable status symbols during the 1950s. Ewen may be interpreted to mean that this was a kind of logical conclusion to the process that had begun sometime in the 1830s, when the idea of design in industry came to denote the decoration of the surface of artefacts with ornaments and other adornments, based on the differentiation between the form and content (or function) of the product. In this process, the technical planning and manufacture of a product became almost completely separated from its decoration. According to Ewen, this separation of form from content was the peculiar paradox of nineteenth-century capitalism (see Ewen 1988: 33).

Contemporaries felt that the paradox was particularly evident in architecture, where the new building technology (the walls were no longer primary structures) had made the façade in a way constructionally unnecessary and thus able to provide a mere surface for ornamentation. Veblen's (1961) criticism of contemporary architecture is characteristic in this respect and still makes altogether hilarious reading:

> This process of selective adaptation of designs to the end of conspicuous waste, and the substitution of pecuniary beauty for aesthetic beauty, has been especially effective in the development of architecture. It would be extremely difficult to find a modern civilized residence or public building which can claim anything better than relative inoffensiveness in the eyes of any one who will dissociate the elements of beauty from those of honorific waste. The endless variety of fronts presented by the better class of tenements and apartment houses in our cities is an endless variety of architectural distress and of suggestions of expensive discomfort. Considered as objects of beauty, the dead walls of the sides and back of these structures, left untouched by the hands of the artist, are commonly the best feature of the building.
>
> (Veblen 1961: 115)

## Why do the standards of the respectability of the leisure class become the general standard of decency?

Veblen agrees with Rousseau that social competition creates something artificial in people. In Veblen's case, the question is not so much the deformation of needs as the corruption of taste and beauty. Social competition produces beauty which is not real beauty, taste which is not good taste, and manners which are not decent.

Veblen's *Theory of the Leisure Class* (1961) is hopelessly obscure in many ways and it combines several different themes of criticism. On the one hand, Veblen seems to share the rather prevalent view that when lower classes and the nouveau riche try to imitate and adopt the manners and taste of the upper class, they can never really do so properly. That is why they become superficial and artificial. Georg Simmel, a contemporary of Veblen's, expressed this concern of many critics of mass society by saying that equalization does not generally mean that the lower classes should come closer to the upper ones, but rather that the upper ones should be lowered (see Simmel 1950). On the other hand, Veblen's basic starting point, that people value wealth and money, makes him conclude that the more expensive an object is the more beautiful and desirable it is considered. In addition to this 'pecuniary sense of beauty', however, people generally have another, inborn sense of beauty, which aims at revealing the fact that pecuniary beauty is not, after all, genuine beauty. This conception of Veblen's becomes particularly manifest in his studies on fashion.

The basic elements of Veblen's thinking are rather simple. According to him, people value wealth and power based on money, or in his term 'pecuniary power'. Rich people are respected by everyone, and this is what their sense of their own worth is based on. Among those whose lot it is to work in order to meet the immediate necessities of life, a hard-working person is also respected, but the more work loses its essential nature, the more necessary pecuniary power becomes. The desire for wealth is infinite, in principle; it can never be satisfied and it surpasses all other motives of acquiring and accumulating goods. Therefore, an individual's moral and aesthetic value is always determined on the basis of his or her wealth in society. However, wealth is not an absolute but a relative measure of value: an individual's value is determined in comparison with that of others.

For wealth to be evaluated and estimated, it must be visible. A mere bank account or share portfolio is not a very good investment in this respect. Traditionally, leisure time has been such a visible indication of wealth. Veblen writes that refraining from work is a conventional sign of high social status. It has also been associated with the idea of a respectable and proper way of life. Another relatively visible indication of pecuniary power is the employment of domestic servants, who, according to Veblen, do not so much carry out necessary tasks and services, as are kept as proof of their masters' wealth and leisure. In the modern middle class, housewives have taken the place of servants as an indication of social respectability. The head of the family's ability to support an idle wife is, according to Veblen, proof of the family's wealth. Veblen may, in fact, be regarded as the originator of an idea (cf., for example, Ehrenreich 1983) which Americans have long persisted in sharing, namely that middle-class husbands are prepared to work themselves to death (at the risk of a coronary) to support a respectable home, i.e. a house in the suburbs, trimmed lawns, a wife who stays at home, and children. All the manifestations of leisure time that aim at showing pecuniary power are called, in Veblen's terminology, conspicuous leisure. They are all forms of waste.

According to Veblen, however, leisure also has a more indirect significance from the point of view of the development and popularity of the standards of social esteem or taste – or respectability. During leisure, by definition, no work is done and, consequently, nothing is produced, but it is not the same thing as inactivity. During leisure, people are busy with quasi-aesthetic achievements and such 'tasks' as have nothing to do with supporting life as such: art, etiquette, sport or even race horses. Knowing one's etiquette and manners as well as taking an interest in art and sport, for example, are in themselves a sign of wealth. They are socially respected, because the acquisition of these hobbies or the skill and ability to know how to behave and dress requires leisure, which again is a direct indication of wealth and as such, as we have seen, the ultimate object of all respect. 'Refined tastes, manners and habits of life are a useful evidence of quality, because good building requires time, application and expense, and can therefore not be compassed by those whose time and energy are taken up with work' (Veblen 1961: 38).

The more time-consuming certain manners or hobbies are, the higher their social respectability and reputability. The idea of the significance – in the system of social distinctions – of manners, etiquette and factors which have to do with outward appearance and which express the individual's habitus was presented by Bourdieu (1984), but it is directly related to Veblen. Even according to Bourdieu, legitimate taste and cultivated manners require time (and this, indeed, is what makes them respectable).

Veblen presents very clearly the way in which the taste and etiquette of the upper class become prevalent in society, a common standard of good taste which everyone tries to adopt. Social groups or classes are, however, so modest and realistic that they do not all aim at adopting the taste and manners of the social elite directly, but rather those of the group directly above them. In this way, a hierarchic, multi-graded system of tastes and manners is created in society. Veblen sums up his own view in the following words:

The leisure class stands at the head of social structure in point of reputability; and its manner of life and its standards of worth therefore afford the norm of reputability for the community. The observance of these standards, in some degree of approximation, becomes incumbent upon all classes lower in the scale. In modern civilized communities the lines of demarcation between social classes have grown vague and transient, and wherever this happens the norm of reputability imposed by the upper class extends its coercive influence with but slight hindrance down through the social structure to the lowest strata. The result is that the members of each stratum accept as their ideal of decency the scheme of life in vogue in the next higher stratum, and bend their energies to live up to that ideal.

(Veblen 1961: 63–4)

In modern society, according to Veblen, people become anonymous and their encounters are often short-lived and sporadic. In these conditions it becomes difficult to notice leisure. Therefore, as an indication of social value, it is increasingly replaced by conspicuous consumption or such buying and accumulation of goods as only serves the 'need' to display. Like nearly all theoreticians of consumption who operate with some notion of luxury, even Veblen becomes confused in his attempts to define what really belongs to conspicuous consumption, luxury and – consequently – waste. First, luxury only belongs to the leisured class. Workers, he claims, only consume what is necessary. But many forms of consumption which appeared as luxury at first, slowly become common and thus, in a way, part of necessary consumption. This would seem to refer to the fact that whatever is considered necessary or at least important in society at any given period of time is, even according to Veblen, historically determined and therefore relative.[1] However, Veblen also claims that even all the consumption that has become common and ordinary is indeed waste and can be historically deduced from the habit of making pecuniary comparisons aimed at creating envy and achieving esteem (see Veblen 1961: 75). Consequently, waste and luxury do not only involve everything that is not shared by all (in shared consumption, obviously, no one can be in a better position than the other) but also everything that, at some time in history, may have been used as an indication of social superiority.

Veblen sets another condition to luxury: it must not serve human well-being as a whole. Colin Campbell (1994) has pointed out how this puts Veblen's example of an American millionaire who donates

37

money to a hospital or university into a strange light: Veblen had thought that this was an example of the same kind of conspicuous waste as keeping a personal servant, for example, or buying a new car every year. The wide scope of Veblen's concept of conspicuous consumption also becomes clear from his other famous example of an itinerant journeyman printer, who only meets people accidentally and for short periods and who for this reason, in Veblen's experience, is particularly generous in buying drinks for his mates at the bar: he, too, is in principle guilty of similar waste as the millionaire mentioned above.

Veblen has often been interpreted as if the objects of his implicit criticism were, in particular, the nouveau riche of the end-of-the-century United States. Like all people who have suddenly become very rich, they tried to find a short cut to a respected social status by acquiring certain visible and conspicuous signs of a high social position (there is the typical example of a millionaire who buys a castle in France and has it put up in the middle of his farmland in Texas) or mannerisms (butlers, banquets, etc.). Veblen's indignation or irony would appear to direct itself rather towards so-called conspicuous consumption than to a life of leisure and good manners, which in fact serve the same purpose. Anyone who has money can buy things, but the matter is not so simple as far as manners and hobbies are concerned: one does not become a good golfer overnight, even if one has the leisure time required for it. Conspicuous waste is a problem, however, because as far as the objects purchased express, or are part of, a more or less comprehensive way of life or style – such as a knight's castle – just buying things is still not enough to guarantee social esteem: you have to know how to consume them and use them: for example, how to use the golf club.

Veblen himself does not, however, pay much attention to such things. We can only guess that something like this must have been going on in his mind. From his own starting point, in fact, it should be only the amount of money and waste that determines who is the most respected and esteemed person in the country. And then it should follow that the one who gets the most respect is the one who uses his money in the most useless, ostentatious, conspicuous and therefore wasteful way. Yet if this is so, on what grounds could Veblen then criticize the 'unnecessarily' ornamental façades of buildings? Why are they not really beautiful, if anything expensive is indeed considered valuable and beautiful?

In emphasizing that the desire for wealth is limitless and in considering any consumption that goes beyond the merely necessary as waste, Veblen does not have to postulate such additional conditions which are typical of many later scholars who follow the Veblenian line of argumentation: as wealth becomes more widespread in society it becomes more difficult to show off with simple amounts. Overeating is no longer waste or luxury if all, or at least a major part, of the population are guilty of it. In a situation like this, it is often thought that small quality-based distinctions become important indications of social respect. As Stephen Mennell says, talking about the development of culinary art, 'when the possibilities of quantitative consumption for the expression of social superiority had been exhausted, the qualitative possibilities were inexhaustible' (Mennell 1987: 389). The popularity and widespread adoption of the cultivated and fine cuisine created by French culinary art in the nineteenth-century 'civilized' world has often been said to be based on this phenomenon.

It is probably no surprise that Northern America, especially the United States at the turn of the century, is considered the epitome of nouveau riche vulgarity, because there was no upper class consisting of old aristocracy which could have acted as the proper role model for good manners. Besides, if we can believe Levine (1988), it was only towards the end of the century that a clearly distinctive upper-class culture was born – or rather, forcibly made to develop – in the United States, to replace the existing relatively homogeneous culture. To use Levine's example: the rich and poor alike once sat in the same tent or saloon – even if on differently priced seats – for a performance of Shakespeare's *King Lear*, which was interspersed with occasional vaudeville song numbers. But now Shakespeare was transferred to separate theatres, which could not be entered just by paying the price of a ticket, but also required the ability to dress for the occasion and display acceptable behaviour when in the presence of such great art.

## In spite of our inborn sense of beauty our objects are not getting more beautiful

As was mentioned above, people have, according to Veblen, two senses of beauty: pecuniary beauty and what could be called genuine or inborn beauty. The more expensive an object is, the more beautiful it is generally considered. Consequently, anything hand-made is not only more expensive but also more beautiful than an object made mechanically. The link between beauty and price is certainly not conscious.

Veblen is not that vulgar. We do not at first look at the price tag and then decide how beautiful a product is. The link is more subtle and more unconsciously made. Veblen has many funny and more or less telling examples of this. If an object has some practical use in addition to its duty to be aesthetically pleasing and ornamental, this immediately reduces its aesthetic value. A lawn mowed by a gardener is more beautiful than a pasture, although it may be difficult to tell them apart with the naked eye. Even pedigree dogs and cats may be of use as domestic animals, which is why we generally consider a race horse as more beautiful. Veblen's examples related to female beauty are more conventional: since it is impossible to work wearing high heels and a corset, such things are beautiful. Fragile, ethereal women with narrow waists are likewise more beautiful than robust women who are capable of work. This difference is, however, losing its importance: as leisure has become common among women of different social classes, the physical characteristics related to it no longer have the same importance as before.

What is expensive, therefore, is beautiful. Veblen calls this concept of beauty pecuniary beauty. Yet besides this, people also have the ability to distinguish something that is truly – as it were, properly – beautiful from this mere 'pecuniary beauty'. This is important from the point of view of Veblen's rather peculiar description of the mechanism of fashion (see also Wilson 1985: 52). In fashion, in fact, it is a question of the interaction of these two different principles of beauty. Fashion is a typical form of waste. It leads to a faster exhaustion of products: when the style is out of fashion, the product is useless even if it is still in perfect condition (see Veblen 1961:132–4). Dressing is a major forum of conspicuous consumption – it is, above all, visible – but Veblen sees fashion in other areas as well. Changes in fashion may, however, result from other things, too. If fashion only followed the principle of pecuniary beauty, the objects we use would become more and more expensive, outrageous and grotesque. If, again, it only followed the other principle of beauty, our natural pursuit of beauty, it would gradually lead to the perfection of beauty. This, obviously, has never happened. Fashion involves a permanent variation between these two principles, which is why natural taste corrects the excesses of fashion from time to time as something inherently repulsive to it:

> Our transient attachment to whatever happens to be the latest
> [in fashion – J. G.] rests on other than aesthetic grounds, and

lasts only until our abiding aesthetic sense has had time to assert itself and reject this latest indigestible contrivance.

(ibid.:133)

All in all, it seems that Veblen's critical comments on conspicuous consumption and waste are fundamentally based on the idea that the principle of pecuniary beauty leads to excess and grotesque manifestations (not only in fashion but elsewhere too) which our natural sense of beauty tends to reject. Although what is expensive is also beautiful and even respectable, it is not really so, or at least not always and everywhere. And apparently the money or time put into learning good manners – when it is not only a question of imitating but of a genuine integration – is valuable and, ultimately, worthy of higher social respect than wasting money in buying all kinds of things. At any rate, leisure and the manners and quasi-aesthetic hobbies related to it are not as clearly an object of Veblen's scorn as a millionaire living in an expensive but tasteless house and offering expensive but tasteless dinners. If this is what Veblen's criticism is actually all about, it is, after all, relatively conventional. As Molière knew, a genuine nobleman is always more honourable than a nouveau riche millionaire, even if the latter has more pecuniary power.

As was pointed out above, Veblen's analysis resembles many later studies of social competition, distinction and valuation (in addition to Bourdieu, see also Norbert Elias and Mennell) – which were probably also directly influenced by his ideas. Veblen's emphasis is, however, slightly different. The others – we might perhaps even talk about a European tradition here – emphasize how the competition over social respect related to different lifestyles is apt to improve and cultivate taste, because the upper class is always committed to distinguishing itself from the lower classes which are trying to imitate it. In this, small differences of quality and style become important, and the result is what Campbell (1987) called aristocratic aesthetics. Veblen, on the contrary, emphasizes another aspect of the same thing. Taste becomes vulgarized as the standards of good taste are lowered in the social hierarchy.[2]

Vulgar taste is born when consumption and consumer goods become more and more important status symbols and yet anyone can buy them – as long as they have enough money; this separates them from their original link with lifestyle. They become in a way freely exchangeable and movable signs of lifestyles and social value (cf. Goffman 1951). This is exactly what creates the powerful impression of superficiality and tastelessness, described by Veblen. We might well say that Veblen has created a theory of kitsch and kitsch fashion.

## Why does the entire material culture of the late nineteenth century create an impression of kitsch?

One way of approaching the rather obscure phenomenon called kitsch is to say that we often have a feeling that almost all the material culture of the nineteenth century – or of the England of the Victorian era at least – was kitsch. 'In various guises our idea of kitsch comprises every article that was ever exhibited in the nineteenth century and signifies our determination that Victorian commodities are no longer capable of performing the cultural work they once did' (Richards 1990: 91). Kitsch would in this way relate to all the objects whose cultural significance has in some way become incomprehensible and strange to us. But why should this have happened to many of the products of the nineteenth century in particular? According to Ewen, kitsch is related to the products of last century, especially those that were imitations of elite style aimed at the middle class and produced by mass production (see Ewen 1988: 64). What makes an object kitsch is that it is a cheap, mass-produced copy of some original object or model which was considered elegant.

For Richards, who analysed the material culture of nineteenth-century Britain, the pure, classic example of kitsch is the so-called Jubilee kitsch, i.e. all knick-knacks and different 'useless' memorabilia produced in honour of Queen Victoria's Jubilee Year, 1887, and decorated with all kinds of symbols and emblems of the queen and her reign. As Richards' examples show, kitsch proliferated particularly in conjunction with the great World Exhibitions of the last century. (Cf. the miniature copies of the Eiffel Tower, which are a classic example of an ornamental object commemorating a particular institution.) In this more limited sense of a souvenir, kitsch can, according to Richards, be characterized as follows: 'Kitsch may be defined as elaborately aestheticized commodities produced in the name of large institutions (church, state, empire, monarchy) for middle-class home use. Kitsch is a short-order charisma . . . ' (Richards 1990: 88).

In their more limited sense, kitsch objects have been designed to satisfy a momentary, suddenly arisen need. They are commemorative and ornamental objects which are useless in themselves; placed on the mantelpiece or shelf, they keep the memory of a ceremonial moment or institution, yet at the same time make it trivial by turning it into an

42

article of daily use (a provincial coat-of-arms reproduced on the handle of a spoon, for example). Richards' more narrow categorization of kitsch makes it possible to understand the phenomenon more widely. Ordinary, mass-produced articles of daily use (such as dinner sets or furniture) which imitate the earlier elegant models and styles also borrow from the 'charisma' attached to the way of life of the nobility, for example, at the same time making it more trivial by making them accessible to anyone who can afford to buy them. This is why they feel like kitsch – somehow artificial and superficial. The impression of kitsch is, however, often simply created by the fact that the models in question have been removed from their original context. As McCracken (1988: 94) has pointed out, it is only relatively few products that act as status symbols at any given time.

### The war against kitsch in the name of democracy

At the beginning of this century, Escoffier, the creator and developer of modern French restaurant cuisine, launched his new style which was more rational in preparation and less ornamental in style. He was clearly inspired by the same spirit as the one found in many better-known representatives (such as William Morris) of fields that were more traditionally perceived as design or arts and crafts. Escoffier, however, was in a sense more realistic and far-sighted than many contemporary artists or designers. He seems to have been better aware of the laws of the marketplace and the importance of fashion in his statement that in modern times, foods and dishes had to satisfy the requirement for novelty and variety above anything else. 'Novelty is a universal cry.' This was generally ignored by the reformers of art, which is one of the reasons why their programmes were never carried out widely enough for them to have been able to change ordinary people's sense of style and consumer habits in any essential way.

These movements of art reform in the nineteenth century can well be seen as an early movement of critique of consumption – or even of consumer policy. Their express purpose was to improve the taste of both designers and consumers and, in this way, to make consumption more democratic. What had destroyed that taste, or at least threatened to destroy it, was kitsch, whose popularity, according to these critics, was based on the belief that consumers, blinded by social respectability, imitated those above them, which led to ostentatious showing off with goods. The *art industriel* movement wanted to turn articles of everyday use into objects of art and, in this way, to make everyday life

43

more aesthetic. At the same time, it was obviously directed against another way of making everyday life more aesthetic – one that it considered wrong. This wrong aestheticization and ornamentation was represented by the typical industrial design of the time and the prevalent style in the production of mass consumer goods: it consisted of ornamentations and decorations freely copied and superficially added to anything from dishes to building façades. As Georg Maag has pointed out, the aestheticization of objects of use was considered possible in two opposite ways:

> When art is attached to concrete, physical needs, its primary manifestation is *l'objet d'usage*, where again beauty may be added either by an ornamentation which hides the function of the object or by giving it a functional form reduced to style.
>
> (Maag 1986:71)

*Art industriel* was also a movement of *art social*, where the cultivation of taste ultimately served the cause of social justice. A typical representative of this cause was Camille Mauclair, an aesthete excellently characterized by Rosalind Williams (1982), and who was active in Paris towards the end of the nineteenth century. According to Mauclair, the beauty of an object could be reduced to three principles: it should be modern, appropriate and democratic. The first thing to do was to liberate consumption from its dominant aristocratic mentality, which craved prestige by means of imitating the style of the elite. It was the appropriateness of the object that was to replace prestige as the general principle governing its design. Popular taste must be liberated from the corrupting influence of the bourgeoisie. Disgust at anything ornamental, fanciful or exotic was in this way not only an aesthetic but also a social question.

According to this thinking, the integrity of objects was based on their ability to satisfy everyday human needs, those that were shared by all and sundry. The basic need of consumers had to be brought to light and they were to guide design (see Williams 1982: 164). This principle of the appropriateness and usefulness of objects was, in its essence, democratic – it did, after all, respect the needs that were shared by all. The purpose of the *art social* programme was a kind of democratization of luxury by means of a democratization of art, or perhaps rather the extinction of all luxury as useless and unnecessary.

What, then, was the power that made the designers continue to design and the buyers continue to buy kitsch? Why did artificial ornamentation often seem to gain the upper hand in the contest over the consumer's soul? According to Mauclair, the final reason was that planning itself was not democratic and, consequently, the models produced by it could not be modern. Mauclair ended up by demanding a completely new, moral art education, one where the consumers themselves could participate in the planning of the products. It is only by making things oneself that one can learn to appreciate beauty. The reason for a corrupted sense of beauty was the separation of both spiritual and manual labour from consumption and production. A mere consumer reform was bound to fail; a consumer, as a consumer, can never adopt an aesthetic taste (see Williams 1982: 177). Even in William Morris' thinking, the separation of manual and spiritual labour had corrupted people's taste. That was the reason why most modern architecture only consisted of 'imitations of imitations of imitations'. This central problem of modern life cannot be solved only by finding a style suitable for the modern era. According to Morris, the whole era had to be redefined in a completely different way and the unity of thought and action, model and its representation, as well as design and material, had to be re-established (see Ewen 1988: 13).

Morris ended up by admiring gothic style and the ancient English community. Mauclair, again, found a very similar solution, as did Emile Durkheim, a contemporary sociologist, in his rejection of social anomie. In addition to that people again had to be able to make their own articles of everyday use in small workshops; the re-establishment of the unity of consumption and production – and the creation of a new morality related to it – required a revival of the trade guilds. Only corporations could control lifestyle and consumption in an effective way. The democratic reform of art, the purpose of which had been the aestheticization of modern mass production and everyday life, thus ended up by demanding, besides a moral education of the modern consumer, the virtual annihilation of all modern mass production and the re-establishment of a secure, decent way of life guaranteed by corporations.

Raising the useful and functionally appropriate to the highest aesthetic principle and seeing it as the guideline of modern design produced results that were paradoxical in two ways. First, as Rosalind Williams (1982) has pointed out, people did not put their money into opting for this kind of beauty. The reformers were repeatedly disappointed in people's taste, which continued to prefer kitsch to modern design. Besides, many of the objects which were in accordance with the new design, and were meant as objects of use, soon turned into objects of art and collectors' items. As such, they again became inaccessible to the ordinary consumer and acquired their value and price from the aura of high culture, as had decorative everyday art before them. Second, there is a major paradox in the basic starting point of the whole art reform. The perspective of object culture which aims at aestheticizing articles of everyday use is the consumer's and not the traditional producer's perspective. By demanding that consumers assume the producer's perspective in their material object environment, the reformers actually came to demand the annihilation of this aesthetic dimension and turned objects into mere instruments in the satisfaction of needs.

## Marketing kitsch

What early ideologists of industrial art and early sociologists criticized in the mass consumption and style of consumer goods of the turn of the century was that it emphasized social hierarchy based on money and wealth even in material culture. Objects were seen primarily as representing social status to the consumer and containing the promise of a social climb. Misplaced social pride corrupted taste.

With the lack of more exact studies of material culture, it is difficult to say to what extent such points of view were really taken into account in planning and manufacturing products, and to what extent the producers actually furnished their products with such status symbols. Those who were responsible for marketing the products, on the other hand, seemed to have adopted the idea quite widely as a useful strategy of sales promotion by the end of the century at the latest. Daniel Pope (1983), a historian of advertising, says, however, that this kind of advertising became more common in the 1920s, when the emphasis was more generally shifted from product-oriented to more personalized methods. Yet it has never been the only or even the dominant form of advertising.

The earliest known marketing strategy based on this thinking dates back to the middle of the eighteenth century. Wedgwood's china factory manufactured its products in different series, offering the first to the upper class as an 'option to buy'. If the product was sold, Wedgwood marketed a less expensive version of the same product to the middle class and bourgeoisie, stating in its advertising that the set already decorated the dinner table of Lord or Lady So-and-So (see McKendrick *et al.* 1982). As is shown by Richards' study, among others, this type of advertising seems to have been fairly common in England at the end of the century, when Queen Victoria herself often appeared in advertisements as the role model of (women) consumers (see Richards 1990: 91–104). But as Richards also points out, many prominent figures who advertised the various products were not all that well known until they became so thanks to the advertisements (ibid.: 84).

## Kitsch as a historical stage between class and mass fashion

As Arto Noro (1991: 66) has pointed out, there is a prevailing conception among sociologists that fashion 'is born as a form of class differentiation in a relatively open class society, where the elite class attempts to differentiate itself by means of visible signs, such as certain distinctive ways of dressing'. The lower class, for its part, tries to identify itself with the elite by adopting these signs, and this is the basis both of the more or less rapidly spreading fashion and the fashion cycles in society.[3]

Herbert Blumer (1969) was one of the first sociologists to emphasize the democratic aspect of fashion and its independence from class hierarchy: the mechanism of fashion even acts against the hierarchies. In fact, Blumer does not emphasize the role of fashion as a mechanism of differentiation at all, as he is obviously afraid that it would only lead to the old vision of class differentiation (see Noro 1991:104). It is, however, evident that sociologists have found it very difficult to consider this simultaneous identification and differentia-tion without considering some kind of hierarchy attached to it. A good example of this is 'imitation without a model', the paradoxical pair of concepts introduced by Gabriel Tarde (1962 [1890]), a theoretician of the turn-of-the-century mass society. When studying the conditions in which fashion may appear in some particular field, Blumer, rather surprisingly, mentions a condition that would seem to be in conflict with his own ideas. The fifth condition of fashion in his list is that there must be such prestige figures in the field that are acknowledged to be capable of evaluating the value and appropriate-ness of competing models (see Blumer 1969: 286–7). Although this prestige does not have to be linked with people's class status, as it may be based on other kinds of models as well (such as film stars or beauty queens), it does inevitably smuggle in a kind of concept of hierarchy even in Blumer's framework. (For a discussion of the role of fashion innovators – or 'fashion change agents' – in contemporary clothes fashion, see King and King 1980.)

Of all fashion theoreticians, the one who has most clearly

emphasized the difference between mass and elite fashion may, in fact, be Horowitz, who speaks of clothes fashion, in particular, but nothing prevents us from generalizing these ideas to apply to other fields as well. According to Horowitz, elite or class fashion is characterized by the fact that it tends to strengthen status differences, as there is a limited number of products (or their availability, at least, is limited) and they have been directed at a selected group of consumers. If they became more widespread, they would inevitably decrease in value. Mass fashion, on the contrary, has to do with products aimed at mass consumption, and expresses a pursuit of conformism. Age groups are often important factors of differentiation in the mass fashion of clothes (see Horowitz 1975a: 289). According to Horowitz, semi-mass fashion can be considered a new kind of phenomenon that has grown on mass fashion but resembles elite fashion in some respects. Examples of this are boutiques which emphasize the uniqueness of the products they sell and the individual nature of those who wear them, even though they are, in fact, accessible to all consumers, at least in principle (see Horowitz 1975a: 290). Although these different types of fashion may exist simultaneously, it is, however, elite fashion that is historically the earliest form. Horowitz emphasizes the different spreading mechanism of this fashion as compared with modern mass fashion. 'The basis of the communication of elite fashion to wider groups in the society was essentially a process of imitation which reflected the social aspiration, of those women who accepted their "betters" as their reference group' (ibid.: 289).[4]

Historically, kitsch can now be interpreted as an intermediary stage between elite fashion and democratic mass fashion. It resembles class fashion in that it operates with status symbols emphasizing social hierarchy, and in doing so, imitates highly valued models. These models, however, do not represent the upper class or elite of society, and the fashion does not imitate the style of any existing upper class. They are as genuine as the King of Denmark's Chest Lozenges in Finland during my childhood.

It is obvious that it is this historically specific form of fashion that has been in the minds of many sociologists and cultural critics who have presented theories of fashion and consumption – and who have been discussed earlier – acting as a kind of general model of fashion for them. It would, indeed, seem that many of those who thought that fashion spreads in society from the top, down the class pyramid, and who were at the same time afraid that this would lead to a vulgariza-tion of taste, were in fact studying kitsch fashion. In thus moralizing modern consumption, we may recognize both the wise old saying that everyone should live in a way that is appropriate to their class (because everything becomes mediocre when spread too widely), and the more modern concern that consumers' choices and judgments of beauty are not, in fact, guided by rational thinking and functionalism, even though that would be possible for the first time now that the old restrictions have tumbled down.

## KITSCH AND LUXURY IN THE SOVIET UNION

### The secret of the caviar sandwich

In the Soviet Union a historically specific culture of consumption was born. Democratic luxury was an essential part of the everyday life of the Soviet people. It was in particular expressed in the numerous public and personal feasts or celebrations that were typical of Soviet life. When and why this luxury was invented is an intriguing problem for researchers. The following considerations are but a preliminary attempt at understanding Soviet consumer culture.

What did this traditional or democratic luxury consist of? What does this paradoxical expression mean? The luxury consisted of such products as champagne, cognac, caviar sandwiches, assorted choco-lates, two specific types of cakes, chocolate and fruit, and perfumes. All these goods are meant to be enjoyed, by eating, drinking, or smelling. They are also very feminine goods, welcome gifts for women. One could add several other items to this list and the place in the process of consumption of every item could be seriously discussed. Many goods sold in special state gift shops in the cities, such as crystal glasses and vases, amber necklaces, scarfs and fur hats, belonged to this group, too. One could add still more, but the important thing is that there existed such a limited group of products which had preserved their status throughout several decades of Soviet history.

These were all products that were especially bought to be consumed at family parties, as birthday presents, or to celebrate a public holiday. Most of them were available in great quantities before public holidays (New Year, May Day, October Revolution) for a moderate price. In the 1960s, before the anti-alcohol campaigns, a worker on his way to work early in the morning could stop at a kiosk and enjoy a glass of champagne and a caviar sandwich – a pleasure of which workers in the capitalist world could only dream. Was the Soviet Union the workers' paradise after all?

The fact that these products could be bought for the same state-regulated price everywhere from Leningrad to Vladivostok, from Archangel to Odessa, and that their range was kept more or less intact from year to year, meant that they were an integral part of state economic planning. Even though the gross value of all the cakes produced yearly within the territory of the Soviet Union was small compared to the value of the produce of bread factories, the reliable and centralized production and distribution of cakes demanded huge investments, factories and transport facilities, building of new shops and cafés, etc. It also meant that someone, somewhere had once made a decision about their production on a mass scale. It was almost self-evident that this was not a question of any continuation of pre-revolutionary traditions or a prolongation of the culture of the NEP (New Economic Policy) period of the 1920s.

These luxury goods were by no means all that was regarded as luxury – in the sense of transcending everyday needs – by the Soviet people. They were not necessarily the most valued or cherished items either. As early as the beginning of the 1930s special shops were opened to serve a privileged clientele. In these shops one could, for instance, buy products of foreign origin. Almost any foreign and imported goods were turned into a luxury, difficult to achieve due to the policy of creating socialism in one country and the strong reliance on its own resources and raw materials. The black market trade in jeans or nylon stockings in the post-war decades are probably the best known examples of this phenomenon. (In the 1930s, Parker pens and imported cigarettes played a similar role in Soviet culture.)

In the 1930s there were already many examples of 'real' privileges and luxury, too, which were enjoyed by a wider circle of people, extending the political elite: directors and leaders had cars with chauffeurs, separate houses, big flats in the centre of the city, summer villas, vacations in health spas on the Crimea, etc. – later even trips abroad and access to *valuta*, foreign currency that could buy practically anything. For instance when a meeting of Stakhanovite workers was held in Moscow in 1936, Ordzhonikidze presented the participants with 50 cars, 25 motor cycles, 500 cycles, 150 gramophones, 200 hunting rifles and 150 pocket watches (see Siegelbaum 1988: 228).

## The old and the new luxury

Since the mid-1930s these real luxury goods and services were part of the lifestyle, not only of the rather narrow political elite, but also of a rapidly growing group of 'privileged' people consisting of educated specialists and top workers. As late as the 1960s such luxury belonged to one's 'office'. At least in principle, it could not be bought with money, but was a reward to be earned by hard work or exceptional talents. (For an interesting discussion of the nature of such 'luxury', see Beriya 1995: 5–6.) It was in the 1960s that it first faced a serious challenge. It became possible to dream of buying a motor cycle, a small family car, a summer cottage, a small private flat, etc. The establishment of the giant Togliatti car factory producing Zhigulis under licence from FIAT marked an important turn in history – and not only symbolically. At the same time, refrigerators, televisions and entertainment electronics in general, portable radios and hi-fi sets began their – at first very slow – intrusion into Soviet homes. New microcities (suburbs) with huge housing complexes were also built at an increasing speed to help overcome the very serious housing shortage which had worsened during the whole of Stalin's reign. The most remarkable change in housing policy was, however, the new target of providing every single family with a private home, a home that could be decorated and furnished according to one's own private taste. New flats were often distributed according to the needs of families, but they could, to some extent, be bought with money (so-called cooperative houses had been built in the 1930s but this programme was rescinded on Stalin's orders).

These new luxuries and the production of modern consumer goods mostly imitated in a rather crude manner the life and consumption model of the middle classes which had become common in the USA and the most prosperous countries of Western Europe after the Second World War. The aim of the peaceful economic competition declared by Khrushchev was not only to 'overcome' (exceed) the production figures for steel, coal and electricity, but also – even though it was not stated explicitly – to achieve the standard and the model of Western consumption – at least in some respects. In order for socialism to prove its superiority, it should be able to produce as many cars, refrigerators, television sets and stereo players as the United States. (In 1940, it was estimated that there were not more than 4.4 million radio receivers in the 38.4 million city households in the Soviet Union. Of these the

51

biggest part were loudspeakers tuned to receive only one radio station.)

It should, however, be remembered that in the beginning of the 1960s this aim was not as far-fetched as it was later. Such 'luxury' products were then still relatively rare in the homes of Western Europe too, and the property of well-to-do people. It was reasonable to believe that the gap could be overcome within a decade or two.

The new ideal of Soviet luxury was based directly on the standard of living of the Western middle class and prosperous workers. In this respect, the old luxury characterized earlier was totally different. Whereas the new was borrowed from the West, the old was home-made and based on a more original conception of a good lifestyle: it did not have any existing models. Therefore one can speak of a genuine Soviet culture and style of material goods, and it is interesting to try to analyse what kind of a conception of a good life or of luxury it expressed.

If the above catalogue of luxury goods is representative at all, they represent a way of life that was lived by rich people sometime in the middle of nineteenth-century Europe – or rather a life which the Bolsheviks thought the rich had lived: champagne, caviar, chocolate, cognac, perfume: only lackeys, horse carriages, courtesans and roulette are missing from the catalogue. On the other hand, it would have been difficult to combine these elements of a 'good life' with the ideal socialist way of life. In any case, it was in principle possible for a Soviet worker to dine *à la* Parisienne under a crystal chandelier and enjoy the services of a butler in a tailcoat, say, in the Metropol, Natsional or Prag restaurants, or in the new Soviet showpiece, the Hotel Moskva next to the Kremlin Wall, built at the end of the 1930s. And the prices were moderate.

It was typical of this Soviet luxury that it was basically home-made and not imported. Chocolate excluded, all the raw materials were produced in Russia. On the other hand, the most popular Russian stimulant, vodka, was not part of this luxury. It was an everyday necessity. Beer is a bit more difficult to classify. Soviet beer was not highly valued but imported beers, like the Czech Urquell, shared the aura of all foreign products. It is easy to see that old and 'genuine' luxury products had acted as models for the Soviet luxury goods, the high value of which was derived from their uniqueness or rarity which in part stemmed either from 'natural' limitations (cognac, champagne or caviar) or from sumptuary laws (perfumes, chocolate). Armenian cognac or Russian champagne naturally had very little in common with the drinks produced in the French *départements* of Champagne or Cognac. They were 'cheap' imitations of products that had been expensive and rare under capitalism and were out of reach of the proletariat toiling under its yoke.

What made the situation rather peculiar was the fact that these were hardly the products that a wage worker living under capitalism in the 1930s dreamed of or was eager to achieve. They could be called Soviet kitsch. They imitated models and artefacts that were thought to be valued or belonging to the world of 'high society'. Their propagandistic message was thus obvious: they were meant to show that every Soviet worker lived like a real bourgeois or aristocrat. At the same time there was a constant deficit of basic daily necessities, including bread. The rationing of basic provisions was cancelled first in 1935 – only to start again after the outbreak of the war! To buy a bottle of champagne certainly was beyond the reach of millions of *kolchoz* peasants: it has been estimated (Gordon and Klopov 1989) that the average wage of a *kolchoznik* – including the income from a private plot – did not exceed 20 roubles in 1940 (in the currency of 1989). But at the same time there were already before the war hundreds of thousands – if not millions – of peasants and workers who were clearly more prosperous.

## The great retreat

When was this new Soviet luxury invented? Even if conclusive proof is not available, there are good reasons to believe that it was in February–March 1934, around the time of the Seventeenth Party Congress during which the Second Five Year Plan received its final form. One can reach this conclusion by reading Timasheff's famous work, *The Great Retreat* (1946), in which Timasheff claimed that a major change took place in Communist Party politics and in the building of socialism in the Soviet Union. This change also meant giving up many of the earlier basic and 'holy' aims of the Bolsheviks.

The First Five Year Plan with its programme of enforced industrialization had been 'successfully' completed. The foundations of heavy industry had been created at great human cost. The deportations and famine following enforced collectivization of farming were also part of history. The First Five Year Plan had been completed in 1932 but the new plan was officially adopted one and a half years later. This was what led Timasheff to claim that a major reorientation had taken place in the politics of the party, during the course of the Party Congress which discussed the new economic plan. According to this version, the minister of heavy industry, Ordzhonikidze, went back on the words of the head of Gosplan, who had made a speech the day before, and set new economic policy tasks and aims, promising for instance more investments in consumer goods industries. Ordzhonikidze would thus have made concessions and promised people some relief, compared with their lives under the First Five Year Plan.

According to Eugene Zaleski's (1980) close examination of the conditions of the birth and realization of the Second Plan the picture given by Timasheff was strongly exaggerated and dramatized. According to Zaleski:

> the revisions made in the draft of the Second Five Year Plan at the Seventeenth Party Congress seem minor. Ordzhonikidze, People's Commissar of Heavy Industry, proposed the reduction of the average rate of growth of industrial production from 18.9 to 16.5 per cent and small reductions in the 1937 goals for machine-building and the principal metallurgical products. The revisions proposed by A. I. Mikoyan for the food industry and by I. E. Lyubimov for light industry were hardly more substantial. Nor were these reductions spontaneous; Molotov announced to the congress that they had been approved by the Party Politburo.
>
> (Zaleski 1980: 129–30)

The change in politics did not include any promise of relief as far as the Soviet consumer was concerned. (As mentioned by Zaleski these figures should not be taken too seriously since the possibility of the full realization of the plan was from the very beginning negligible. If all the planned investements were summed up, the total yearly national product would hardly have been enough to cover them all.)

The standard of living did not improve during this five year period, either. Such beliefs, still common enough in Western analyses, are obviously wrong. According to Barber:

> In the mid 1930s the atmosphere appears to have improved. Higher living standards, the end of rationing, the three good years of 1934–6 in industry, a series of better harvests, together with a temporarily more relaxed political atmosphere, produced a more positive mood.
>
> (Barber 1990: 9)

54

On the other hand, it is obvious that the standard of living of many – if by no means all or even the great majority – improved remarkably due to the consciously promoted increase of income differentials. The general atmosphere might also have become more optimistic and relaxed. Had not Stalin himself promised in 1935 that life would become better and happier?

It is thus obvious that Timasheff, whose information was mainly gained from the contemporary Soviet daily press, was exaggerating and dramatizing the general importance of this Party Congress and the new Five Year Plan. But the revisions that were made and the discussion waged about the new plan still prove there was some kind of insecurity of orientation, and express a need for reorientation on behalf of the party leadership and economic planners.

Timasheff is, however, much more convincing in showing that around the year 1934 a crucial change took place in the cultural politics of the party and more broadly in the conception of a proper Soviet way of life. The end of the 1920s and the beginning of the 1930s were dominated by the conception of proletarian culture and the ideal of the ascetic self-sacrificing Soviet worker. (The famous leather jacket of the commissar was the fashionable garment of the 1920s.) In this sense the year 1934 signalled an almost total about-turn.

In the autumn of 1934, the party leadership condemned all kinds of asceticism (self-induced pauperism) and libertarianism (free love). What is even more important, the doctrine of egalitarianism which had dominated the party ideology faced the same fate. It was now strongly condemned as a petit bourgeois deviation opposed to real socialism. School reforms were also stopped the same year, and the old regime was rehabilitated, a regime reminiscent of the system that had been established during the most reactionary period of Russian cultural policy in the 1880s and 1890s. The authority of the university professors had been reactivated a bit earlier: they, and not the party, were entitled to give credits to students. The school reforms of the proletarian phase were now criticized and shown to be a total catastrophe – backed by research data according to which university students could hardly read or write when starting their courses.

In 1933 the Central Committee of the Party declared socialist realism to be obligatory in art, thus cancelling the ideals of proletarian culture. Richard Stites (1992) has aptly summarized the meaning of this turn in art as follows:

they canonised classical music, ballet, and architecture, realistic theatre, and didactic painting. At the same time they helped fashion a 'mass culture' of socialist realist fiction, state-sponsored folk lore, mass song, military bands, parades, movies, and radio – accessible to all.

(Stites 1992: 65)

It was a culture bearing 'solemn hallmarks of high culture'. It was as if the history of literature, music and art had stopped sometime in the mid-eighteenth century – all the newer developments were declared to be incomprehensible and condemned as damaging to human values and taste. It is characteristic of the abruptness of the change that whereas one could, in 1933, declare that Tolstoy was almost useless because of his classless attitude (see Timasheff 1946: 264), in 1937 a festival of Russian art was celebrated, reaching its climax in the centennial of Pushkin.

## The new happy life

Once classical music was declared as the prototype of Soviet music, folk art and music were also rediscovered. On the eighteenth anniversary of the October Revolution (1935) Stalin attended an evening of popular music and dances. After the show he applauded eagerly. The following day an article was published in *Pravda* in which it was claimed that folk art is 'the great source of inspiration of our artists'. That such had not always been the case is demonstrated by a fact mentioned by Timasheff (1946: 272): the production of accordions now recommenced. There were very few musicians who knew how to play the accordion, but some were found. They were then given the important task of teaching the young generation how to play this previously popular instrument (see Timasheff 1946: 272 and Stites 1992).

Recordings of popular music were also published on a new scale. After a short period of Soviet jazz, the breakthrough of tango and folk music followed. Finally the eclectic Soviet 'mass song' was born: 'Schlagers' written and composed by adopting popular folk melodies and styles. Blanter's 'Katyusha', for instance, was the great 'top ten' hit of the year 1938 (see Stites 1992: 75–8).

By the end of the 1930s the basic elements of the new Soviet Culture were thus created. It was a mixture of light classics, adopted folk art and Soviet popular songs, a combination that was still easily

56

recognizable a few years ago to anyone visiting the Soviet Union or listening to the 'Mayak' radio station.

It was furthermore characteristic of the period that in the middle of the 1930s dancing was not only allowed but actively encouraged by party politicians. It was regarded almost as the duty of every Komsomol boy or girl. Numerous dance schools were opened up in Moscow. To learn to dance became obligatory for officers of the Red Army. Voroshilov and Molotov set a good example by learning to dance the tango!

As many reminiscences of the 1930s recall, 'joyous life' was not only allowed but positively encouraged. The Soviet citizen was supposed to be happy. The abruptness and unexpectedness of this change in party politics is well documented in a letter cited by Timasheff (1946: 314–15) which was sent to the editor of a youth journal by a group of Komsomol members living in the countryside. They asked whether it really was now allowed to visit friends, play the accordion and have fun. Their leader, obviously loyal to the old politics, still demanded that they should stay at home and listen to instructive programmes on the radio.

Now it was allowed to be different and to distinguish oneself from the group without getting into trouble: 'We endorse beauty, smart clothes, chic coiffures, manicure.... Girls should be attractive. Perfume and make up belong to the "must" of a good Komsomol girl.... Clean shaving is mandatory for a Komsomol boy' (cited in Timasheff 1946: 317). Such recommendations could be found frequently in newspapers and journals in 1934–5. The importance of washing one's hands and cleanliness in general was a continuous theme in youth papers. A new journal of fashion was also established in Moscow which gave instructions on how to dress and how to furnish one's own home.

### 'Happiness lives in the country of plenty'

*Merry Boys*, the famous film by the threesome Dunayevsky, Aleksandrov and Orlova, as well as the somewhat later *Volga, Volga*, showed how this idea of having fun was central to the new cultural policy. *Merry Boys* was a conscious imitation of Hollywood musicals accompanied by Soviet jazz played on accordions. It caused a minor 'cultural war' but was soon released and became a great success. The comedy *Volga, Volga* describing the journey of a village orchestra along the river Volga to a folk music olympiad in Moscow, a journey full of amusing occurrences due to misunderstandings with local bureau-crats, compressed all the themes of the period together into a harmonious whole.

It is also characteristic of the period that from the mid-1930s carnivals and popular festivals were organized in the cities. Rosalind Sartorti, who has published an interesting history of these festivities, described the carnival organized in August 1936 as follows:

> In the night of 5th to the 6th of August, a hundred thousand participants in costumes and masks were dancing waltz and tango, slow and fast fox-trot, they were enchanted by the torch processions of the carnival heroes, by the Ferris wheel, the fountains which resembled burning asters, by the nightly sky brightened by the play of projectors, by the fireworks and the rockets, and they went down the river Moskva in boats decorated with pennants.
>
> (Sartorti 1990: 41)

These carefully planned and organized carnivals were something totally new in Soviet society. They tried to transmit an atmosphere of Soviet society 'characterized by a holiday mood which knows nothing of scarcity, tension or necessity, but quite the contrary, a world of overabundance, amusement and forgetting' (ibid.: 42).

At these carnivals food and drinks were usually plentiful. The following is a report of the May Day celebrations in Moscow in 1936 published in *Komsomolskaya Pravda*, 4 May 1936:

> It is hard to describe how Moscow enjoyed itself in these joyous days of the May Day celebrations. . . . We have to talk about the garden of the plenty behind the Manezha building, this garden where sausages and *Wurst* were growing on the trees. Where a mug of foaming beer was accompanied by delicious Poltava sausages, by pink ham, melting Swiss cheese, and marble white bacon. . . . Walking across the square one could get a giant appetite.
>
> (cited in Sartorti 1990: 66–7)

As Sartorti also said, these carnivals were organized under conditions of a huge deficit of many basic foodstuffs and consumer goods. Where, for instance, did they get all the textiles to make the carnival outfits? How did this 'Garden of the Plenty' of the Stalinist carnival relate to Soviet reality at the end of the 1930s? Was it after all the carnivalesque world turned upside down, an unconscious parody of Soviet reality?

(See Sartorti 1990: 70.) But this was not the case: they were simply typical examples of socialist realism, the task of which was to show concretely how a grain of the future had already been sown in the present. The festivals were, after all, very disciplined and absolutely no expressions of spontaneity were allowed.

## The coming into being of the new middle class

In the analyses of Stalin's times it has been common to interpret the 'value transformation' in cultural politics which started in the middle of the 1930s and continued well into the 1950s with occasional periods of tightening cultural climate, as an indicator or proof of the increasing weight of a new middle class in Soviet society. According to Vera Dunham's famous interpretation, the Soviet political elite made a 'big deal' with this new middle class by yielding to its demands and aspirations in cultural politics and lifestyle and received as a reward its undivided political loyalty (Dunham 1976). As many observers witnessed, Stalin seemed to be enjoying great popularity among the citizens of the time (see e.g. Volkogonov 1989).

Stalin's programmes of industrialization had, in the 1920s and 1930s, for the first time given rise to a large working class that was young and of rural origin. The city population increased dramatically: millions of people moved into Moscow and Leningrad alone from the countryside. A ruralization of cities and city culture became evident. At the same time a new group of experts and specialists was schooled by the Soviet system itself. They often originated from among the ranks of poor peasants and workers. The Stalinist terror, enforced collectivization and deportations, which were responsible for the deaths or removal of so many people, offered a possibility of social ascent to millions of others – and education was a central channel of this ascent. It was offered almost cost-free to talented and industrious young people.

The condemnation of the principle of egalitarianism which had dominated the First Five Year Plan was a result of the pressure exercised by these young and industrious peasants and workers and the new specialists. The ideal of equal pay was given up. With the help of various systems and after many experimentations the system started to reward industriousness, talents and skills that were thought to be useful in building the socialist society. Economic stimuli were taken into account. Income differentials increased greatly. (The Stakhanovite movement was an expression of these emerging trends.) As a result, a new Soviet middle class was being born, 'non-party Bolsheviks', educated professionals, Stakhanovite workers, artists, scientists, etc., who did not belong to the party hierarchy as the old political elite did but who could still earn and live well. According to Sheila Fitzpatrick (1979: 252–4) who has studied the relation between education and social mobility in the Soviet Union, the upwardly mobile parts of the population wanted a well-ordered society with stability, traditional channels of mobility and easily recognizable symbols of success and achievement as well as rewards in the form of traditional goods which could be consumed and displayed. Once again a gentleman was allowed to look like a gentleman!

This new way of life was characterized by a special cultural consciousness, 'kulturnost' (see Boym 1994 and Volkov forthcoming, 1997). It was good to display and make use of one's prosperity – otherwise material stimuli would have been of no use – but it would have been indecent to 'show off', which was proof of not being sufficiently cultured. A large part of all rewards were still being paid *in natura* and not in cash: holiday trips, summer cottages, private homes or houses, etc. But the new middle class also appreciated cosiness and a homely atmosphere, which it could create by itself. This atmosphere was characterized in a condensed form in a now famous citation from a popular novel according to which 'tea was served under an orange lampshade in red, polka-dotted cups. In this small, gay and bright paradise, everybody was pleased with life and discussed how good it was that work in the club was becoming well organized . . .' (cited in Dunham 1976: 43).

As Stites (1992: 65) argued, these newcomers appreciated privileges. They were expected to develop decent manners and good taste, to act in a cultured way. The new elite had its own tailors and barbers and it liked to put its status symbols on display (such as Parker pens and imported cigarettes) in order to show its social status and prestige. Those who had been promoted from among the working class were encouraged to wear a black suit and carry a briefcase: 'the newcomers were invested with privilege and expected to develop respectable habits and tastes. . . . They thirsted for old high culture as a badge of distinction; for entertainment they enjoyed sentimentalism, fun, uplift, and an affirmation of their values' (Stites 1992: 65).

According to this interpretation, Stalin bought the loyalty of the new middle class with 'trinkets' – as taught earlier by Adam Smith – but also with real privileges and by allowing for widening status differences. This new middle class had been produced and demanded by the structural changes taking place in the society. It adopted light classical arts as its status symbol, together with an eclectic collection of symbols of middle-class normality, such as a happy and harmonious family life, and invested in the future of its children and their education. The personal – even the most personal, the happiness of a man and woman – was no longer in contradiction with the happiness of the state (cf. in particular the sentimental popular wartime songs, 'Dark is the Night', 'In the Dugout', etc.).

In her study based on the analyses of popular literature of Stalin's times, Vera Dunham (1976) has shown how the possession and acquisition of goods and services was a pertinent moral problem that was discussed time and time again in these books. Dunham wondered why many authors who quite obviously adopted a positive attitude to these new values of life also showed a clear distaste for material possessions and condemned Soviet citizens who were all too eager to possess such material goods. As Dunham claimed, the theme seemed to be a particularly acute and perplexing one among contemporaries. Most literary examples presented and quoted by Dunham could, however, be interpreted to demonstrate that any luxury that was not deserved was to be morally condemned, as a result of corruption alone. On the other hand, all such luxury possessions which had been rightfully earned by one's own labour, talent or effort, were well deserved. (Thus, for instance, the use of the director's office car by his wife for shopping trips was to be condemned. Even more morally indefensible was the behaviour of the smooth-tongued and well-mannered student who seduced an innocent young female colleague, and stole the manuscript of the doctoral thesis of an older, more experienced and industrious colleague in order to get a promotion – the plot of a novel by young Yury Trifonov from the year 1951). The corrupting influence of unearned and undeserved luxury was a permanent theme in Soviet art and media in the years after the war.

The morals of the new Soviet middle class could thus be summarized as follows: inequality, the aspirations of higher income and better material living standards, and a better life, are legitimate insofar as they are righteously earned by one's own labour and/or talents. The last mentioned reservation is important in particular because the 1930s, and the whole period of Stalin's regime, generously rewarded artists and scientists. (The winners of the Stalin Prize were handed, in the eyes of their contemporaries, enormous sums of roubles. The Jewish-Ukrainian leader of a Moscow jazz band, Tsfasman, was rumoured to have been one of the richest men in the pre-war Soviet Union.)

## Democratic luxury and the pleasures of the few

As has already been pointed out by Vera Dunham, the problems of decorating and furnishing a home were hardly the problems with which most Soviet people were struggling daily in the 1950s. Such luxuries clearly were out of the reach of ordinary people living in *kommunalkas* or in country shacks without any modern conveniences at all. They were only ideals, or the dream worlds of popular literature. But on the other hand, it is obvious that many more prudent objects of 'the good life' were already within the reach of vast sectors of the population. Happiness did not only consist in collective feasts and celebrations, in which any poor but respectable Soviet citizen could in principle take part and enjoy, for instance, a glass of foaming beer with *Wurst* before returning to his or her communal kitchen, full of the smell of Sauerkraut. A lot of beautiful, fine, but inexpensive, artefacts were available to ordinary customers.

It is worth questioning whether these consumer goods can be analysed as status symbols or as signs of belonging to the 'better classes' in the Soviet Union. The taste expressed in them certainly is petit bourgeois in the classical meaning of the word: conservative, safe and stable. This was a Biedermeier culture. But this taste did not imitate anything better than itself – or if it did, it only imitated imagined historical ideals or models. The word 'kulturnost' captures the inner meaning of this taste. These are people full of good cultural will. They want to distinguish themselves from the masses but do not dare to be too different from their neighbours or colleagues, too individualistic. The material culture of their 'good life' is therefore best characterized by the seemingly paradoxical concept, democratic luxury.

This democratic luxury consisted mainly of food and drink, table utensils and other modest domestic or personal decorations. In addition elements of a more collective nature were part of it too: restaurants with music and dancing, concerts, theatre and ballet performances, public festivals and feasts. These were all parts of the imagined 'high life of the past'. The only thing that was new was the art and entertainment produced by means of new technology: radio, cinema and gramophone.

Why did not the industry producing consumer goods supply the country in a similar way with, say, gloves, silk stockings, neckties, pocket watches, evening gowns and costumes, etc.? To some extent they had already been available in the late 1930s. There were attempts to re-establish more refined ways of dressing and behaviour. Ladies' and gentlemen's ateliers were opened in big cities to provide an alternative to the cheap, ugly, ready-made garments mass-produced by the clothes industry. Beautiful furniture and other artefacts of domestic interior decoration belonged probably more to the post-war period of Soviet life. Pocket watches, the classical sign of a prosperous worker in Western Europe, were regarded with suspicion as signs of bourgeois mentality, but in 1947 the production of wristwatches (trade mark 'Pobeda') was started on a mass scale. (Watches had been a cherished war souvenir or loot among the Soviet troops returning from the Western front.)

There are some general features common to all these items of luxury. First, it was part of the very nature of this democratic luxury that it included only a limited number of items. In addition, they did not change much: novelties were rare. Second, they should be cheap enough and quotidian enough so that anyone could at least sometimes think of being able to buy them. In this sense, a new evening gown was still for most women a dream not within reach, but almost anyone could think of buying at least occasionally a bottle of perfume or a make-up kit, not to mention champagne or caviar or a box of chocolates. In a country in which there was an almost permanent deficit of the most basic foodstuffs, it was easy to understand the function of champagne and caviar as a 'promise of a better future already realized in the present', a socialist utopia come true. (On the other hand, one could just as well regard them as a cynical joke: 'Why don't they eat cake?' ) Third, these items were associated with festivals or parties: they were concrete proof of the fact that everyday life in the Soviet Union was a feast.

## Was there any Soviet design?

Democratic luxury was already *per definitionem* kitsch, cheap imitations of real or imagined finer models. In the autumn of 1954, the year following the death of Stalin, when the whole culture and philosophy was under scrutiny in the Soviet Union, an interesting article about style and design – or the total lack of them in the Soviet Union – appeared in the cultural journal, *Novy Mir*. The author, N. Zhukov (1954), used his keen eyed judgment of taste on the whole of Soviet material culture: furniture as well as women's wear, the toys and cakes sold at the famous children's department store, Detsky mir, as well as the new shop windows and neon signs of Moscow. The author referred to the authority of the philosopher Alexandrov, who for some time acted as the minister of culture and who recently had emphasized that everything that surrounded people in their daily lives was an essential part of their culture and had a decisive influence on their taste. According to Zhukov

> we, the men living during the age of the building of a Communist society, are faced with the task of elaborating a new style of material culture which would better answer the demands of the masses or population and express better the character of our great times.
>
> (Zhukov 1954: 159)

The author implied that no aesthetics were adequate to the building of communism as far as consumer goods were concerned – moreover, no one seemed to care. Zhukov compared in an ironic tone the industrial aesthetics of cars and railways with the anachronistic aesthetic of the goods sold in the shops in Moscow: sofas with pompoms, marital beds with flower and fruit decorations, imitations of the mirrors and decorations of the Restaurant Savoy, a fashionable restaurant during the old regime (ibid.: 165). As a model for new and better designs Zhukov – not surprisingly – offered both the new streamlined industrial aesthetics and folk decorative art inspired by Russian fairy tales.

Henri Lefebvre, who in the preface to the second edition of his *Critique of Everyday Life* (published in 1958) referred – without mentioning the name of the author – to Zhukov's article, could claim that

> the Soviets are thus discovering problems which we, who live in a capitalist country, have been aware of for a long time (which does not mean that we have solved them). As far as the style of everyday life is concerned, the Soviets have not progressed far beyond 1900. They are discovering *social needs* which are already known and which have already been explored (which is not the same thing as saying that they have been satisfied or fulfilled). They have attained petty-bourgeois mediocrity as though that were progress. How easily and quickly will they leave it behind? Today the latest stop is the 'industrial aesthetic', an old chestnut

which is liable to involve them in more than one lapse of taste . . .

(Lefebvre 1991: 45)

Today we can only try to guess what this new socialist design and taste longed for both by Zhukov and Lefebvre could have been – hardly the streamlined industrial design of machine aesthetics, which did not satisfy Lefebvre who already knew the dead end this style had led to. It remains a simple fact that neither in the Soviet Union nor in the other countries of the socialist bloc was much attention ever paid to the design of consumer goods, not even in countries like East Germany and Czechoslovakia, which within the mutual socialist division of labour were more specialized in producing consumer goods and which were held up by Zhukov as ideal models for future Soviet design. The Czech art historian, Jan Michl, could still write in 1989 that 'moderately said, socialist countries are not well known for the quality of their producer goods. Extremely seldom have these products reached the highest standards on the international market' (1989: 69). The explanation for this lack of style and design given by Michl is not very surprising: there is no economic competition nor any freedom of enterprise in socialism. More interesting are his other observations concerning the fact that it is not – or at least was not during the period dominated by ideology – regarded as decent to emphasize and show off one's own social position if it violated the principles of egalitarianism which were widely shared in the society.

## The socialist way of life: decency and small delights

If the above thesis concerning the increasing importance of the educated middle class in the Soviet Union from the late 1930s to the early 1950s is true – that it was inclined to distinguish itself from other people, thought to be more 'common', and display its own prosperity with status symbols – then one would imagine that there would have emerged a more acute social demand for a new 'design industry of taste', at least since the 1950s. It is thus obvious that one should have some reservations concerning this thesis and its general importance in the development of material culture. The product differentiation in socialism was not only restricted by the inflexibility of the system of production or by the fact that there was a guaranteed market for most products under the conditions of relative scarcity created by low prices. The development of the Soviet culture of

65

commodities was also – and probably to an even greater extent – restricted by the very rigid system of social distinctions with its inherently imposed self-limitations. Distinctions were not totally forbidden by common morality, but only distinctions that did not violate respectable and cultured manners were allowed. The resulting modest demand for the signs of distinction was satisfied by the supply of goods characterized as democratic luxury and by the consumption of cultural goods. The system promoted mediocrity and decency under the banner of 'kulturnost', which could almost be translated as conformism, more than cultural dynamism, innovation and differences. A good Soviet citizen did not show off or experiment with life. He or she preferred to live in conformity with the general standards of the society – just like all the other good comrades.

With only slight exaggeration one could claim that in the Soviet Union there existed just one single class, a huge middle class, consisting both of well-to-do workers and educated specialists, the so-called intelligentsia. It included all the people who had adopted a rather homogeneous conception and ideal of what was a good life, with its limited luxuries. All the rest of the population were without a culture: criminals, drunks, wasters, gypsies, bohemians, etc., a single mass of the lumpenproletariat. Even though it was increasingly possible to aspire to a good private life, people did not ask for too much – not for much more than their comrades had. Thus the good life of a Soviet citizen was stable and conformist. In many respects it conformed to the stoic ideals of humanistic education predominant in Europe since the Renaissance. Everyday life usually held few great surprises, and was from time to time – quite often, in fact – enlivened by small delights and indulgences such as visiting the ballet or a concert of popular music with an occasional glass of champagne and a caviar sandwich enjoyed during the interval. Everything else, anything more demanding, was apt to corrupt a man.

Of course there were those who were different, who had a car and a summer villa and the right to travel abroad, but in the 1960s and 1970s these were still exceptional people, artists, scientists, high civil servants or party bureaucrats, kosmonauts, etc.

The above interpretation was based on the role of the caviar sandwich and other popular luxuries in the Soviet culture. According to this interpretation, Stalin's 'Great Retreat' or the 'Big Deal' did not yet mark the end of socialism but rather the beginning and the development of a particular lifestyle and taste which was, indeed, adequate to socialism. An original conception of socialist 'good life' was being born. It is possible that the contradictions inherent in such a regulated and planned lifestyle, which was almost identical to the rigid lifestyle of the old estates, in turn led to the gradually deepening crises of commodity culture which since the 1970s had helped to weaken the authority of the Soviet leadership.

## Consumers and the end of socialism

A new period of Soviet middle-class culture began in the 1960s when the new aspirations and standards adopted from the Western capitalist world began their slow but victorious procession through Soviet society. These aspirations were no longer derived from an imagined past, from the history of 'high society', as those of the 1930s and the 1950s were, with private chauffeurs and bespoke tailors, champagne and caviar. A private flat, however small, with modern conveniences and set in a new suburb, became the central symbol of this new 'luxury'. Refrigerators, television sets and even private cars (without a chauffeur) were gradually coming within the reach of ordinary citizens. After the 1960s the development of the commodity culture in the Soviet Union followed well-known paths. Western habits of consumption, in a strictly regulated manner, gradually penetrated the everyday life of Soviet citizens. The only classical European luxury, which gradually became popular during the 1960s, was coffee, most often Turkish-style coffee – although American instant coffee has lately taken its place.

The old conception of luxury survived right up to the present day, alongside the new one. For instance, the kiosks of Russia now all have an abundant variety of liquor and wine, of chocolates and cigarettes, of cosmetics and cheap decorations; new imported brands that still to some extent enjoy the 'aura' of rare Western imports have largely been substituted for the old Soviet brands, but the assortment has otherwise remained more or less intact.

In a recent article 'Communism: a post mortem' (1990–1) Zygmunt Bauman suggested that the main reason for the collapse of the East European socialist states was the incompatibility of socialism with a modern consumer society. In Bauman's opinion, socialism was relatively competitive in mobilizing national resources in the service of industrialization and in organizing and planning economic growth. But it faced a serious and insurmountable problem as soon as it had to answer the increasing demands of the population. In other words, socialism was still capable of satisfying people's basic needs relatively effectively, but it was unable to cope with the rapidly increasing diversity of demand. Along with Agnes Heller (1976), one could say that socialism led to the establishment of a dictatorship over needs. One could probably even claim that socialism was functional as long as the logic of needs in general was concerned. It could, in principle, satisfy such demands, which were universal and common to all. Once it was faced with the, in principle, insatiable and individual demands of a modern consumer (the self-illusory hedonist, cf. Campbell 1987) it was doomed to failure.

It was central to Bauman's argument that in socialism the state took full responsibility for the gratification of the consumer. Any disappointment experienced by any consumer could be interpreted as resulting from the inability or negligence of the government and the state to run the economy properly (see also Pastuhov 1991). Once consumers' demands and wants multiplied and diversified in earnest, the government could not, even in principle, satisfy them any more. A socialist society of mass consumption is a *contradictio in adjecto*. The reasons for its failure were not technical ones, neither did they result from the inability or corruption of its politicians and leaders. A planned economy can only follow the logic of needs, not that of desires. Only capitalism, which leaves it to the private initiative of the individual, can live with the individuality of demands. As a consequence, a socialist society is unstable and very politicized, whereas in the West the state cannot usually be blamed for disappointments experienced by the consumer. Consequently, the bourgeois political order is very stable (see Bauman 1990–1: 268). In this sense, the emergence of socialist states did not end the era of revolutions. Rather, this era was inaugurated by their emergence.

As has also been discussed above, a socialist society shared many features related to consumption which made it particularly resistant to change and prevented any possible disappointments being directed towards state power. As students of the economy of scarcity have pointed out (see Kornai 1982), during scarcity the most important problem for the consumer is how to get information about the existence and the whereabouts of a commodity (cf. Srubar 1991). Anyone who knows how to get hold of a particular good is in possession of valuable 'social capital'. Under such conditions, money is a necessary but not a sufficient condition for getting hold of goods.

Under such conditions, a shadow economy emerges out of necessity, consisting of various, unofficial and more or less complicated networks for distributing provisions. A great proportion of all products simply 'disappear' into these networks and are distributed anew through unofficial channels. Such networks may be based on family or friendship networks, but their basic activities are the mutual obligations created by gifts and services.

The workings of such networks can in many respects be compared with the primitive institution of gift. They tie their members into a network of mutual obligations and loyalty. As Srubar has pointed out, their morality is a morality of egalitarianism characterized by resentment. It opposes any change which promotes rewards based on individual achievements. It also effectively prevents the development of a new, strong individual identity. In Srubar's opinion, the social identity of a socialist individual was strongly tied to its own 'clan' or 'family'. A clear and strong distinction was therefore made between 'us' and 'others' (see also Vinnikov 1994: 1229–30).

Srubar's interpretation of the development of a specific socialist individuality would thus give further support to the above thesis about the basic decency and conformism of the Soviet consumer expressed in the material culture as the dominance of democratic luxury. The demands for change caused by the emergence of modern consumers in socialism, as postulated by Bauman, are thus open to serious doubt. Since most citizens believed that the prosperity and higher standards of living of other groups could only have been gained through corruption and criminal deeds – and other people's wealth was usually thought to be achieved by wrongdoing – the dissatisfaction of consumers is by no means directed first towards state power but can just as easily be channelled into hatred and bitterness against alien privileged groups. This conclusion is supported by the fact that the fight against corruption was one of the most permanent and pertinent features of the Soviet political system.

On the other hand, as the above preliminary analysis of the development of the material culture since Stalin's times has, I hope, shown, even in the socialist world there gradually emerged elements of a new middle-class culture with its more individual patterns of consumption which at least to some extent allowed and even promoted possessive individualism and private acquisitions. The main historical turning points in this transition were the new cultural politics adopted by Stalin in 1934, the new housing policy of the 1960s and the simultaneous, very slow and unsteady turn towards producing some basic durables which were generally regarded as symbols of the Western way of life (private cars in particular). Thus, probably since the 1960s, one could speak of a very slow erosion of the socialist collectivist culture in the Soviet Union. However, even today one can easily observe many remnants of the old democratic luxury living in peace side by side with the new and more individualistic consumption patterns.

# FASHION AND PLENTY IN THE POST-INDUSTRIAL SOCIETY

## Consumer society as an abundant society

Paradoxically, since the latter part of the last century, there has been a strong trend of cultural criticism in Western society that has blamed modern society for the very thing which, according to Bauman (1990–1), actually proved victorious. According to these critics, modern commercial society continuously encourages, or even forces, people to exceed or overstep their needs. It creates 'artificial' or unnecessary needs, and – to use an old expression – the demand for luxury. People are persuaded to consume more than they really need, and this is a cause of much of – if not all – the misery in modern society. The critics seemed to fear that once the limits set by the 'natural' or real (as opposed to artificial) needs (traditionally set by the sumptuary laws or standards of the estate to which they belonged) are by-passed, there are no limits at all to people's demands. In other words, modern commercial society is not to be blamed because it leaves the basic needs of the greatest number unsatisfied and permits them to live in misery, as the early socialists believed; but rather should be blamed for its tendency to make them continuously exceed their needs. As has already been shown, at the turn of the century this theme can be found in various disciplines among the pioneer critics of the consumer society: in early modern nutrition science in its efforts to understand the problems both of overeating and malnutrition, and related health problems; in the various democratic arts reform programmes – *art social* or *art industriel* – propagating a reform of industrial design which – at least in its more extreme forms – would have eliminated all 'useless' decorations not functional to the satisfaction of needs (i.e. democratic needs, common to all). At the same time, social reformers understood many social problems to emerge from the fact that people were tempted by false and artificial needs which they could not satisfy – and some of which could never be satisfied. If only people would learn to regulate and recognize their genuine needs they would not only be able to live a more satisfying life, but – as the early utopian socialists thought – to get rid of money, capital and private property, and the inequality which accompanied these social evils.[5]

Implicitly at least, Zygmunt Bauman seemed to suppose that sometime during the last 70 years in Europe a major change or even a rupture in the functioning of modern commercial society has taken place. In early industrial society consumption was still predominantly oriented to needs, whereas now there are no limits to the demands and wishes of a consumer. One could also say that industrial society has been transformed into post-industrial or mass consumption society (Bauman even speaks of a post-modern society). These changes have somehow even influenced the development of socialist societies, too. And the main characteristic of this new type of society would seem to be that consumer demands have become much more difficult to predict and, in principle, impossible to satisfy. In the analyses of the early critics of consumer society, a similar break was usually associated with the end of scarcity (hunger and disease) and it was thought to have taken place much earlier in Europe. But on the other hand, the demands of this early modern consumer were, even though already in a state of continuous growth, still somehow thought to be limited or regulated by the consumption pattern set by the example of the upper social strata which it was supposed to imitate. In this sense there was a limit – even though this limit was never totally rigid.

In the theories of post-industrial society of the 1960s and 1970s (and in their radical critiques) consumption does not seem to have played a very important role. Post-industrial societies were certainly supposed to be societies beyond scarcity – or affluent societies. Most people would enjoy high living standards and would have more free time – to use, among other things, for consumption. The expected changes were more of a quantitative character: higher real income, higher living standards, more free time. In his comprehensive study of the theories of post-industrial societies, *Prophecy and Progress*, Krishan Kumar (1983: 195) has pointed out that the general idea of an economy beyond scarcity was shared both by the radical critics of the consumer society like Herbert Marcuse and Christopher Lasch, its technocratic propagators like Herman Kahn and Anthony Wiener and the ecologically-oriented anarchists like Murray Bookchin. They all agreed that the progress of productivity had created a historically unique situation, an age of abundance and plenty. For the first time in the history of humanity, the leisure and culture of a small minority was not dependent on the toil and misery of the great majority. The forecast presented by Keynes in the 1930s had thus become a reality.

71

What these authors disagreed about were the possible cultural and social consequences of this state of affairs.

As far as the character of modern consumption was concerned, these visions were rather vague and not at all concrete.[6] The development of consumption was mainly described in quantitative terms. In 1987 Herman Kahn and Anthony J. Wiener, for instance, in their famous *The Year 2000* (1967: 149–60) classified societies according to the level of their GNP per capita. In their opinion industrial societies would be followed by mass consumption or advanced industrial societies, which in their turn would be superseded by post-industrial ones. In 1965 only Western Europe and the USA – and perhaps Japan – had reached the mass-consumption stage, but by the year 2000 Kahn expected twelve nations to have reached the 'visibly post-industrial stage', and nine others would be knocking at the door. To Kahn, post-industrialism held a promise of more leisure for all and an economy of abundance which could sustain everyone in comfort and economic security whether or not they engage in what is commonly recognized as work.

If one reads these modern utopias it becomes clear that it was widely presumed that somehow the role of consumption is bound to become more important in the future – at least in quantitative terms – and at the same time people need no longer be bothered with the economic problems of their daily life. In these visions, the role of consumption in future society remained, however, rather vague – in fact, one could almost claim that consumption had been a more important target for the critics of modernization (ever since Veblen, Vance Packard and Herbert Marcuse) than for its protagonists. Somehow it did not pose any problem for these utopias until more recently. To take a more recent example: according to Eva Etzioni-Halevy's *Social Change* (1981), before modernization people lived close to subsistence level. Since then real wages have risen remarkably and almost continuously. Consequently, the standards of living and of consumption have been rising drastically. There are other changes in the consumption patterns, too. More specifically, consumer durables have gained in importance: 'There was a marked proportional increase in expenditure on consumer durables stretching from stoves to iceboxes and sewing machines' (Etzioni-Halevy 1981: 105). (One could easily continue the list: cars, video recorders, CD-players, etc. – J. G.) As a general conclusion, Etzioni-Halevy stated that 'western societies have indeed become affluent' (ibid.).

It was Daniel Bell, one of the initiators of the whole discussion about post-industrial societies, who more sharply than most others formulated the basic dilemma of an affluent or mass-consumption society. According to Bell, we can speak of a society of abundance only in a very limited sense: the problems of hunger and disease need no longer exist. But as Bell also argued, only basic needs are satiable and, consequently, in this sense only 'the possibility of abundance is real'. No imaginable economic system or society can ever solve the problem of scarcity: our resources will always be scarce relative to our desires or wants. As Bell formulated it in economic terms: 'Scarcity is a measure of relative differences of preferences at relative costs' (Bell 1974: 466). To Bell the economist, abundance essentially means not that goods are more plentiful in physical terms, but that they are cheaper. In other words: abundance is always a relative state of affairs.[7]

Bell's *The Coming of Post-industrial Society* also included some amusing considerations about the possible scarcity of free time in the future due to increasing consumption. A man who owns, for instance, a complete set of golf clubs, a tennis racket, a sailing yacht and a summer cottage has to hurry during his summer vacation in order to have time to make use of or consume all these articles and goods, in particular if their proper use demands, as is often the case, training or schooling. Bell, however, does not further develop this last-mentioned fact, which is particularly important in Bourdieu's analyses of lifestyles and 'habitus'.

It seems to be rather difficult to find any interesting comments concerning a possible change or rupture in the nature of consumption in modern society in the theories of modernization discussed above. This is partly predetermined by the nature of their argumentation: their predictions often are based on quantitative extrapolations of present tendencies. We live in an age of plenty, instead of want, or there is a change from material production to the supply of services. These studies do not, thus, have much to offer to a sociological understanding of modern consumption. Yet, at least intuitively, many commentators seem to think that even some kind of a 'qualitative' change has taken place in the nature and role of consumption in the advanced industrial societies since the Second World War or during the last few decades – a change which Zygmunt Bauman seemed to take for granted in his analysis of the collapse of socialism.

# 4

# TASTE AND FASHION

## FASHION AS A SELF-DYNAMIC SOCIAL PROCESS

### The modern fashion pattern

Many analyses of modern society share the idea that some crucial change has taken place in the action orientation of the modern consumer. A new hedonistic consumer has come into being, whose demands are no longer regulated by an 'economy of needs' but by an 'economy of desire and dreams', or the longing for something new and unexperienced. In characterizing the new middle class as the main carrier of the hedonistic ethos of consumption, Bourdieu (1984: 365–72) emphasized that the new consumer wants everything at once and without having to sacrifice anything. The ethics is an 'ethics of fun'. The emergence of this new ethos of consumerism has often, especially in the American tradition, been thought to have resulted from transformations in the emotional make-up of the family (e.g. absent fathers), the cultural importance of youth, or the growing importance of free time and the subsequent erosion of the work ethic.[1]

Usually, there is no mention of fashion in the theories and utopias of post-industrial society. It seems to have been too ephemeral and frivolous a social phenomenon to have been taken seriously in such rational analyses of social change. However, fashion does offer a natural explanation for the fact already problematized in economic terms by Daniel Bell: the crucial characteristic of the abundant or affluent societies cannot be comprehended simply through the contrast between plenty and want. The wants of modern human beings *are* different, but what is even more important, the consumer in the affluent society is no more satisfied than were the suffering poor of earlier times.

As is well known, the fashion mechanism was to Georg Simmel, as well as to the leading literary prophet of modernity, Charles Baudelaire, an important social phenomenon as far as the experience of modernity was concerned. Through it we can comprehend the contingent and ephemeral nature of modernity. To Simmel (1981), fashion was a mechanism of social distinction and identification and offered a provisional shelter from the threatened levelling influence of money. In a modern society with a money economy it helped the individual to cope, at least tentatively, with the tension which emerged between principles, and demands of equality and difference, or between the principles of positive or negative freedom (in other words, between self-realization and independence).

As Quentin Bell wrote in his classical treatise on fashion, *On Human Finery* (1992: 63), 'it is we in the west who are peculiar; fashion is probably our invention. At all events we and we alone have given it that dizzy speed which we now take for granted.' It is generally thought that the modern fashion mechanism started in the West sometime during the Renaissance or early modern period; it was also an essential companion to the process of individualization of the Western world which started with court society. As Lipovetsky formulated it:

> it has been a vector of narcissistic individualization, an instrument for enlarging the aesthetic cult of the self, even at the heart of an aristocratic age. The first major mechanism for the consistent social production of personality on display, fashion has aestheticized and individualized human vanity; it has succeeded in turning the superficial into an instrument of salvation, a goal of existence.
>
> (Lipovetsky 1994: 29)

In the clothing industry, in which the fashion mechanism was institutionalized earlier, it became a regular pattern, sometime during the early part of the nineteenth century, to expect biennial changes. The hundred-year reign of Paris-based haute couture, during which the French fashion houses played a leading role, also generally acted as the ideal model for the classical sociological or philosophical analyses of fashion. The

> mechanism combining mimesis and individualism occurs over and over at various levels, in all the spheres where fashion operates; still, it is manifested nowhere more strikingly than in

75

personal appearance, because dress, hairstyles, and makeup are the most obvious signs of self-affirmation.

(Lipovetsky 1994: 33)

Jennifer Craik has recently criticized the conception common in fashion studies according to which fashion is a peculiarly Western and modern phenomenon:

> Symptomatically, the term fashion is rarely used in reference to non-western cultures. The two are defined in opposition to each other: western dress is fashion because it changes regularly, is superficial and mundane, and projects individual identity, non-western dress is costume because it is unchanging, encodes deep meanings, and projects group identity and membership.
>
> (Craik 1994: 18)

In Craik's opinion one can recognize fashion-like changes in outer appearance in various cultures and ages – whenever and wherever people express their individuality in decoration and an openness to change. The main difference between our modern age and traditional cultures would thus not be the very existence of fashion but rather the rapidity and regularity of these transformations. The difference would thus be more of a quantitative than qualitative nature. Following Lipovetsky's (1994: 35) suggestion one could, however, claim that, in earlier times and other cultures – despite the fact that one certainly can identify changes and even novelties in dress and decorum which deviate from the standard costume and which resemble our fashion mechanism – these changes are deviations from a pattern and do not form a pattern of their own as is the case with the modern Western fashion pattern: 'An individual might vary and combine figures, but only within the bounds of an intangible repertory fixed by tradition: there were plays of combination and permutation, but there was no formal innovation' (Lipovetsky 1994: 35).

According to Renate Mayntz and Birgitta Nedelmann (1987) such a fully-fledged mechanism of fashion is a typical – and as such a particularly good – example of self-dynamic social processes ('*eigendynamische soziale Prozesse*'). It is typical of such processes that they are kept in motion without any causes that are created or originated outside the system itself. From the point of view of the social actors involved in such processes the motivations which keep them going are continuously being born and strengthened within the very same process. It is further typical of processes like these that it is difficult for

76

any individual or social institution to regulate or to foresee their outcome in advance because it is part of their very nature that they are realized despite, and often against the will of, the individual actors involved in them – as if they were following some hidden plan unknown to the individuals. In this sense they resemble the economic market for which Adam Smith's 'invisible hand' and Immanuel Kant's '*Naturabsicht*' were metaphorical expressions. Mandeville was the first to believe that private vices could, in fact, be public virtues. To individual actors such processes appear socially coercive while, paradoxically, also giving them a free hand to act or choose as they want.

As Mayntz and Nedelmann claimed, fashion, as recognized and analysed by Georg Simmel, is a typical self-dynamic (or autopoietic, cf. Luhmann) process. In Simmel's opinion, there is a question of both social identification and distinction in fashion. The activity of individuals is motivated by two opposing social forces or goals. On the one hand, they are willing to be integrated into a social group by imitating others; on the other, they are willing to distinguish themselves from others and emphasize their own individuality and uniqueness by adopting something new, not shared by others. As Mayntz and Nedelmann (1987: 654) understood it, the resulting process is self-dynamic because these opposite stages of making a distinction and emulating others automatically follow each other, and in so doing give rise to one another. A novelty adopted by everyone is no more a novelty and has to be supplanted by another 'real' novelty. Thus, innovation and imitation constantly and eternally follow one another, always giving rise to a new cycle of imitation and innovation. The mechanism of fashion is like a merry-go-round or, rather, a *perpetuum mobile*.

The merry-go-round of fashion which Mayntz and Nedelmann described (developing Simmel's ideas) does not, in fact, realize all the criteria of a self-dynamic process. Even though the actors' motives emerge from the process – in the sense that imitation always gives rise to a new phase of distinction and the subsequent stylistic innovation – the basic social motivations behind imitation and distinction cannot be explained by this process alone. According to Simmel, they seemed to be something which belonged to the very sociability of human nature.

## The pleasures of novelty

The fashion pattern satisfies the demand for novelty. As Immanuel Kant (1980: 572) knew, it is the demand for novelty, in the sense of experiencing something new, which is essential to fashion. As Appadurai (1986: 22) pointed out, fashion 'suggests high velocity, rapid turnover, the illusion of total access and high convertibility'. The 'novelty mania' (cf. Barthes 1983: 300) is a desire which can never be fully satisfied: 'The desiring model constitutes a state of enjoyable discomfort, and wanting rather than having is the main focus of pleasure seeking' (Campbell 1987: 86). The hedonism of the modern consumer is inherently self-illusory because total fulfilment can never be achieved (cf. also Falk 1994: 129–45).

In fashion, the demand for novelty is satisfied over and over again, despite – or because of – the fact that fashion often only repeats and varies old styles and models. There cannot be any progress in fashion. As economic historians have shown, the demand for novelty was characteristic of the markets for mass consumption goods from the very beginning. All the commodities were 'new' and they were advertised as such. As McKendrick et al. (1982: 332) have pointed out, during the eighteenth century at the latest, 'improvements', 'produced according to the latest method' and 'latest fashion', became guarantees of a good product and were widely used in advertising and marketing. During the eighteenth century, the demand for novelty assumed almost manic features. Everything, even the products of nature, had to be new. The potential of nature and man to produce endless variations was not doubted for a moment: florists offered new plants and flower seeds. Even dogs and horses had to be new. McKendrick et al. even referred to the fact, well known from other sources of the history of ideas, that contemporaries shared the common consciousness of belonging to a new age. As the authors said, 'no consumer society could exist without the belief in modernity' (McKendrick et al. 1982: 334).

It is thus quite feasible to claim, as Campbell did, that the new hedonist was born during the eighteenth century, at the latest. Even Campbell identified the new consumer with the middle classes, which formed the main market for the new mass products in England. It is, however, not possible to try to reduce the determinants of these new classes to any well-defined social positions. Members of the middle classes were understood to be people – certainly with a generous income – who adopted the new lifestyle or, in other words, who were modern people.

One could claim tentatively that the main characteristic of a modern consumer society is that in it the extension and social influence of fashion has greatly increased. In such a society new collective tastes are being born – and are dying – at an increasing tempo. 'Good taste' is always being followed by another 'good taste' creating order in an increasingly individualized and aestheticized (cf. Schulze 1992) modern society. Mayntz and Nedelmann shared Simmel's opinion that it is the novelty in fashion which enchants. The more rapid the transformation of fashion the more enchanting and seducing it becomes. However, together with other similar self-dynamic processes fashion has a tendency to become routinized and formalized. As such it can also lose the charm it exercises over consumers. Once it has been institutionalized, fashion becomes, at least partly, independent of an individual's will of distinction and imitation and, in general, of his or her subjective motivations. Such a fashion resembles a formal scheme. Originally fashion was not consciously created; it was born as a side-product of purposive social action which had totally different aims of its own. The actors can, however, gradually learn to recognize and make use of this 'objective' formal mechanism. In such a case, fashion is created intentionally by designers and producers. Under the influence of a fashion industry, fashion can be experienced and lived as a mechanism of social coercion. The desire for change can become a duty.

The main purpose of Campbell's study, *The Romantic Ethic and the Spirit of Modern Consumerism* (1987), was to find the intellectual origins of the spirit of modern consumerism. He put forward the provocative thesis that it emerged from the same source as Max Weber's spirit of capitalism, from the inner tensions of the Protestant ethic of the seventeenth century. Following Campbell's argumentation, one could thus claim that the modern hedonist was not born during the period of late capitalism but had already played an important role in the genesis of this modern economic system. Just as capitalism could not have emerged without the ascetic spirit analysed by Weber, it cannot be conceived of without the spirit of modern hedonism. Werner Sombart was an early critic of Weber who paid attention to this fact (see Sombart 1986 [1913]). To paraphrase Weber, the early puritan did not just want to be a devoted professional, '*Berufsmensch*', he wanted also to be a self-illusory hedonist.

There are some interesting problems related to Campbell's thesis.

Even if his interpretation of the intellectual origins of the modern consumer was adequate, he did not analyse in detail the possible future destiny of this romantic ethic. In fact, the Weber parallel could even be extended to question whether the commodity market and fashion mechanism, once firmly established as a self-dynamic process, could completely do without this spirit. If this ethos was institutionalized in the market of mass consumption goods in the same way as the spirit of capitalism was thought by Weber to be institutionalized in the functional mechanism of the capitalist firm, would it not imply that it would be transformed into a purely mechanical principle? Fashion would become an objective mechanism alien to the individual and forcing him or her repeatedly and eternally to consume the latest thing – and the same article as all the others – irrespective of personal desire. Fashion could therefore increasingly get rid of all individual subjective motivations and aspirations. In this case, the whole analysis would end up in the rather common and trivial conception of manipulation which explains consumer behaviour in terms of – more or less automatic – responses to the demands and imperatives of a capitalist economy. Or is it possible that the hedonistic ethic still needs to be revitalized from time to time and emerge anew as the ethic of a 'new' middle class?

In Mayntz and Nedelmann's opinion, such a fully developed fashion mechanism can provoke a counter-reaction as is the case if, instead of a fashionable set of clothes, an ordinary outfit is chosen by the consumer. In other words, consumers can get tired of continuous change and 'eternal' novelties and resort to something which is known and safe. By doing so, they can feel 'at home' in their clothes and oppose the alien social forces which tie them to a mechanism of perpetual change. (See Mayntz and Nedelmann 1987: 654.)

In the above example concerning the possible reactions to fashion one should, however, distinguish between two different alternatives. First, one can understand Mayntz and Nedelmann to be arguing that consumers do not want the marketing and advertising agencies to force novelties on them by excessive persuasion and manipulation, thus depriving them of the personal joy of invention and the chance to express their own genuine choice. Such complaints of manipulation certainly are common enough in popular criticisms of advertisements. Second, it could be a reaction to another and theoretically more interesting phenomenon: one could imagine that the consumer simply gets tired of the eternal 'Sisyphus' labour of fashion. But this would presuppose that every fashion style returns eternally in more or less exactly the same form. Then the new would not, in fact, be new and would lose its power to enchant and seduce. Following Simmel's social psychological formulation one could express the same thing as follows: either there can be too many stimuli and they can change too often, or novelties are too few and predictable. In the first case irritation and withdrawal would follow as a natural consequence, in the second, only dullness would reign.

What is then the opposite of fashion, anti-fashion? According to Simmel as well as to Mayntz and Nedelmann it would be a uniform, a unified dress worn by all. In principle, it could just as well be a totally individual set of clothes worn by every single person alone. Those who love a uniform long for reason and order, those who prefer uniqueness are afraid of losing their individuality. The first case would be synonymous with total lack of individuality, the second would make everyone a completely separate personality, unconnected by any social ties at all. In the same way as Rousseau thought that a person should grow up in social isolation in order to be able to recognize his real needs and develop his sense of true self-love, the ignorance and avoidance of fashion would demand the restriction of all social interaction to its minimum.

As Arto Noro (1991:110–13) has pointed out, anti-fashion is not the only and not even the most convincing reaction to the modern fashion mechanism and to the over-excitement or the threat of repetition alternately associated with it. As retro-fashions have taught us (see also Matthiesen 1988) fashion is hardly ever repeated in totally the same way, but seldom is it presented as something absolutely new either. When it repeats the old, the old is never exactly the same and, in any case, it is presented in another and new context. By doing this retro-fashion can increase our sense of history and – in the best cases – make our relation to fashion and change more reflexive. The proper reaction to coercive and forced change is 'a combinatory self-styliza-tion' (Noro 1991: 112) or the free and creative combination of the various elements offered by contemporary fashion at any one time. Highly individual styles emerging from this process can thus be transformed into ideals or models of new fashions and targets for further stylization, as has been proved, for instance, by the contem-porary 'street fashion' which takes its designs from the modern 'dandies' of the street. Thus, fashion can never be petrified. It continuously gives birth and demands perpetual self-criticism and innovation.

Even though Mayntz and Nedelmann are cautious in their

evaluations they seem to think that such self-dynamic processes as fashion are due to become more common in the modern, functionally differentiated society, characterized as it is by many ambivalences concerning social goals and aims. Both on the basis of Simmel's visions and her own empirical studies about fashion, Ann-Mari Sellerberg (1994: 60) has listed six dualisms characteristic of modern fashion:

1 Fashion reduces social complexity and at the same time, due to its way of functioning, it generates complexity, e.g. more subtle distinctions.
2 Fashion contains very precise rules and regulations regarding what is 'in'. In its functioning, however, fashion is subversive of every convention and authorized rule.
3 On the one hand, fashion is indifferent to the material and practical. On the other hand, fashion feeds on and lives through the concrete.
4 Our attitude towards fashion today consists both of intense involvement and detachment.
5 Fashion involves responsibility as well as freedom from responsibility.
6 Fashion is both accessible and inaccessible.

In a preliminary manner, one could say that the very intensification of fashion, both its spread into new fields and the increase of its influence in old fields, is the most typical feature of a consumer society. Thus, a consumer society – or an abundant society – is a society of fashion and mass fashion in particular (cf. Horowitz 1975a). What separates us from the previous centuries is that the cycle of fashion has become more rapid; the new and functional is exhausted and transformed into old and useless in an increasing tempo. New styles follow one another, and these styles are formed without any earlier models or ideals. Such a society cannot actually recognize and has no answer to the problems of excessive or superfluous consumption, because there cannot possibly be any objective criteria which could determine what is really needed or what is superfluous. Furthermore, a consumer society conceptualized along such lines is, of necessity, always a society of scarcity, because its members can never be satisfied. Consequently, modern consumer-hedonists have a positive attitude towards fashion and its eternal supply of novelties; they are both willing and eager to approve and consume the 'newest' article in the numerous fields of commercial life.

# THE SOCIAL FUNCTION OF STYLE AND FASHION

## Immanuel Kant and Georg Simmel on fashion

Georg Simmel's idea of a formal sociology was, in many ways, influenced by his reading of Immanuel Kant's aesthetic writings, and *Critique of Judgment* in particular (see Frisby 1992 and Davis 1973). Less attention has been paid to the fact that many of Simmel's essays on various social phenomena can also be understood and read as extended commentaries on Kant's ideas or suggestions – often not forming any essential part of Kant's own thinking and mentioned only in passing. This, in particular, is the case with Simmel's famous essay(s) on fashion.

Immanuel Kant made a short comment on the significance of fashion in his writing on anthropology (Kant 1980 [1798]: 571–2), but obviously this social phenomenon was not considered to be worth any extensive treatment. Kant's ideas cannot be said to be very original either. Rather, he shared an attitude towards fashion common among learned men of his time (cf. Gadamer 1975: 34).

Kant discussed fashion in the context of taste. According to him, fashion has nothing to do with genuine judgments of taste ('*Geschmacksurteil*') but is a case of unreflected and 'blind' imitation. As such it is opposed to 'good taste'. It stems only from man's vanity and social competition in which people try to get the better of each other and improve their social standing. Still, it is interesting to note that Kant shared Simmel's opinion that it is far better to try to follow fashion than to try to avoid or totally neglect it – an effort as futile as it is impossible ('It is better to be a clown of fashion than to be a clown without fashion' – Kant 1980: 572). As Kant also knew, fashions are transitory – otherwise they would be transformed into traditions. Fashion regulates only things that could just as well be otherwise or, as Herbert Blumer put it, 'the pretended merit or value of the competing models cannot be demonstrated through open and decisive tests' (Blumer 1969: 286; see also Gadamer 1975: 34). It is, moreover, the principle of novelty which enlivens fashion and lends it its special charm (Kant 1980: 572).

There is, however, no hint in Kant's treatment of fashion to suggest that he would have thought the social significance of fashion to be even nearly as important as Simmel later thought it to be. To Simmel, fashion helped to overcome the distance between an individual and his society and it was a phenomenon of modernity par excellence (Simmel shared Baudelaire's idea about fashion as 'contingent, transitory and fugitive' (cf. Frisby 1985: 40–1)). It is, however, fruitful to read Simmel's essays on fashion as critical commentaries on Kant's *Critique of Judgment* or as ironic comments on his ideas about taste and beauty. Fashion is a living antinomy: it does not have to make up its mind whether to be or not to be, because it can both be and not be at the same time.[2]

As Colin Campbell (1987) has suggested there is an important affinity between fashion and taste. Fashion can be understood to be a *de facto* solution to the main – and theoretically unsolvable – problem inherent in the aesthetics of taste of the eighteenth century. Fashion offers a socially valid standard of taste which is only based on the individual preferences and choices of the members of the 'community of tastes'. In order to avoid misunderstandings it should be pointed out that fashion obviously does not share the ideal, and in a sense exemplary, character of 'good taste', but still can be said to be equally binding or obliging in relation to the individuals concerned. In the most general terms, it can be said to form a universal standard of taste which, however, allows for the singularity and subjectivity of individual tastes. There is strong evidence that Simmel was aware of this parallel, even though he did not formulate it in quite the same terms or quite as explicitly.

Simmel's analysis of social formations often aimed at showing how they all offer – at best – provisional societal solutions to a problem which, in his opinion, was obviously the main problem facing people in modern society. Sociology could thus make an invaluable direct contribution to the philosophy of life. In *The Metropolis and Mental life* (1950 [1903]: 423), the modern city offered an ideal arena for the two principal ways – which are always in opposition to each other – of allocating roles to individuals. According to the first principle, all men are equal and share a common substance of humanity, whereas the second principle dictates that every human being is unique and irreplaceable as such. Both principles are logically exclusive – but their opposition is overcome daily in modern society. In the same way, fashion is a societal formation always combining two opposite principles. It is a socially acceptable and secure way to distinguish oneself from others and, at the same time, it satisfies the individual's need for social adaptation and imitation:

> Fashion is the imitation of a given example and satisfies the demand for social adaptation; it leads the individual along the

road which all travel, it furnishes a general condition, which resolves the conduct of every individual into a mere example. At the same time it modifies to no lesser degree the need for differentiation, the tendency towards dissimilarity, the desire for change and contrast on the one hand by a constant change of contents . . .

(Simmel 1981 [1904]: 6–7)

In Simmel's opinion it was Immanuel Kant who, more clear-sightedly and more profoundly than any other before him, had in his *Critique of Judgment* formulated this great problem facing every modern individual. In this sense Simmel read Kant in the same spirit as Terry Eagleton today. But Simmel was not an ideology-critical thinker. To him Kant was not a bourgeois ideologist who tried to reconcile the unreconcilable: on the contrary, he had, in fact, posed a real and serious problem. Kant's aesthetics try to show how it is possible for the individual to be genuinely free and autonomous without degenerating into a state of isolation and lawlessness (Simmel 1905a: 168–9): 'In any case, it is one of the first and one of the most profound attempts of reconciliation in the aesthetic sphere between the indispensable individual subjectivity of the modern man and the equally necessary overindividual community.'

As Simmel tried to show in great detail, the modern fashion pattern constitutes a social formation which operates like an over-individual scheme through which an individual can express his loyalty to and strengthen his social ties with the 'norms of his time' without losing his 'inner freedom' (see Simmel 1986: 57). Expressed in the most general terms: 'Two social tendencies are essential to the establishment of fashion, namely, the need of union on the one hand and the need of isolation on the other' (Simmel 1981: 8).

## The antinomy of taste

As Howard Caygill has recently shown (1989), the two parallel traditions of thought (German *Polizeiwissenschaft* and British empiricist aesthetics) which Kant confronted in writing his *Critique of Judgment* and which, in a sense, he tried both to unite and to overcome in formulating his famous antinomy of taste, can be understood to be dealing with exactly the type of questions emerging from Simmel's reading of Kant. Aesthetics were not in any straightforward manner understood to be dealing with a political question. Still, the

85

opposition between individual autonomy and social order could not only be discussed but was obviously also thought to be felt and experienced in the most tangible form in the aesthetic sphere.

As argued earlier, the old saying '*De gustibus disputandum non est*' did not originally mean that every man had a taste of his own which was of no concern to others. On the contrary, matters of taste were thought to be self-evident and judgments of taste, at least in principle, generally shared by all. There could, thus, be no reason or ground to argue about them. A false judgment of taste was caused either by ignorance or error. According to this interpretation, judgments of taste concerning the beauty of objects were ultimately based on feelings of pleasure and displeasure: what felt good was both right and beautiful (see Hooker 1934 and Campbell 1987).

In these discussions, the physiological or gustatory sense of taste often acted as a model for the aesthetic judgment of taste. As Dr Armstrong wrote in 1702: 'As of beef and port, judge for yourself, and report of wit'. In particular, making judgments of taste, and distinguishing beauty from ugliness, was as self-evident and easy as telling salt from sugar. As Edmund Burke (1987) quite seriously claimed in his treatise concerning the beautiful and the sublime – probably the best-known work on aesthetics during the eighteenth century – once the possibility of error had been overruled, only a fool could fail to make the proper judgment.

The representatives of this tradition, for example Hume, Hutcheson and Addison, were by no means so naive as to think that people's choices and preferences actually tended to converge. On the contrary, even people of similar origin were seldom seen to agree on their judgments. Good taste was a *Bildungsbegriff*. It was something which, at least potentially, could be shared by all regardless of social origins, even though it had to be admitted that its proper exercise demanded practice and the presence of suitable examples to be followed. And practice obviously demanded time. Thus, only men of considerable wealth could be expected to show good taste in their daily manners.

Still, the revolutionary nature of the standard of 'good taste' should not be forgotten. For the first time it was now possible to think that all human beings had similar taste: the hunger of a king did not, in principle, differ from the hunger of a beggar.

There was, however, a problem inherent in the tradition, of which its representatives were only partly aware. It was explicitly formulated first by Kant: how could something which was exclusively based on the subjective feeling of pleasure (see Kant 1987: §31) be universally valid? The feeling of beauty requires that it be shared universally. In his *Critique of Judgment*, presenting his famous antinomy of taste, Kant said that there are two commonplaces: (1) everyone has his own taste and (2) there is no disputing about taste. The first amounts to saying that any judgment of taste is merely subjective, whereas the second claims that the basis determining such a judgment cannot be expressed in any determinate concepts. We can dispute about taste but not present reasons for or against it.

According to Kant's definition of (pure aesthetic) taste, it is the ability to judge or choose in a universally valid way ('*allgmeingültig zu wählen*') (Kant 1987: §20). But what kind of universal validity of judgments is it which shares only the universality of a single judgment ('*die Allgemeinheit eines einzelnen Urteils*') and cannot, consequently, be equal to any logical and conceptual universality, and for which there cannot possibly be any *a priori* grounds of acceptance (ibid.: §31)? The universality cannot be gained by means of a concept that deals with the contents of the judgment of taste (see Lyotard 1988: 37). In Kant's own words, we are dealing here with something which can be referred to as 'non-conceptual subjective universality':

> We want to submit the object to our own eyes, just as if our liking of it depended on that sensation. And yet, if we then call the object beautiful, we believe we have a universal voice, and lay claim to the agreement of everyone . . .
>
> (Kant 1987: §8)

In particular, there cannot possibly exist any general standards or criteria according to which one could judge an object to be beautiful. The power of judgment operates 'as if' with examples (see ibid.: §18).

Kant emphasized time after time that this subjective universality had nothing to do with the empirical generality of a belief or a preference: 'Since a judgment of taste is in fact of this sort, its universal validity is not to be established by gathering votes and asking other people what kind of sensations they are having' (ibid.: §31). The fact that something is generally liked does not justify our calling it beautiful. The universality of aesthetic judgments which Kant had in mind is totally of another kind. In his opinion, we should be equally careful not to blend genuine aesthetic (disinterested) pleasure with sensual pleasure: it is, in principle, a different matter to say that one likes oysters than to say that Titian's paintings are beautiful.

## Kant's community of the united tastes

As Kant pointed out, in presenting an aesthetic judgment, despite the fact that it is ultimately based on our subjective feelings alone, we cannot avoid expecting others to join in our appreciation of the object of beauty – otherwise, the judgment would not be a real judgment of taste. The judgment of taste must have a 'subjective principle, which determines only by liking rather than by concepts, though nonetheless with universal validity, what is liked or disliked' (Kant 1987: §20). But how can such a claim to universality be justified? Kant's 'solution' to the problem is the postulation of a 'sensus communis', a communal sense, or a community of feeling and taste. Every time we make a judgment of taste we are, in fact, presuming that such a community exists. It is this idea of a community of taste that makes Kant's discussion especially interesting as far as a sociology of fashion is concerned, even though Kant would without doubt dismiss the whole question by saying that a community of fashion is only empirical and, as such, it cannot possibly have anything to do with the universality expected from aesthetic judgments.

The different characterizations of this *sensus communis* given by Kant are rather problematic and difficult to interpret, as evidenced by the long history of commentary. At some points, Kant seemed to define it in purely negative terms: such a community must be postulated, otherwise judgments of taste would be impossible; but, on the other hand, it is only constituted if the judgments – or feelings – are, in fact, universally shared (see Kant 1987: §20). At first glance, Kant's argument would seem to be almost a circular one.

The idea of a communal sense, '*Gemeinsinn*', obviously gets some support from the fact that we are indeed able to communicate both our knowledge and feelings (ibid.: §21). In the traditional interpretation which was presented by Georg Simmel in his lectures on Kant, the question of the possibility of a shared '*Gemeinsinn*' was reduced to the rather metaphysical idea of a community of souls. Aesthetic experiences. find a common basis of resonance in all human beings because they all, in the last instance, have a soul with similar spiritual functions:

> And this vague awareness, that the most basic functions of our spirit are here in operation, functions that are identical in all souls, lets us believe, that these judgments are not ours alone. As a matter of fact, we do believe that every one would judge in a

similar way, if only he could approach the object (*'das Object zulassen'*) in the same way.

(Simmel 1905a: 168)

There are some formulations in Kant's own writing which certainly would lend support to such an interpretation:

> A judgment of taste is based on a concept... but this concept does not allow us to cognize or prove anything concerning the object because it is intrinsically indeterminable and inadequate for cognition; and yet the same concept does make the judgment of taste valid for everyone, because... the basis that determines the judgment lies, perhaps, in the concept of what may be considered the supersensible substrate of humanity.

(Kant 1987: §57)

There is, however, another possible interpretation which is less orthodox but more interesting and which has recently been suggested by Lyotard, in particular (see Lyotard 1988; see also Weber 1987 and Santanen 1991). According to this interpretation, Kant's community of taste is only a regulative idea or, rather, a promise which can never be realized. The community can never come into being:

> The aesthetic community, therefore, remains, as Kant puts it, only an idea, or as I would say, a horizon for an expected consensus. Kant used the word 'promise' in order to point out the non-existent status of such a republic of taste (of the united tastes?). The community concerning what is beautiful has no chance of being actualized. But every judgment carries with it the promise of its universalization as a constitutive feature of its singularity.

(Lyotard 1988: 38)

The universality should be sought only in the form of the demands (ibid.). Or, as Kant put it, in making a judgment of taste we do not, in fact, postulate that everyone agrees with us on the matter; we only, so to speak, propose that everyone joins in the same community of feeling.[3] Everyone else must, at least, be able to experience the same aesthetic feeling. When we call an object beautiful we make a call to the other and 'believe ourselves to be speaking with a universal voice and lay claim to the consensus of everyone' (Kant 1987: §8). In Kant's own words:

> The judgment of taste itself does not *postulate* everyone's

agreement (since only a logically universal judgment can do that, because it can advise reason); it merely *requires* this agreement from everyone (*sinnet jedermann*), as an instance of a rule.... Hence the universal voice is only an idea.

(ibid.)

## Fashion and taste

If asked, Kant – and Lyotard too – would certainly hasten to add that this kind of a 'non-existent' consensus or harmony of feelings has absolutely nothing to do with the universality of fashion which is always 'only' empirical by its nature. Still, Simmel's characterization of the fashion pattern includes features resembling, to an amazing extent, Kant's idea of *sensus communis* as interpreted by Lyotard:

The kind of consensus implied by such a process, if there is any consensus at all, is in no way argumentative but is rather allusive and elusive, endowed with a special way of being alive, combining both life and death, always remaining *in statu nascendi* or *moriendi*, always keeping open the issue of whether or not it actually exists. This kind of consensus is definitely nothing but a cloud of community.

(Lyotard 1988: 38)

Like Kant's consensus of taste, fashion, too, is in a perpetual state of coming into being and dying. It never actually exists. 'To be in fashion' is constantly transformed into being 'out of fashion'. There is a tendency towards universalism inherent in every fashion, but this tendency can never be fully realized. As soon as a fashion permeates everything, it stops being a fashion:

As soon as the example has been universally adopted, that is, as soon as anything that was originally done only by a few has really come to be practised by all – as is the case in certain portions of our apparel and in various forms of social conduct – we no longer speak of fashion. As fashion spreads, it gradually goes to its doom.... Fashion includes a peculiar attraction of limitation, the attraction of simultaneous beginning and end...

(Simmel 1981: 9)

Colin Campbell (1987: 154–60) suggested – without explicitly referring to Kant's antinomy – that there is a problem inherent in the aesthetics of taste which cannot be solved theoretically:

Fashion became the *de facto* answer to the problem which none of the eighteenth-century writers on taste would solve; that is, how to find a commonly agreed, aesthetic standard which, while catering for people's real preferences, could also continue to serve as the basis for an ideal of character.

(ibid.: 158)

The only solution available is a practical one: the contemporary fashion pattern. Taste always refers to the preferences and choices of an individual and is totally private by its very nature. Everyone is supposed to choose what feels good. At the same time, the ideal of good taste is meant to be beyond the individual, and to be socially binding. It offers a universal standard, potentially applicable to all members of a society. It is an ideal which everyone is supposed to follow. Furthermore, it is a standard which is socially communicable even though it can never be conceptually determined.

Campbell, whose main preoccupation was the search for the intellectual origins of the self-illusory, hedonistic, modern consumer, made it sound almost as if the social pattern of fashion had, in fact, been invented in order to satisfy the theoretical need to solve the antinomy of taste. One would be on firmer ground by claiming only that fashion is a functional equivalent to the principle of good taste. But, in other respects, Campbell was able to catch something essential in the role played by fashion in modern society: fashion does function as a substitute for the standard of taste, without actually being one.

Strictly speaking, the fashion pattern cannot satisfy all the criteria presented by Campbell. It cannot possibly 'serve as the basis for an ideal of character' in the sense demanded by the tradition (cf. Gadamer 1975: 34–5; also see Simmel 1981). Fashion does not share the same ideal and, in this sense, obliging, nature as the principle of good or legitimate taste. Campbell's thesis should rather be read to claim that, in modern society, fashion fulfils a social role similar to the one originally expected from the standard of good taste. Thus, they are functional equivalents (cf. Appadurai (1986: 32) who compared the role of fashion with that of sumptuary laws). Fashion provides a socially binding standard of taste which effectively influences and directs individual consumer choices. Thus, it can be said to create order in the modern, fragmented world (cf. Blumer 1969).

If Campbell is right, it also means that, despite his autonomy and freedom, the modern consumer – or modern eater – does not necessarily live in a state of permanent anomie, as suggested by

Claude Fischler (1990: 204–17). To a great extent, contemporary fashion plays a role similar to traditional norms – or standards – of good taste in guiding the modern consumer in the perplexing task of selecting proper meals and socially accepted foods and drinks. These guidelines offered by fashion are not fixed. On the contrary, they are transitory and constantly changing. The world of fashion is full of ephemera. However, as far as the individual is concerned, the norms can still be felt to be almost equally binding and obliging as were traditional norms – or eating habits and table manners.

The parallel between fashion and judgments of taste goes even further. Fashion is a thoroughly aesthetic phenomenon in the Kantian sense. The charm of novelty and transitoriness offered by fashion (see Simmel 1981: 47) is a purely aesthetic pleasure. Simmel certainly shared the prejudice of his contemporaries (cf. Veblen 1961) in believing that the creations of fashion were more often ugly and, from an aesthetic point of view, disgusting. But it would be impossible to defend such a stance once Simmel's other and more principal formulations about fashion are taken into account. To Simmel – as well as to Kant – fashion only regulates things that could just as well be otherwise. In other words, fashion does not recognize any objective criteria or reasons. In Simmel's understanding, this necessarily means that all such considerations which have to do with the usefulness or purposiveness ('*Zweckmässigkeitsbeziehungen*') of objects are totally out of place in fashion:

> This is clearly proved by the fact that very frequently not the slightest reason can be found for the creations of fashion from the standpoint of an objective, aesthetic, or other expediency. While in general our wearing apparel is really adapted to our needs, there is not a trace of expediency in the method by which fashion dictates, for example, whether wide or narrow trousers, colored or black scarfs shall be worn.
>
> (Simmel 1981: 7)

In the quotation presented above, Simmel, curiously enough, identified aesthetic with 'other' objective expediency. If fashion does not obey the criterion of objective reason, it shares precisely that peculiar feature which was suggested by Kant to distinguish aesthetic pleasure from both sensual pleasure and every utilitarian consideration: 'Beauty is the object's form of purposiveness insofar as it is perceived in the object without the presentation of a purpose' (Kant 1987: §17). Kant also dismissed the relevance of such classical criteria of beauty as

harmony and perfection. The objects of beauty have a form
as if they had an objective end, either serving an outer purpo$
or an end dictated by its inner nature, but they do not have e₁
only the form of finality (see Kant 1987: §§11–15).

Fashion, as characterized by Simmel, seems also to have such a form
of finality without satisfying any needs. As a matter of fact, fashion
does have a 'purpose' – or function – but it is a purely social and, hence,
'formal' one (see Simmel 1981: 7). It is, furthermore, the function of
the whole fashion pattern, and not of any single object of fashion. But
Simmel also seemed to think that consumer goods are used to satisfy
the 'social-psychological' need of individuation or distancing oneself
from others. The usefulness of objects as markers of social distinction
is obviously different from, say, their ability to satisfy needs. But still
it would offer an independent criterion according to which one could
judge their merits, a criterion which, in principle, is of a different kind
than any judgment of their aesthetic worth.

It is, however, a different thing to say that people enjoy fashionable
consumer goods because of the feeling of novelty associated with
them, than to claim that they consciously make use of them in order to
promote their own social standing. It is also a different thing to say
that fashion has consequences for social stratification, than to claim
that individuals consciously make use of objects of fashion in order to
climb up the social ladder. And it is not always clear whether Simmel
has in mind the first or the second process or mechanism.

### Class fashion or mass fashion?

Simmel's essay has dominated much of the sociological discussion
about fashion up to now to such an extent that Herbert Blumer (1969)
made him responsible for the generally held conception that fashions
are class fashions. In Blumer's own opinion, modern mass fashion
operates in a rather different way. The whole secret of fashion consists
of the process of collective taste formation. Blumer obviously was only
familiar with Simmel's first essay. But even though one can find in
Simmel's later essays formulations and ideas which make it clear that
he did not think that the only distinctions making up the dynamics of
fashion were class distinctions (see Noro 1991: 70–5), it still cannot be
denied that he shared with many of his contemporaries the model
according to which fashions have their origins in the upper strata of
society from which they then descend – more or less slowly – the social
ladder:

the fashions of the upper stratum of society are never identical
with those of the lower, in fact, they are abandoned by the
former as soon as the latter prepare to appropriate them.... 
Fashion, ... is a product of class distinction...

(Simmel 1981: 7)

Following Simmel's ideas, it has been typical to think that fashions
unite members of a social class while demarcating classes from one
another. The dynamic of the fashion pattern has been understood to
result from the fact that once the lower classes have succeeded in
adopting a new style or mode of social conduct, the upper ones have
hastened to abandon it in order to find new styles to mark their
superiority and distinctiveness. (For a recent discussion, see Jones
1991.)[4] Simmel's idea of fashion as combining the opposite motives of
distinction and imitation is thus often understood as if the first motive
would operate mainly between, and the second mainly within, classes.
Such a view is certainly supported by historical evidence concerning
the operation of fashion in earlier capitalism. Contrary to what
Herbert Blumer (1969: 277), among others, has proposed, Georg
Simmel did not see fashion only in this way. What was primary in
fashion, according to Simmel, was its form, the simultaneous movement of social identification and differentiation, which does not in
principle require a class hierarchy. Blumer is, however, right about
Simmel in that he, too, certainly studied the movement of fashion in
the class hierarchy from the top down in most of his examples. In his
remarks concerning the latest development of contemporary fashion,
Simmel also laid special emphasis on how fashion abides in the middle
stratum of society. It is only the middle stratum – the vast middle class
– that follows and initiates the rapid changes which characterize the
movement of fashion (see Noro 1991: 72–3).

In at least one respect, Blumer's (1969) analysis of fashion comes
closer to Kant's idea of a *sensus communis* than Simmel's does. Whereas
Simmel strongly emphasized the demarcating role of fashion, the
function of which is to accentuate one's individual uniqueness – a
tendency becoming more important because of the great levelling
impact of money in modern society – Blumer, who used the Paris
fashion market and fashion shows as empirical examples, was mainly
interested in the process through which a collective and uniform taste
was distilled out of numerous individual tastes.

The main problem with Blumer's characterization of the fashion
pattern is that he does not give any reasons for its continuous

dynamics: once the collective taste has been reached there would not actually seem to be any reason to break away from the consensus. On the other hand, the opposite version, which emphasizes the logic of distinctions in fashion formation, often leads to the conception that the actors in this game are closed social groups which set themselves strictly apart from other social groups (see Simmel 1983: 63). If one reads Simmel's writings on fashion through Kantian eyes one could suggest that the 'need of differentiation' does not only include a 'tendency towards dissimilarity' but also a 'tendency towards similarity'. As Simmel (1981: 10) wrote, 'while fashion postulates a certain amount of general acceptance, it nevertheless is not without significance in the characterization of the individual, for it emphasizes his personality not only through omission but also through observance'. In setting themselves apart in order to emphasize their individuality and uniqueness, individuals also expect others to approve of their choice and share their taste. And the impetus to set oneself apart as an individual by choosing differently is already given by the fact that once a taste has been generally adopted it becomes impossible to recognize it as one's own and to identify oneself with it. It has become completely anonymous. A metaphor for the spread of fashion, more apt than that of the social ladder, would be the dissolution of a drop of liquid in a basin containing a liquid of a different colour.

## Lifestyle, style of art and fashion

Niklas Luhmann, in an article written in 1986, suggested that style makes art a distinct functional social system. Without style there would not be any separate system of art at all. Art objects as such are characterized by a high degree of autonomy. They are understood to be closed and self-sufficient entities that only have a goal in themselves. Once works of art are appreciated for their novelty and surprise value – as is increasingly the case in modern art – the problem becomes even more accentuated: what makes an object a work of art? Style is something that is common to different works of art, shared by many. Thus, style makes it possible to determine which objects are to be regarded as art, and what is their special contribution to the system of art:

> It is the style of a work of art which makes it possible to recognize what it owes to other works of art and what is its

95

importance to further, new works of art. The function of style is to organize the contribution of a work of art to the autopoiesis of art, and to a certain extent, against the intention of the very work of art, which aims at the closure of a single work. The style both corresponds to and contradicts the autonomy of a single work of art.

(Luhmann 1986: 632)

Luhmann's characterization of the function of style could have been taken from Simmel. In his little known essay 'The Problem of Style' Simmel presented what are, in many respects, similar ideas:

By virtue of style, the particularity of the individual work is subjugated to a general law of form that also applies to other works; it is, so to speak, relieved of its absolute autonomy. Because it shares its nature or a part of its design with others it thus points to a common root that lies beyond the individual work...

(Simmel 1991b [1908]: 64)

However, Simmel's concept of style differs from Luhmann's in one important respect: Simmel thought that genuine works of art could not share a common style (cf. Simmel 1985). Only works of applied arts (arts and crafts) or designed products can have a style. In Simmel's words, 'Instead of the character of individuality, applied art is supposed to have the character of style, of broad generality...' (see Simmel 1991b: 67). Because objects of applied art are always meant to be used, they cannot be unique. They already have something in common: they all serve a specific useful purpose and satisfy a need that is common to many people (ibid.: 65).

Simmel quite obviously would not have wanted to deny the usefulness of the concept of style in art history. He must have been well aware of the common use of the concept of style which became established in the middle of the eighteenth century by Baumgarten. But Simmel's own concept of style is more ambitious. In some respects it comes closer to the older concept of *'maniera'* traditionally designating the way to make things (see Link-Heer 1986). In order to share a common style objects of applied art – or any objects – must have been produced in a special manner: they must be stylized. Genuine works of art, on the other hand, can never be stylized, otherwise they would lose their uniqueness and individuality. One could then perhaps venture to say that 'style', to Simmel, is something more than a mere thought abstraction. To use a concept taken from another tradition of thought it is a 'real abstraction' ('*Realabstraktion*').

Simmel's discussion of style is sociologically particularly inter-esting because he draws a direct parallel between the style of objects of use, and lifestyle. In his opinion, in the same way as one can speak of a personal fashion (see Simmel 1981: 13–14), one can also speak of a personal style. Such a personal style is, however, a borderline case, the possibility of which is reserved only for strong personalities (like Goethe). We common folk have to be satisfied with something far less ambitious. An attempt to try to surround oneself with objects that would have a strong personal flavour of their own would only end in total stylelessness (see Simmel 1908: 314; see also Noro 1991: 92–3): 'anyone who is not that strong must adhere to a general law; if he fails to, his work fails to have style...' (Simmel 1991b: 70).

What makes Simmel's comment so remarkable is the fact that he does not seem to think that the whole life of a person (say, a member of the modern middle class) should be stylized in order to obey a common law and to be shared by others. In other words, Simmel does not postulate the necessity of any general principle, criteria or disposition which would regulate his behaviour, in most, or even all, fields of life. Neither does he think that members of a society have to share a common lifestyle with other members of their class or other social group. On the contrary, even though their lives are stylized, all individuals are able to retain both their full individuality and uniqueness and to share a common style, or rather many different but common styles. How is this possible? The suggested solution is a typical 'Simmelian' societal solution to a theoretically unsolvable antinomy.

As has already been pointed out, Simmel's concept of a style has more to do with objects of consumption: the objects or com-modities are stylized and not the way of life or the individual taste in themselves. Simmel's own example of furnishing a room can here serve to illustrate what he had in mind. The furniture of a living room should, in Simmel's opinion – at least in an ideal case – consist of a compilation of pieces of furniture all representing different but generally approved and common styles, of stylized objects:

> as soon as the individual constructs his environment of variously
> stylized objects; by his doing the objects receive a new centre,

which is not located in any of them alone, but which they all manifest through the particular way they are united.

(Simmel 1991b: 69)

If the room of a contemporary house consisted only of items representing a single style it would create a very sterile impression and the individual would not find any natural place in it. It would be an equally big mistake for a person to try to produce all the furniture totally according to his own private taste in order to create a private style of his own. Only a genius of Goethe's calibre – to use Simmel's favourite cultural idol – could succeed in such an effort. Otherwise, the result would only show total lack of taste and find no response among his peers (see Simmel 1991b: 69–70).

Simmel did not explicitly discuss the relation between style and fashion. However, he obviously understood both style and fashion – in their particular fields – to make their contribution to solving the great problem of our times: how to unite or bridge the gap between something which is totally individual or private on the one hand, and universal and general on the other (ibid.: 70). How can an individual belong to a 'higher' totality without losing his individuality? One could also imagine Simmel agreeing with Luhmann in arguing that style and fashion are, indeed, functional equivalents. In the end, Luhmann even has to admit that it is difficult – especially as far as the modern art world with its rapid stylistic innovations is concerned – to find any difference between style and fashion at all:

The autopoiesis of art should thus resemble the change of fashion, and one should not ask so much what is the contribution of a work of art to a certain style, but rather: how does the style of a fashion provoke the next one

(Luhmann 1986: 655)

The only difference that remains is the fact that art does not tolerate copies, whereas copies make a fashion even more striking (see Luhmann 1986: 656). But once the world of art is abandoned and the styles in applied art or of consumer goods are considered, the difference is of no consequence: in producing consumer goods, models are copied and style is something that characterizes the unifying features of both the copies and their original models.

## The community of fashion

Simmel's analysis of fashion – read through the correcting eyes of both Kant and Blumer – has taught us how a person can be a homogeneous part of a mass without losing his individuality – or how he can both stick to his own private taste and expect others – who also have a taste of their own – to share it. But to Simmel all such solutions to the conflict between the principles of individuality and sociability are only provisional. Social harmony is never within reach. As Lyotard said: the community of the united tastes is only a 'cloud of a community'. The bridge crossing the gap between the individual and his society has to be built over and over again.

In Simmel's opinion the concept of style should be reserved only to the objects of design. Objects of art are always unique. Otherwise Simmel's and Luhmann's conceptions of style do not differ from each other: in the modern society of mass consumption, in particular, they are functional equivalents. The concept of style has more to do with the characterization of the objects of consumption, whereas fashion characterizes the whole social pattern of distinction and adaptation.

In discussing the social theories of Giddens, Beck and Bauman, Alan Warde claimed that they all share the common idea that people living in a modern society are relatively free to choose and, at the same time, almost forced to construct their own identity, and that in this process consumption plays a significant role ('people define themselves through the messages they transmit to others through goods and practices that they possess and display', Warde 1994: 878), Warde came to the conclusion that in general these currently dominant approaches to consumption assume far too individualistic a model of a consumer (ibid.: 892). Left to himself the modern consumer, operating without any guidance or rules, would be faced with anxiety. Warde compared the situation with Durkheim's famous study on suicide: it almost seems as if the modern consumer were a suitable candidate for the role of would-be suicide today.[5] Fortunately, in Warde's opinion, there are compensatory mechanisms, processes and institutions which reduce the anxiety arising from personal consumption. Warde mentioned five different compensatory mechanisms from the advice given by mass media and personal contacts and networks, to the persistence of conventions, the symbols of respectability and all kinds of rules of etiquette. Finally, there is the role played by complacency: 'Many people appear content with their self-image, or even will assert their sense of personality against the trappings and fripperies of display and presentation' (Warde 1994: 892). The importance of such conventions, contacts and influences cannot be denied, and they are not only remnants of a more traditional way of life, either. Warde does not, however, mention or pay any attention to the fashion mechanism, which is by far the most important standard-setter in modern consumption, offering guidelines and models of orientation to the consumer, who is still free to choose what he or she likes, and can use the world of goods to help build and express his or her own identity.

Simmel's suggestion of the necessity for a 'stylized lifestyle' in modern society can equally be seen as a further development of the idea concerning the role played by the various objects of consumption in the life of a modern person. Even though their lives are stylized, members of a society are able to retain their full individuality and share a style or styles with others. The individuality of individual taste is expressed in the relative weight which objects of different styles or fashions have in a compilation of objects. The idea of style as 'bricolage' (see Hebdige 1983) would not then be restricted to modern youth culture but would rather characterize the whole of modern consumption culture from the very beginning. The taste expressed in a collection of goods surrounding a person is always both private and universal at the same time. Such a solution is in line with Simmel's more general idea about modern individuality as an intersection of many spheres of life (see Noro 1991).

The development of a stylized lifestyle can be seen as a concrete example of the attitude of superficiality which, in Simmel's opinion, was a possible and even typical response to the problems caused by the increasing fragmentation of modern society. In Simmel's understanding, the division of labour – or social differentiation in general – had created a situation in which the individual is faced with conflicting demands, interests, needs and hopes. Social differentiation threatens the totality of the individual's life by pulling it in opposite directions. If one were to get involved with equal seriousness in every field of life, one would simply lose one's social integrity (see Lohmann 1992:352–3) It is not surprising that a recent characterization of the consumer in post-modernity in *Advances in Consumer Research* (Firat 1991) could equally well be read as a 'modernized' summary of the results of Simmel's analyses of fashion and style:

> The consumption life of the consumer is segmented, fragmented into separate moments which are not or only superficially linked. Each instance may well be cultivated to represent a

different image of oneself.... The catch in the capitalist market
system is, however, that to represent the different images people
will be acquiring and consuming the same products...and
adopting the same consumption pattern represented by these
products.... So what appears to be difference at the level of
symbolic culture turns out to be an underlying uniformity.

(Firat 1991: 71)

The only thing that Georg Simmel would probably consider somewhat strange in reading the above quotation would be its slightly
moralizing overtone. He would probably be tempted to remind the
reader that 'the difference appearing at the level of symbolic culture' is
just as real and important a characteristic of modern consumer culture
as its 'underlying' uniformity.[6] In consuming goods people are both
expressing their own aesthetic preferences and sharing a collective
taste with others.

## TASTE AND THE PROCESS OF COLLECTIVE SELECTION

### Fashion as *Zeitgeist*

In his seminal article of 1969, 'Fashion: From Class Differentiation to
Collective Selection', Herbert Blumer analysed the formation of a
collective taste based on his personal observations concerning the
women's fashion industry and the great fashion houses in Paris shortly
before the war. According to him (Blumer 1969: 284), 'the origin,
formation, and careers of collective taste constitute the huge problematic area in fashion'.

In his opinion, there were three matters in particular which seemed
to provide the clues for an understanding of fashion in general (ibid.:
278). First, the setting or determination of fashion actually takes place
through an intense process of selection. This selection process can best
be observed at the seasonal opening of major fashion houses. At the
beginning of such openings, there may be a hundred or more designs
of women's evening dress before an audience of from 100 to 200
buyers. The actual selection of about six to eight designs is usually
done by the buyers representing sellers of designer women's wear.
What is even more important for the sake of Blumer's argument, the
managerial corps of the fashion houses are generally able to point out
as potential successes about 30 of the original lot of 100 or more

designs presented to the audience, but they are typically unable to predict the smaller number on which the actual and final choices converge. Furthermore, according to Blumer, these choices are made usually by buyers independently of each other and without knowledge of each other's preferences.

Second, the amazing convergence of these independent choices is explained by Blumer by the fact that 'the buyers were immersed and preoccupied with a remarkably common world of intense stimulation' (Blumer 1969: 279). Because of this 'intense immersion' the buyers developed common sensibilities and appreciations and expressed a common taste in their preferences. According to Blumer, they all were actively participating in 'a world of lively discussion of what was happening in women's fashion, of fervent reading of fashion publications, and of close observation of one another's lines of products' (ibid.). One could also say that these people were experts or insiders in the social world of fashion (cf. Becker 1982). At the same time these buyers were, in a sense, 'the unwitting surrogates of the [much broader – J. G.] fashion public'.

The third observation made by Herbert Blumer pertained to the dress designers themselves. Blumer was interested in the sources of their new ideas. According to the designers' own testimony these ideas came mainly from three sources: from historical fashions, from the exotic costumes of people in far-off countries, and from the reflection of more recent and current styles of dress. The third source was, in Blumer's interpretation, the most important one. The insiders had developed 'an intimate familiarity with the most recent expressions of modernity as these were to be seen in such areas as the fine arts, recent literature, political debates and happenings, and discourse in the sophisticated world'. According to Blumer's interpretation, designers were, in fact, engaged in translating these areas and media into dress designs (Blumer 1969: 279). The shared influences and common experiences explain why the designers themselves create – independently from each other – remarkably similar designs. Thus the process of collective selection, as described by Blumer, takes place not only among the buyers but among the designers themselves.

Blumer summarized the three results of his analysis as follows:

they [the designers – J. G.] pick up ideas of the past, but always through the filter of the present; they are guided and constrained by the immediate styles in dress, particularly the direction of such styles over the recent span of a few years; but above all, they are seeking to catch the proximate future as it is revealed in modern developments.

(ibid.: 280)

For the sake of Blumer's argument it is important that the buyers still have far more alternatives from which to select than the number they actually are buying. In this sense, despite the earlier process of selection, they are free to choose from among a greater variety of models and designs.[7]

During this process of collective selection there is somehow established 'a relation between, on the one hand, the expressions of modernity to which the dress designers are so responsive and, on the other hand, the incipient and inarticulate tastes which are taking shape in the fashion consuming public' (ibid.: 280). The analysis of this relationship or homology is the most mysterious or obscure part of the understanding of the whole process, which in many ways resembles the treatment of the problem of taste in the classical aesthetic discourse to which Kant's 'sensus communis', discussed earlier, was the most subtle answer. It looks almost as if the various expressions of modernity in culture, fashion among them, were all, in fact, expressions of some deeper and, unavoidably vague, Zeitgeist.

Blumer's description and understanding of the formation of collective taste and its relation to the mechanism of fashion has been criticized for its vagueness and unspecificity (see Davis 1992: 119). Blumer certainly does make the process of catching the core of the Zeitgeist look rather mysterious and obscure – evidently he thinks that it is, in principle, impossible to describe the process more concretely. It is, however, not totally justified to claim, as Davis did, that this is the same problem as identifying the different stages in fashion process or the problem of the identification of the key actors in the process. It is true that Blumer does not pay much attention to the fashion cycle or to the different stages through which fashion has to pass. It simply does not belong to the task he has set himself. The key actors of this process are, on the contrary, at least in the concrete process under examination, clearly described and identified by him. In the case of the Paris seasonal shows they consisted of the designers, the administrative staff of the fashion houses and the international buyers who worked for big department stores and were, in a way, representing the larger public.

Davis' critique is more justified concerning Blumer's failure to consider the 'palpable influence of the elaborate institutional apparatus surrounding the propagation of fashion in the domain of dress' (Davis 1992: 120). The realm of dress is today, as Davis points out, extremely institutionalized. There are evidently other fields in which fashion is equally operative but where one cannot find such elaborate and tightly organized institutional apparatuses of creating, propagating and distributing fashion (see for instance the case of first names in Lieberson and Bell 1992). Obviously, as Davis himself admits, the phenomenon of fashion cannot simply be reduced to the effects of manipulation by the economic apparatus to promote its interests even though there is no doubt that fashion is functional to the economic system of capitalism. Fashion is, after all, an ideal and extreme case of waste, by transforming otherwise perfectly useful (in the narrow functional sense of the word) objects into totally useless ones (in the aesthetic sense). As such, without doubt, it promotes sales and accelerates the turnover of capital.

Lipovetsky (1994) has recently formulated this dilemma – without explicitly referring to this particular discussion – in an elegant way which gives credit to the relative validity of both Blumer's and Davis' positions. According to Lipovetsky, fashion, in the form in which it appeared in the classical haute couture represented by the French fashion houses, inaugurated an era which combined the domination of the bureaucratic apparatus of institutions with mass democracy. In this sense, fashion can be said to present an early paradigmatic example of such social processes which came to characterize our society even more generally during this century:

> Programming fashion while remaining unable to impose it, conceiving of it as a whole while simultaneously offering an array of choices, haute couture inaugurated a new type of supple power that functioned without issuing rigid injunctions and that incorporated into its processes the unpredictable and varied tastes of the public. This mechanism had a bright future: it was to become the preponderant form of social control in democratic societies . . .
>
> (Lipovetsky 1994: 80)

Despite, or rather alongside, bureaucratic regulation, fashion offered guidelines that left enough room for personal choice and encouraged personal initiative:

> instead of stylistic uniformity there is a plurality of models; instead of prescriptive programming and minutiae of rules,

104

there is an appeal to personal initiative; instead of regular, constant, impersonal coercion, there is the seduction of the metamorphosis of appearance . . .

(ibid.: 78)

Lipovetsky's formulations refer to the early stage of fashion which came to an end before the 1960s (see also Horowitz 1975b and Craik 1994: 210–11) and which was dominated by the haute couture, and more concretely by the great Paris fashion houses. Later, during the more democratic stage of mass consumption of cheap ready-to-wear clothes and with the increasing importance of product brands, some of the great fashion houses (Chanel, Lagerfeld, etc.) were transformed into companies marketing not only women's wear but other goods as well, and the role of these bureaucratic institutions as taste setters has somewhat diminished. Even though dresses are designed, marketed and advertised by economically more powerful enterprises, the democratic character of fashion has become far more accentuated and evident. There is no longer any hierarchical structure in the fashion mechanism with models originating in haute couture and gradually descending lower in the hierarchy, finally reaching street fashion. There are professional designers working in the mass fashion industry who take ideas and models directly from the street. This transformation, often described by observers of the fashion process since the 1960s, does not make the role of designers obsolete. On the contrary, in order to satisfy a mass demand for novelty their creations must still be stylized by designers and offered to the buying public at an increasing tempo.

## The Finnish study of fashion design

In the autumn of 1992 we conducted interviews among Finnish fashion designers.[8] The themes of the interview were inspired mainly by Blumer's article even though we were fully aware of the differences both in the historical and geographical setting of our objects of research.

Finnish fashion designers in the 1990s seemed, to an amazing degree, to be responding to the question about the possible sources of new ideas along similar lines to the Parisian designers interviewed in the late 1930s by Blumer. Fashion was generally understood to be a visual and remarkably compressed expression of various streams of modern culture. It was thought to be influenced by almost anything that is taking place in the modern world: politics, wars and catastrophes as well as major cultural events and happenings. As such, it is a mirror of our time. In general, then, fashion was understood to be an expression of a *Zeitgeist.*

Fashion was thought to be influenced also by other forms of art, movies, theatre and literature, from where new ideas and images that need to be visualized were often received. Alternatively, observation of street life, 'people walking in the city streets', was mentioned as an equally important model or source of inspiration. Amazingly, other forms of mass media or popular culture are hardly mentioned at all: only music, television and videos are occasionally mentioned. This could probably be explained more by the fact that television and other forms of mass media are understood to be part of the same world as fashion. They are already inhabited by 'fashion models'. As such they cannot possibly provide inspiration in the sense of idols or models but rather as competitors or accomplices in the same trade. Some even felt that in the world we live in, we receive so much information all the time that it has become increasingly difficult to identify the sources of new ideas or models. To live in this permanent flow of information is as self-evident as it is important to follow international fashion magazines. Today it is more difficult to avoid the 'touch of the *Zeitgeist*' than to try to grasp it. You do not have to bother to keep up with the times, the time keeps up with you! But, of course, you still have to be sensitive to the message of the media in order to be able to interpret it actively. This is even more the case if one is trying to translate this media message into the visual language of fashion.

For a successful designer it is not, however, enough just to be able to feel and interpret the pulse of the time. As one of the interviewed designers formulated it, a successful design is based on the happy coincidence when consumers are willing to identify with and adopt the 'trend' which was interpreted and visualized by the designer. The task of the designer would thus be to sketch and concretize in visual and easily recognizable images the loose and vague ideas shared by the larger public. According to Blumer (1969), collective taste is initially

> a loose fusion of vague inclinations and dissatisfactions that are aroused by new experiences in the field of fashion and in the larger surrounding world. In this initial state, collective taste is amorphous, inarticulate, vaguely poised, and awaiting specific direction. Through models and proposals, fashion innovators

sketch out possible lines along which the incipient taste may gain objective expression and take definite form.

(Blumer 1969: 289)

If the whole secret of the trade simply consisted of being able to follow the common 'trend', it would be a relatively easy profession to learn, in particular since there are professional agencies and trend setters from which you can buy your 'weather prognosis'. In the contemporary situation, the main problem for a fashion designer is rather to know when to distinguish him or herself from the trend followed by others and when to follow it. In other words, in order to be successful you have to be able to see further than others and already be able to 'smell' the next trend or the next cycle of the trend, otherwise you only repeat the present fashion. The trend prognosis can tell you whether or not hemlines are rising or falling, but designers are time after time taken by surprise when the whole 'look' is totally changed or the trend reversed. In other words, there is no single reliable method or device to prognosticate the fashion of tomorrow. Despite all the methods of following trends and new ideas in various fields, the secret of final success – to be just one step ahead of others – always remains a mystery – or is finally determined by chance and by contingent factors.

In the discussion conducted with Finnish designers Blumer's two other sources of new ideas, exotic or historical clothes, were not mentioned. (Even though travelling and tourism were often mentioned as important sources of inspiration.) This could be explained both by the peripheral position of the Finnish fashion industry – on the whole it is on the receiving end of international influences – and by the fact that Blumer's historical study had as its target the great Paris fashion houses creating articles of haute couture which were more or less unique creations, whereas the experience of the Finnish designers was received mainly from industrially produced mass fashion.

In the study conducted by Horowitz (1975b) in the 1950s in England, one of the main questions concerning the self-image of the designer, or the perception of his or her role, was to what extent the designers understood their position in the way suggested by C. Wright Mills in an article with the same title as Horowitz's: 'The Man in the Middle' (1963: 378): 'His art is a business, but his business is art.' Among the designers interviewed by Horowitz (1975b: 29), 'about half regarded their occupation as an art, while the other half preferred to regard it as a craft'. Even among those designers who were occupied with haute couture and understood their occupation as creative art, commercial success was still often regarded as the main sign or criteria of a successful career as had been envisaged by Mills.

Horowitz's designers, at least a good part of them, were among the last occupied in the traditional haute couture and employed by the great fashion houses who acted as trend setters in relation to mass markets. As noted by Horowitz, by the time of the publication of the article the situation had totally changed and haute couture had lost its hegemonic position in relation to the mass market which now received its ideas directly from the street and had its own professional designers who designed directly for the mass market without any finer models to imitate.

The question whether fashion design is an art certainly had occupied the minds of the Finnish designers – as a matter of fact, it had been an important issue in their trade association a few years earlier but by the time of the interviews it seemed to have been, at least provisionally, resolved. Whereas some quite evidently thought of their profession as real art others just as evidently regarded it as a craft. There was not, however, such a big contradiction between these views: designing was considered by all to be a creative occupation, and in this sense it was close to 'real' art. At the same time, in most cases designers did not aim at creating unique objects of art, but industrially produced objects of use. The self-evident nature of these responses could possibly be explained by the fact that all the Finnish designers had a long formal schooling behind them at a school of industrial design and consequently shared a strong professional identity which set them apart both from pure craftsmen and artists.

In general, the designers felt that they were relatively independent in their creative work. Despite some organizational and commercial restrictions they were relatively free to choose the proposed models through their own best understanding and liking. From the dress designer's point of view, in addition to the more obvious commercial interests and restrictions presented by the managerial staff of the firms that employed them, there were also some interesting preconditions which they had to take into account in planning the models of a coming fashion. First, the producers of textile fabrics and threads offered new products to the market each year, and the variety of their supply was naturally limited. Thus, in designing clothes and dresses one usually had to use whatever was offered by these producers. Second, you had to take into account the forecasts of the trend agents. (*Promostyle* was the agent most often mentioned.) Their guidelines were often felt to be too vague and general, but the colours of the new designs were often said to be determined, at least to some extent, by these agencies. Thus, given the typical patterns and colours of fabrics it was, to put it crudely, left to the imagination and creative capacity of the designers to create the final models or patterns and the final cutting or shape of the garment.

Obviously, the trend agents as well as the textile and thread manufacturers, with their own professional designers, had to propose their ideas and designs a year or a year and a half earlier than the dress designers. They had a fashion cycle of their own which had to be synchronized with the latter. In a similar way, the fashion designers themselves felt strongly that their 'fashion' was different from the 'fashion' of the buying public. They had to 'know' or to be able to determine it one or two years before their public. Professional fashion is different from street fashion and precedes it by a considerable span of time. Designers' fashion is the innovation which still is in the process of coming into being and only some parts of which are generally adopted by the buying public once finally offered for sale in department stores and boutiques. Designers' fashion also naturally includes many more varieties and models than are offered to the buying public, or are then bought and consumed by it, or finally become really fashionable.

In a sense, one could say that today the social institution of fashion design – or the world of commercial fashion and trade – consists of several different layers or steps. At each step the variety of possible items or models from which to choose becomes more limited from the perspective of the next step. The guidelines offered by garment manufacturers or the trend agencies' advice (the colour for the autumn or spring season) restrict the fashion designers' freedom of innovation and choice only in certain respects. On the other hand, the buying public has to be satisfied with the assortment of clothes finally offered for sale each season at the shops. But even to consumers a large assortment of goods is offered, only some of which find a demand big enough to become economic successes. At least the buyers always have the freedom of a combination of different clothes, shoes and hats, and, consequently, of their contextualization.

In this respect the mechanism of the selection of models that finally are presented to the customers, and the associated formation of a collective taste, resembled the Paris fashion shows as analysed by Blumer. The main difference is that a further division of labour has taken place in the process. Instead of two (designers and buyers) or three (if the managerial staff is included) different influential actors or groups of actors taking part in the process of collective selection, there are now, in the industry of ready-made clothes, at least five or six different sets of key actors. First, textile fabrics and threads are designed by manufacturers; second, trend setters present the results of their efforts of coming to grips with the collective taste of the time (e.g. of colours); third, the fashion designers make their suggestions and propose their sketches of future models; fourth, they are discussed with the managerial staff who pick their own favourites and take them into the final process of production, to be presented to department and chain store buyers; and finally, the buying public with its money power makes the final selection, thus evolving and expressing its own collective taste. Each of these stages precedes the earlier one by several months or even a year or two. At each of these stages the potential array of choices is further restricted. The final crucial test of the commercial success of the product proves whether all the processes of the formation of a collective taste have been synchronized well enough. What is important in the sociological analyses of this social formation is that, in principle, the process taking place at each of these stages can be described along the lines already presented by Herbert Blumer: somehow, in an almost mysterious way, a collective taste, in a more or less compressed and clear form, is distilled out of a myriad of individual tastes, and expressed in a concrete form in the models presented to the market by the designers and the producers, and in the choices made by the buyers.

The belief in the total autonomy and freedom of the customer is an ideologically distorted conception. No one can act in the market of today without previous limitations restricting his or her choices, or create a personal style in total isolation with unlimited possibilities, according only to his or her own individual taste. Customers can choose only from among the, often very limited, number of items that are at the moment offered in the shops. Even though the new and advancing technologies of production would make it possible to mass produce individually designed products, as is the case already, for instance, in the car industry, the difference between this new flexible mode of production and the old more rigid mass production is still only one of degree and not of kind. The customer can choose from among a greater number of possible combinations but still the parts are predesigned and the possible array of choices always consists of a limited number of items.

It is, however, equally distorted to believe that all our choices, as autonomous and independent as they often seem to be, are, in the final instance, more or less totally predetermined by alien social and commercial influences, like marketing and advertising. Modern customers are free to choose, to accept or to reject, the products offered to them and since these choices and customers' preferences obviously do not fall randomly on all the possible goods offered, but, on the contrary, are often clearly and strongly concentrated, favouring one or another model or item, one can with confidence say that a process of collective taste formation is taking place in everyday consumption. A modern fashion mechanism is constantly created and kept going. Following the formulation suggested by Lipovetsky (1994), ours is a society in which bureacratic control, represented by big institutions like the whole fashion world, and big organizations like the fashion industry (which has already become much more multi-faceted since the days of haute couture), is more or less successfully combined with democratic aspirations, leaving room for numerous expressions of the individuality of taste and the creative initiative of the customer. As Simmel noted, only in a society of people wearing uniforms or in a society consisting of totally unique and isolated individuals not sharing any common characteristics or features, could this process ever come to an end. In modern Western societies such alternatives are not in sight at present.

## FOOD FASHIONS AND SOCIAL ORDER

### The confusing picture of modern food culture

It would be quite trivial simply to claim that there are fashions in the modern food market and in the culinary culture in general as in almost any other commercial field of human activity. However, frequently repeated food scares follow exactly the logic typical of fashions. It is easy to point out several recent and good examples of the appearance of food fashions: for instance the rapidly changing popularity of various national cuisines or the life history of many convenience foods on the shelves of a supermarket. They are often first introduced as a delicacy, then become part of the daily menu and often – if they do not share the destiny of a fad – finally become part of the 'traditional' diet.

In the following, however, a more demanding position is defended according to which the role of fashion is crucial in understanding modern food culture. The major changes in diet, like that towards a 'healthier diet', are essentially changes of fashion.

Harvey Levenstein (1988) summarized some of the results of his study of changing food consumption patterns in the contemporary United States as follows:

> Perhaps as a result of confusing signals being emitted by the 'experts', a few middle class Americans seem to stick to one set pattern of eating. Buffered from food scare to food scare, enticed by the convenience (and, let it be said, the taste of) fast food, unable to resist snack foods and 'grazing', yet still relishing occasional Julia Child-like triumph in the kitchen, *Homo Americanus* and family present a confused picture.
>
> (Levenstein 1988: 209–10)

Levenstein's work is titled *Revolution at the Table* and it is mainly concerned with the changes in American diet influenced by the development of modern nutrition science. The testimony of another contemporary observer of American food culture is even more striking: American society – and the observation could well be extended to other Western societies – has become increasingly 'confused about what is food and what is not food, what is real and what is imitation' (Schwartz 1986: 267). According to Schwartz, 'very strong forces are at work' in such a society.

Levenstein's and Schwartz's conclusions about the general confusion reigning in food culture are shared by many experts, and are certainly confirmed by many of our own everyday experiences. Following Stephen Mennell's (1985) suggestion, one could also claim that the increasing homogenization of eating habits (diminishing national and class differences) has been followed by a greater differentiation and individualization: the increasing supply of food has made possible the formation of various subcultures, from vegetarians and macrobioticians to connoisseurs of French cuisine, as well as the 'anomic' situation facing every individual and family in their food choices, as characterized by Levenstein: vitaminized corn flakes in the morning, vegetarian health food for lunch and hamburgers in the evening; the whole menu crowned with an occasional gourmet dinner with friends on Sunday afternoon.

Despite the confusing picture offered by modern food culture, Levenstein is willing to argue that there is at least one permanent factor which definitely – and more than others – has helped shape our attitude towards food. The development of scientific knowledge about nutrition – and the parallel numerous pseudo-scientific schools of thought – have permanently transformed our ideas about food and eating, and created a situation where we feel:

that taste is not a true guide to what should be eaten; that one should not simply eat what one enjoys; that the important components of food cannot be seen or tasted, but are discernible only in scientific laboratories; and that experimental science has produced rules of nutrition which will prevent illness and encourage longevity.

(Levenstein 1988: 210)

## The ideal diet of the Finns?

As has been shown in a recent comprehensive study conducted by Ritva Prättälä and others (Prättälä *et al*. 1992; Karisto *et al*. 1993) the Finnish diet has become much 'healthier' during the last twelve years:

Both men and women displayed a shift towards healthier food consumption patterns in 1979–1990, yet women's food choices were consistently more health oriented. The observed absolute change in the proportions of men and women spreading butter on bread was most dramatic: in 1979 63 per cent of men and 56 per cent of women preferred butter; in 1990, the figures were 17 per cent and 12 per cent respectively. Trends in other individual food consumption patterns were similar: consumption of sugar in coffee and high-fat milk decreased, and weekly consumption of vegetables increased.

(Prättälä *et al*. 1992: 282–3)

As the authors admit, the report deals only with a limited number of nutritionally relevant food consumption patterns or factors (butter, high-fat milk, vegetables and sugar in coffee). In the authors' opinion, the results are still very promising since the relatively high consumption of butter and high-fat milk are generally regarded as among the main risk factors in the Finnish diet (e.g. causing cardiovascular disease). Not only did the average diet become more healthy, the relative differences between the social (educational) groups diminished remarkably during the study period (see Prättälä *et al*. 1992: 284; see also Prättälä *et al*. 1993). Even so the diet of the higher social classes is nutritionally better than the diet of the lower groups, and women eat on the average better than men do. The diet of Finnish women is now approaching the 'ideal': 'particularly in the highest social class, practically all women now have a "good diet". The middle- and lower-class women are approaching the level of the upper-class women' (Prättälä *et al*. 1992: 285). These results are in line

113

with the results of several earlier studies, but the social differences obviously first started diminishing in the 1980s (cf. Prättälä *et al*. 1986).

In Finland, as in many other European countries, nutrition education and nutrition-related health campaigns (the so-called North Carelia project has been the most spectacular one in Finland) have been an important part of the public health policy during the last decades. There is thus a strong temptation to interpret these results as giving support to the thesis that the 'message' of the health educators has reached its public. The widespread use of butter and high-fat milk ('unsaturated fatty acids') has been the main target of these propaganda campaigns in Finland. They have traditionally been regarded as valuable nutrients in the Finnish diet, and it has been very difficult for their producers, the farmers in particular, to admit that their consumption could have more detrimental than beneficial effects.

These results are even more spectacular if one keeps in mind that at the same time changes in other health-related habits (smoking, drinking and the frequency of physical exercise) have been much smaller, or almost negligible (Karisto *et al*. 1993: 194). Smoking, in particular, has increased despite several very visible anti-smoking campaigns. Moreover, in this area of 'health-related habits', women are mainly responsible for the deterioration of the situation (see Karisto *et al*. 1993 and Rahkonen 1992).

## Health sells, but education is needed

Many observers would certainly agree with Joseph R. Gusfield's general conclusion that 'beginning sometime in the 1950s and continuing into the present, there has been a quickening of interest in nutrition as a means to achieve good health and prevent illness' (Gusfield 1992: 91). This interest in the nutritional value of food is, in the opinion of many, part of a more general orientation in which health has become something of a super-value or 'a common sieve prism of well-being, through which the values of different things, e.g. quality of food, are passed' (Karisto *et al*. 1993: 187). The new ethics of health appears to offer a universal and generally accepted norm to the modern consumer, mainly because it conceals its moralizing tone behind a pseudo-scientific analysis of everyday practices (cf. Bourdieu 1984: 384–5).

If the representatives of the food industry are to be believed, health sells too. New products can best be marketed if they can claim to make an important contribution to a healthier diet: 'A decisive factor in the wider acceptability of novel proteins may be their contribution to a healthier diet in the form of new products which fulfill some perceived nutritional needs' (Richardson 1990: 149).

On the other hand, 'irrational habits of eating' and scientifically unsound beliefs about nutrition are general among the public as is perhaps best evidenced by the numerous and repeated 'food scares' which can sometimes gain 'alarming measures'. (According to Richardson (1990: 150), 'in the UK worries about food have become something of a national preoccupation'.) As many nutritionists seem to think, the general health orientation of the public can have dangerous side-effects. The public's interest in health can often become too intensive and be led in the wrong directions. 'Only through extensive efforts of health education will scientists be able to convince the American public that good nutrition is easily obtained from a wide variety of foods readily available from our grocery stores,' as the American nutritionists Stare and Behan wrote in 1986. The natural scientists often tend to believe in the power of scientific knowledge to change people's habits for the better. In this respect nutritionists certainly are no exception: 'Everything would change for the better, if only people knew...'

## Scientific and folk models of nutrition

Obviously, health matters. There are unfortunately relatively few studies on what people living in a modern society think, know and believe about food. Unfortunately there is no data about Finland that could be compared with the general development of the diet discussed above. But from the rather modest sources of information at our disposal one can draw the conclusion that people increasingly care about their health and physical fitness. They are aware of the fact that the food they eat can have a decisive effect on their future health. In discussing eating and food in the family, Finnish women regularly refer to the nutritional value of foodstuffs and meals (see Mäkelä 1994). Laymen also seem to have relatively clear ideas about which foods are good, which bad and why they are so. However, these ideas do not, or only incidentally, coincide with the prevalent scientific orthodoxy. However, the practical guidelines which people say they follow in selecting their daily menu often are in line with the recommendations of the experts.

115

In a Finnish study about the consumption of milk fats among girls it was found out that 'health motives' had relatively little to do with the reasons given for their eating habits. However, the older the girls grew, the more important these motives became. In particular, girls who experienced weight problems were more eager to avoid milk fats (see Rimpelä *et al*. 1983: 129).

In a study based on interviews conducted with mothers living in East London, Gail Wilson (1989: 179) reported that 'nearly two thirds of the women spontaneously said that they were influenced by health considerations when they chose food'. Wilson also found out that women were more amenable to dietary change than men were. The women interviewed would also often have liked to change the eating habits of their families but they felt themselves to be 'subject to a range of constraints' (ibid.: 177). However, the women also felt that they could exercise an influence on what was eaten at home (cf. similar observations in Sweden, in Ekström 1990).

Women often felt that primarily they had to please the other members of the family. In particular, women living on a 'tight budget' reported that they did not dare to buy any new foods not normally eaten in the family. They simply could not afford to experiment with food and buy items that could be rejected (Wilson 1989). This would seem to support an observation made also by Karisto *et al*. (1993): it is easier to add something new to the diet than to take something away. An expanding economy in which consumption is increasing promotes change. New items are more easily accepted if they are served as something 'extra' or 'luxury', not necessarily competing with the traditional items on the menu.

The 'folk models of nutrition' or layman's beliefs about good diet were the explicit object of Claude Fischler's study (1986). He interviewed French mothers about the food that is good for children and compared the results with 'scientific dietetics'. At first glance the mothers studied seemed to be influenced to a high degree by scientific knowledge about nutrition and had adopted many knowledgeable ways of talking about food. The fact that they were speaking about the food they thought was good for their children probably further emphasized this tendency: they obviously felt very strongly that they were responsible for the well-being of their children. In particular, when speaking about infants' diet the nutritional emphasis was even stronger. Babies were treated as living organisms whose nutritional needs must be satisfied, but the mothers tended to speak in a similar way about food in general:

'calories' and 'vitamins', 'starches' and 'fats' were pervasive in discourse on child feeding. . . . Instead of hunger and appetite, 'needs' or 'requirements' were discussed, which had to be met by providing appropriate 'nutrients'. Statements rarely mentioned 'food' (*nourriture*) as such, they rather discussed 'diet' (*alimenta-tion*), stressing that it must above all be 'balanced'.

(Fischler 1986: 948)

In many respects the practical recommendations made by laymen were similar to those of scientific nutritionists, but the reasons given often differed. Fat was never mentioned as a dangerous substance by the mothers, whereas meat was conceived 'as a somehow special food, overconsumption of which was seen as self-indulgence or conspicuous consumption' (ibid.: 952). In the mothers' opinion, starches were mainly responsible for children's obesity. Vegetables were valued equally by laymen and experts, but again for different reasons. The vitamins they possessed were seldom mentioned by mothers, but vegetables and 'greens' had an important function to fulfil in their diets. They helped to restore the 'balance'. They symbolized something ('freshness') that was opposed to meat. Thus, their function in the diet was a strategic one. Milk products were valued for their calcium, but milk as a drink, even for children, was treated with suspicion. (In Fischler's interpretation, it was neither a proper drink nor a food.)

The need for a balanced diet was the overall criterion by which French mothers tended to evaluate the contribution of different foods to the diet of their children. In Fischler's opinion it has become a quasi-ethical value or a meta standard of a proper diet. When asked to explain what they meant by 'balance', the mothers often referred to the rule of the golden mean: 'Eat a bit of everything and not too much of anything!' The demand for a balance could be used as an argument in favour of an ingredient that was felt to be missing in the diet (say 'greens') as well as against any item that was felt to take up too big a portion of it (say starches or meat).

In an earlier article (1980) Fischler had already suggested that our modern culinary culture is in a state of a crisis. Since the traditional food rules have lost much of their power to convince, the modern society is in a state of gastro-anomie. In such a society there is a need for new norms to guide our eating habits. In Fischler's opinion, the standard of a balanced diet – for lack of anything more concrete – served exactly such a function: 'What was perceived as necessary was in fact some form of order, rules or criteria, reliable principles for behavioural organization and food choices' (Fischler 1986: 962). The desired balance would then take another, wider meaning, 'that of a cultural construct reducing anxiety-producing symbolic disorder' (Fischler 1986: 963).

Even though she does not draw the same conclusions, Carole M. Counihan's results would seem to support Fischler's thesis in many ways. Counihan's study is based on the analysis of the 'food diaries' kept by her students in the USA. One of her main results was that 'rules for good food involve the notion of a "balanced" diet ... in terms of the basic four food groups' (Counihan 1992: 57). As was the case with French mothers, American students were concerned about their health and physical fitness and – not surprisingly – bodily thinness, which according to Counihan is the crucial criterion of attractiveness in the peer culture (ibid.). They also often spoke about food in terms of its nutritional value and often formulated in scientific terms the rules to be followed in selecting food. In general, these rules favoured restraint in eating.

As Counihan observed, the students were not much upset by their regular failure to follow these rules and to eat in a nutritionally proper way (ibid.: 58). They could often give a number of possible excuses or special conditions under which it was thought permissible to break the rules (such as to grant a reward to oneself for what one had accomplished or to comfort oneself). The rules were almost made to be broken. One of the possible reasons suggested by Counihan for the relative ease with which the rules could be broken, was that the students seemed to think that there were no real consequences, an observation obviously supported by everyday experience (ibid.: 59). The possible detrimental health effects take a long time to manifest. This could be one of the reasons why openly utilitarian arguments ('it's in your own best interest') in favour of a healthier diet or against smoking often do not sound very convincing.

## Health food ascetics and the management of the body

If the argument or the criterion of a balanced diet (also often used in official health propaganda in the form of the nutrition circle with a sector of one's own for all the basic nutrients a human body needs) does, in fact, figure as a general quasi-ethical value or meta value for choosing food, it is worthwhile comparing this 'spontaneous rule of dietetics' with the arguments of the 'religious virtuosi', the founding fathers and representatives of health food movements. In the words of Friedrich Nietzsche (1990: II §3), an ascetic is a man who singles out just a couple of rules and makes them 'stable, everpresent, unforgettable and fixed' ('*unauslöslich, allgegenwärtig, unvergessbar, fix*'). The ascetic procedures and exercises serve the purpose of absolutizing these ideals and making their following an automatic process not to be questioned. To a health food virtuoso, to eat wholesome food and to avoid all the numerous dangerous substances food can contain becomes the major occupation of his life and a means of achieving the supreme moral goal of his life.

Joseph R. Gusfield (1992) compared the philosophy of the earlier and contemporary American health movements, the ideals and goals of the Grahamite movement of the 1830s with the new health food movement which began sometime in the 1950s. As a result, he suggested that the main preoccupation of these – often nostalgic – movements is to teach people the exercise of self-restraint in eating. In particular, the older movements often looked for a 'more natural society' in which men could live in harmony with themselves without the temptations offered by the modern society. A balanced diet was an essential component of such a state of harmony. As Gusfield noted:

> the excitement that certain foods created was dangerous to the body. The refined flour [the main target of critique for Graham, the inventor of Graham biscuits – J. G.] produced in commercial agriculture deprived the body of needed coarse fiber. But it was not only the direct effect of diet on the body that alarmed Graham. It was also the effects of sexual desire and sexual intercourse on health. Limits to lust were essential to human health, as were limits to gluttony.
>
> (Gusfield 1992: 83)

In Gusfield's opinion, Graham equated the moral and the medical, health and good character: 'The self-discipline demanded by healthy diet was itself an act of moral virtue. It was a paradigm of the nineteenth century' (ibid.: 84). To Graham the exercise of self-discipline was a quasi-religious exercise and health was both a reward for the pilgrim's progress and a sign of his moral superiority.

Quite obviously this was not only a paradigm of the nineteenth century, but has deep roots in European intellectual history. It is a paradigm that can, for instance, be found in the teachings of the famous society physician, George Cheyne, the inventor of the 'English

Malady' (gluttony) in the middle of eighteenth-century England (see Falk and Gronow 1985). Carole Counihan identified the basics of this paradigm very much alive in the writings about food of present day university students in the USA. In her opinion, the pseudo-scientific rules adopted by the students favoured restraint in eating 'because it is a path to personal attractiveness, moral superiority, high status, and dominance' (Counihan 1992: 60). (The emphasis of the modern students was, no doubt, often more utilitarian and hedonistic, but this would seem to be a difference of degree only.)

The modern health food movement which began in the 1950s is, in Gusfield's opinion, in many ways different from the older one. Sexual desire is no longer a source of danger. The 'rational' fear of AIDS, surprisingly not mentioned at all by Gusfield, is a recent phenomenon and not an integral part of the ideology of this health food movement. Since the 1960s at the latest, the movement has been part of a broader ecological movement. The new movement is also more populistic (anti-science) by nature. Whereas the Grahamites still often referred to science in support of their principles, in the present movement 'the philosophy of self-help is accompanied by the rejection of medicine and often of academic and scientific writings' (Gusfield 1992: 96).

As Gusfield has pointed out, the philosophy of both of these movements can best be understood as a response to a world in which social norms are in a rapid change:

> In a society in which the institutional controls of family, church, and work are declining [as in the USA of Grahamite times] the body is an area of struggle between the tempting forces of market and city, which draw the person into immediate physical gratifications, and the laws of God and nature, from which the causes of good health and right living are derived.
>
> (ibid.: 89)

Gusfield (1992: 99–100) is certainly also right in emphasizing that the outcome of these anti-modernist movements was paradoxical. By emphasizing the ideas of self-control, restraint and individual auto- nomy to the utmost, they helped to create 'a body brought under the control of the rationalized soul, the central symbol of modern life'. In the Grahamite philosophy the emphasis was put on the temptations and excitement emanating from the outside, from market and city, i.e. the modern commercial society. George Cheyne concretized such temptations to the 'alien products' of a rapidly increasing colonial trade which aroused Englishmen's appetite: i.e. the civilizing process described by Adam Smith was turned upside down, into a critique of civilization. In the contemporary movement the dangers and temptations of indulgence and overeating also threaten every individual, but still the righteous have more reason to worry about other kinds of influences which threaten the balance of their body and their health. The willingness to exercise self-control has not disappeared, but the very foundations which make it possible are threatened. Gusfield probably had the same thing in mind in writing somewhat cryptically: 'What is signified and symbolized in the contemporary health movement is a return to control over one's body. What is signified and symbolized in the Grahamite movement is the attempt to restore moral authority' (ibid.: 98).

The representatives of the contemporary health movement obviously think that the development of science and technology has led us into a situation in which the individual has no independent way of knowing or testing the value of the things he is eating. He has to rely blindly on the judgment of experts and the scientific institutions. According to Sellerberg's (1991) observation,

> the real difficulty is, however, that no formal rules possess the fundamental ability to draw limits for the general public between the food it should trust and those that are less trustworthy. This is because, in the final analysis, trust per se is impossible to produce according to plans.
>
> (Sellerberg 1991: 199)

The situation is reminiscent, to a certain extent, of the situation in Britain in the nineteenth century, when adulteration of food was so common that the Cooperative Society hired a lecturer to tour the country giving advice as to what genuine food should really taste and look like (see Burnett 1966: 202). Only now, in the eyes of the public, science and modern technology, and not unscrupulous businessmen, are chiefly responsible for the 'adulteration' of food. The rules made by science are often not felt to be valid and legitimate. The contemporary movement would thus seem to be mainly occupied with the task of avoiding risks which one cannot, even in principle, foresee or control. One simply has to try to avoid everything the 'purity' of which has been spoiled by the touch of modern technology. To take an example, a modern health faddist would avoid bread made of refined flour mainly because of its negative (almost poisonous) nutritional value, whereas in Graham's thinking the danger lay more in the fact that such bread tasted too good to be resisted.

The purpose of the above discussion about the philosophy of the health food movements has not been to claim that they could, in fact, reveal – in an accentuated form – the truth about modern food culture and the dilemmas facing the modern eater. 'Ordinary' eaters are not simply less devoted ascetics who are all still going in the same direction, even though struggling on the lower stages of the pilgrim's progess. There is, however, an interesting lesson to be learnt from the life and philosophy of health food ascetics. The interesting thing about ascetics is not so much whether or not they have succeeded in reaching their ideals (their ideal diet), which, in fact, they almost never do. Neither is the health food ascetic necessarily consuming less food and drink or using less money in order to buy them. The main thing is that their minds are constantly preoccupied with eating and food. They are continually monitoring, testing, controlling and transforming their eating habits, using the standards they have elected as the unquestionable principles to guide their lives ('to eat only living food', 'to avoid eating refined flour', 'not to eat animal fats', etc.). Total balance or harmony is never within reach. Life is an eternal struggle.

For instance, according to Mildred Blaxter's (1990) results, smokers are even more aware of the perils of smoking than non-smokers. And it certainly is no joke that today the majority of women – probably as many as 80 to 90 per cent – are constantly monitoring their daily calorie intake and eat less than is required to stop them feeling hungry (Mennell *et al*. 1992: 51–2). Most women also perceive their own figures to be heavier than the figure they consider attractive. However, in the advanced capitalist countries women in general, or on average, have by no means lost weight.

## Vitamin deficiency and the 'hidden hunger'

At the beginning of the century, the major issue – besides protein consumption – in the discussion over dietary needs was mainly concerned with hygiene and dangerous additives or surrogates used by the food processing industry. The Pure Food Act, approved in the USA in 1906, was the main result of these concerns. The major task of the nutritionists was to control and prevent the use of dangerous foodstuffs, and to prohibit the sale of alcohol and other drugs widely used in patent medicines. The invention of vitamins, minerals and other micro-nutrients changed the scene in many respects. Since the 1920s, new laboratory experiments have been able to prove the vital importance of many new vitamins to the functioning of the human organism. This marked a crucial change in the practical role of nutrition science and in nutrition consciousness. In public discussions the need for vitamins, and later various micro-nutrients, is not often determined in terms of the maintenance of the balance of the body, nor as a remedy for a disease or a deficiency: their permanent use is rather understood to be necessary for the maintenance of good health in general; they mainly promote longevity. Strictly speaking, the new consciousness concerning the effects of vitamins no longer follows the logic of a discourse of needs (see Falk 1990).[9] At the same time, vitamin products became ideal commodities, not unlike the old patent medicines, for a new mass market, and exemplary products of a new kind of marketing and advertising (cf. Falk 1994: Chapter 6).

According to Levenstein's (1988: 152) interpretation, vitamins became ideal products for a food processing industry once the consumption of food ceased to increase in quantity. With the help of vitamins, the same essentially homogeneous goods could be differentiated into different products or brands. Advertising and marketing could now refer to such properties which, in terms of their use, were rather inessential. The amounts of different vitamins needed were often difficult to quantify and measure, and their effects were often hard to evaluate. In this respect, they could take the place of the old patent medicines (which had been banished shortly before) as ideal commodities.[10]

One could thus claim that vitamins and vitaminized food were among the first modern commodities of consumption in a market where fashions could now freely follow one another. One fashion criteria, suggested already by Georg Simmel (1981), was that there are no crucial (e.g. scientific) tests which can decide whether one commodity is better than another. One of the early advertising successes in the 1920s can be used to illustrate this point (see Marchand 1985: 18). Fleischman's Yeast had been losing markets due to the diminishing interest in home baking. Supported by a forceful advertising campaign, it was then introduced as an important source of vitamins, to be ingested daily. It was alternatively advertised as a remedy for vitamin deficiency and as a laxative, an ideal cure for the 'American disease', dyspepsia. In Marchand's words, Fleischman's Yeast combined 'the necessity for frequent purchase and the almost complete absence of quickly apparent results' (ibid.: 18).

Vitamins – and products like Fleischman's Yeast – also helped to transform the scientifically grounded argument in dietary recommendations. Although laboratories learned to measure and determine the vitamin need more accurately, and even though no vitamins are totally tasteless – in this respect, some minerals and other micro-nutrients have taken their place in promising more or less mysterious effects – there is a decisive shift in nutritional argumentation. Vitamins do not satisfy a 'hidden hunger' and help to recover the disturbed balance of the human organism. If one were to believe the advertisers, their recurrent use would have a preventive function and be necessary for the maintenance of the body in order to keep oneself in good health – the criteria of which are, in principle, always vague and indeterminate. It is always practically impossible to decide whether the goods ingested have kept their promise of general well-being and alertness. In this respect, the circle is completed. If a good and long life is the prize for following recommended habits of eating and diet, the promises of modern science do not differ all that much from those of classical dietetics. The new dietetics, however, has one major drawback compared to the old one: the promise of a good life has become increasingly abstract and empty of meaning unless longevity is regarded as valuable as such (see Falk 1990). The new scientific dietary instructions, with their promises of a good life, have increasingly to compete with advertising and other popular media about the soul of the modern consumer as well.

In speaking about 'good and bad food' the representatives of the natural food movement as well as ordinary eaters are defining themselves as moral subjects and delimiting that part of themselves that will form the object of their moral practice, in the same sense as in the discourse on sexuality in Greek and Greco-Roman antiquity reported by Foucault. In the philosophy of ascetic dietetic movements as in sexual discourse, 'moral conceptions were much more oriented towards practices of the self and the question of askesis than towards codifications of conduct and the strict definition of what is permitted and what is forbidden' (Foucault 1987: 30). As Foucault pointed out, 'the accent is placed on the relationship with the self that enabled the person to keep from being carried away by the appetites and pleasures, to maintain a mastery and superiority over them . . . ' (ibid.).

Even though health matters to most people today, eating and the question of food selection can hardly, in most cases, be regarded as the principal area where 'the individual delimits that part of himself that will form the object of his moral practice and decides on a certain mode of being that will serve as his moral goal'. In the women's views on food discussed above, there is a balance to be maintained – self-control

124

is an important value to a human being – but hardly any need to win back any lost area of individual autonomy. The spontanous ethical rules and precepts to be followed are often an esoteric combination of scientific and folk dietetics, but they are presented without any particular anti-modernistic and anti-scientistic zeal. Most of us are not health ascetics, just ordinary believers.

## The product as the real ascetic

Fortunately, in the recent decades, the food industry has done a lot to relieve us of any further need to struggle and from the burden of all moral responsibility. It has produced foods and foodstuffs that help us live according to the ascetic ideal without hardly having to change our eating or drinking habits at all. We can go on eating just like before and still our diets become almost 'ideal'. One could for instance say that the remarkable change in butter and whole milk consumption observed by the Finnish nutritionists during the 1980s was not caused by any conscious acts of abstinence. People could still go on eating their *voileipä* (bread and butter – the Finnish national dish) as before. And they could still go on drinking milk with it. What changed was that instead of whole ('red') milk they now drank low-fat ('blue') or skimmed milk and spread margarine (in daily parlance often still referred to as butter) or a butter mix on their bread.

These changes were certainly not easy to accomplish. The struggle between butter and margarine went on for decades and is not totally over yet. It took, for instance, decades to convince the Finnish people – some still express strong doubts – that margarine was as good or even better than butter (see Pantzar 1992). As we all know, margarine is not really the same as butter. It tastes different, and in changing from butter to margarine people often felt that they were forced to abandon their earlier eating habits and transform their diet drastically. But still the introduction of butter mix or margarine as a substitute for butter – or even as an improvement over butter – in many ways allowed people to maintain their old cherished habits of eating. One could at least try to convince oneself that one did not have to 'abstain' from anything important.[11]

As a matter of fact, there are now 'health', 'light' or 'low-cal' alternatives to almost every imaginable food or drink. The list compiled by Richardson (1990: 151), a nutritionist employed by Nestlé, is convincing even though far from complete: 'calorie-controlled recipe dishes, low-calorie soups, yoghurt, salad creams, dressings and spreads, table top sweeteners, soft drinks, wines and beers are now widely available as attractive alternatives to conventional food items'. In this substitution industry there are many success stories, low-calorie drinks in particular (low-fat milk is a good example), but in many areas the resistance offered by traditional tastes and the public's suspicion has been difficult to overcome. The early introduction of soya meat after the Second World War never succeeded. It will be interesting to see whether the recent technological innovations and improvements of new protein products can accomplish what soya meat could not. (The totally 'artificial' shrimp sticks produced with the help of this new technology have already proved to be a success, but they are more children's food.)

It is also interesting to observe that, contrary to the claims made by many nutritionists and health researchers (e.g. Karisto *et al.* 1993), a major change has taken place in cigarette smoking, too: from strong non-filter to filter and finally to 'light' cigarettes. In many respects this transformation has been more total than, for instance, the substitution of margarine and vegetable oil for butter, even though the motivation has been largely the same. The reason why much less attention has been paid to it in the studies of 'health-related habits' probably is that the estimated benefits of 'light' cigarette smoking for national health are not very high. These examples would seem to suggest that the process of substitution has been successfully accomplished primarily in cases where the public has become more or less convinced that the new product has at least as many benefits as the old, and the only element missing from the new product is one that is worth avoiding.

## Marketing the 'fashion for health'

Strong doubts have been expressed whether a direct reference to the health-promoting qualities of a new product really does sell to a wider public. Earlier studies about the promotion of soya meat as a healthier alternative to meat do not support it (see Woodward 1945, cited in Rozin *et al.* 1986: 86). As Päivi Lehto (1993) pointed out in her analysis of Finnish margarine advertisements, it is difficult to combine pleasure with health, but there are many examples to the contrary (cf. the advertisements for many low-calorie drinks and sweets, see Falk 1991). On the other hand, it is easy to point out many changes in the consumption of food commodities in which the products that are successfully marketed are anything but health foods.

Sweetened yoghurts (nowadays admittedly often 'light') which have become extremely popular since the middle of the 1960s are a good example. As Somogyi (1990: 106) has shown, potato consumption has diminished drastically in Switzerland during the last decades. At the same time, the loss of the market share has been almost totally compensated by convenience potato products, like French fries, chips and – in Switzerland – *rösti* (covering almost 27 per cent of the total market value). People also eat (snacks, sweets and fruits) more often during the day than before.

The analysis of contemporary food discourse would seem to indicate that the logic of the food market is such that only some items or some nutritional ingredients, like vitamins or other micro-nutrients, can come into special focus at any one time.

This seems to be true about food scares in particular. In such cases there is a widely shared belief that some single item is responsible for all the perils of the whole nation. Or alternatively, a newly invented nutritional wonder-stuff can save future generations from the plague of illness. The lack of selenium in food in Finland or the sudden fear of getting an overdose of vitamin A by eating pigs' liver are good recent examples. The popular interest in food is often rather casual: new worries seem to follow each other at regular intervals and whenever a new topic of discussion is introduced the old is soon forgotten. The overall result of these changing moods would be rather difficult to predict.

## The role of fashion in food culture

Herbert Blumer (1969: 286–7) named six conditions for the appearance of fashion in any possible area. Blumer studied the Paris fashion market, in particular, but there is no doubt that most of these conditions are also present in the modern food culture and market. First, the area is open for recurrent presentation of models and proposals of new social forms, the presence of which introduces a competitive situation and sets the stage for selection between them. Second, there is a relatively free opportunity for choice between the competing models. The area is obviously also open for the emergence of new interests and dispositions in response to (a) the impact of outside events, (b) the introduction of new participants into the area, and (c) changes in internal social interaction. The opening of national borders and general social mobility should take care of most of these conditions in any modern society. According to Blumer, the last condition, in particular, is chiefly responsible for the shifting of taste and the redirection of collective choice which together constitute the lifeline of fashion.

Two of the six conditions mentioned by Blumer are more problematic in the case of food culture. As he argued (1969: 286) 'the area in which fashion operates must be involved in change, with people ready to revise or discard old practices'. In any area where there are strong traditions or things believed to be sacred, fashion cannot operate. As is well known, in any culinary culture and practice there are many strong traditions and even things considered to be sacred (cf. the notorious meatballs, often mentioned in jokes about married couples in Scandinavia, which only the husband's mother knows how to cook), which effectively resist change. On the other hand, if scientific nutrition is to be believed, there are also objective tests through which the relative merit of the competing models can be demonstrated and evaluated. In Blumer's opinion (ibid.) fashion cannot survive in such an area either.

Paradoxically, the increasing importance of scientific knowledge and technology – which is supposed to be acting against fashion – in deciding what food is good to eat, is one of the decisive factors that have promoted the appearance of the first of the above two conditions. By questioning traditions and destroying 'sacred' beliefs (e.g. in earlier times butter was a highly valued – almost a sacred – commodity to most Finns), the science of nutrition opens the area to change. But what about the other condition? Have the results of objective scientific tests increasingly been substituted for traditions as reliable guides to food choice, in which case there would again seem to be less room for fashion to operate?

As has already been mentioned, Claude Fischler (1980, 1986 and 1990: 204–7) suggested that scientific rules have increasingly taken the place of traditional guidelines in modern food culture. As has been pointed out by Sellerberg (1991), a society in which there is a general distrust of food and no reliable guidelines could not survive for a long period of time. As the data collected by interviewing the representatives of modern culture referred to earlier would seem to suggest, scientific knowledge of nutrition is as good, or even a better, candidate to fill the vacuum as any.

There are, however, two reservations that should be made about the possibilities of the science of nutrition taking the role of the new religion of modern society. First, science does not give us very good advice as to what foods to eat. At best, it can advise us to avoid eating some – poisonous – foods, but there cannot, in principle, be any objective tests with unambiguous results to decide what foods are good to eat. Many foods and foodstuffs have practically the same nutritional value. Most diets are good enough. Thus, science leaves too much room for individual choice.

The second argument is more important: people do not eat nutrients but food. Hence, there cannot possibly be any single criterion to determine the relative merit of various foods. In other words, the advice given by science is simultaneously too liberal and too authoritarian. Furthermore, if it is true that the means to achieve the goal of health are not easy to name, nor is the goal itself by any means unambiguous. (In most cases one could probably simply substitute physical attractiveness or even slimness for health.)

According to Blumer (1969: 289), the function of fashion is to introduce 'order in a potentially anarchic and moving present'. Furthermore, 'fashion nurtures and shapes a body of common sensibility and taste' (Blumer 1969: 290). If Blumer was right, then it means that the modern consumer – or modern eater – does not live in a state of anomie, as suggested, for instance, by Fischler (1990: 204–7; cf. also Schwartz 1986: 267). As Fischler understood it, a society in which food selection and intake are increasingly a matter of individual, not social, decisions, faces the danger of a food crisis. But despite the lack of firm traditions or norms, the modern eater is by no means left alone in deciding what to eat and drink in a rapidly changing modern world. To a great extent fashion plays a role similar to traditional norms – or standards of good taste – in guiding the modern eater in the perplexing task of selecting proper meals and socially accepted foods and drinks. These guidelines offered by fashion are not 'fixed' (see Campbell 1987: 157). They are, on the contrary, transitory, contingent, constantly changing. Fashion is an elusive social formation and the community of taste is only a 'cloud of a community'.

From the contingent and transitory nature of the standards of fashion it does not by any means follow that people do not give good reasons for their food choices. Even in the area of clothing, the classical area of the appearance of fashion, reasons are constantly given, even though they are often rather empty of meaning ('I like it because it is fashionable'). As we have seen the reasons given for the selection of food are nowadays often expressed in the vocabulary of science. Neither does it mean that one could not identify stylistic changes in eating habits and interpret them in the light of broader social and cultural developments. For instance, Fred Davis (1992) has recently presented an interesting interpretation of contemporary styles of clothing and recent changes in sartorial manners. He suggested that the main trends in contemporary fashion are a result of the increasing ambivalence of sexuality and gender (cf. the recent masculinization of female fashion). In the same way one could probably interpret the observed changes in health-related habits as expressions of the changing and ambivalent role of women in modern society. Women have taken up many of the traditional masculine habits, like drinking and smoking – although at the same time making them 'lighter' and more 'civilized'. It would, however, seem that in the area of food the feminine influence has been a particularly dominant one.

The principal contingent nature of fashion means that there cannot be any progress – once poverty is overcome and the age of abundance has begun – in food culture. Science is not making our food culture more rational – whatever that means. As suggested by Mayntz and Nedelmann (1987), fashion is a self-dynamic social process which continuously creates its own social conditions. 'Fashion nurtures and shapes a common sensibility and taste' (Blumer) and obviously health has become an area of common sensibility. There is a taste for health in modern society. The rules of scientific nutrition compete among other models as candidates for the formation of this collective taste. That they are taken by many as the only possible and natural ones only proves the point. The naturalness and self-evidence of the present fashion is always contrasted to the oddness and incongruity of past fashions. This also means that these choices are aesthetic. They are predominantly based on taste. As such they are a particularly good example of a wide and important social phenomenon: the aesthetic dimension inherent in practically all social interaction.

# 5

# THE BEAUTY OF SOCIAL FORMS

## SIMMEL ON SOCIAL FORMS

### Can a taste or a smell be beautiful?

In the *Journal of Aesthetics and Art Criticism*, William B. Fretter claimed that wine, almost self-evidently, can be an art object just as much as can a painting or a piece of music. In Fretter's opinion (1971: 100), we cannot reach any other conclusion if we apply the criteria that feel natural in the case of an art object: 'The beauty of wine is a controlled abstract beauty expressing the intentions of the artist.' Fretter does not hesitate to call wines beautiful since

> they give me maximum aesthetic satisfaction. They are complex and rich in the varieties of sensual impressions they make.... And for full appreciation they require a competent observer who can fuse the meanings of past experiences into a present experience.
>
> (Fretter 1971: 100)

The classical guide book of wine tasting written by Amerine and Roessler (1976: xii) is almost as unreserved in this respect: 'In the proper balance, these sensory characteristics combine to stimulate the one sense that provides the most enduring pleasure and appreciation – the aesthetic sense.'

In discussing the aesthetics of wine in the introduction to their work, Amerine and Roessler formulate in an almost classical manner the question about the relation between mere sensual pleasure and pure aesthetic pleasure. They have no doubt that the pleasures of wine are not only sensual and subjective:

> Our first reaction to an aesthetic object such as wine is apt to be

131

purely subjective: we like it or dislike it. For a more lasting judgment however, we apply certain objective criteria, consciously or unconsciously.... Our enjoyment of wine is thus essentially a learned response and is a complex mixture of intellectual and sensory pleasures.

(Amerine and Roessler 1976: 5)

The fact which Fretter as well as Amerine and Roessler regard as self-evident has by no means been self-evident in the European aesthetic tradition. In fact, both Fretter and Amerine and Roessler are implicitly polemizing against the 'traditional' stance. For instance, Immanuel Kant, who was a great friend of white wine, would not have approved of describing a taste or smell as beautiful; even less would he have approved of wine as an art object. He does not even acknowledge a single colour or a single tune as a proper source of aesthetic pleasure.[1]

Kant shared with many of his contemporaries a reserved attitude to 'lower' senses and the pleasures associated with them. As he argued in his anthropological writings, both taste and smell are subjective because they only function when objects are near to them: in the former case the sensory organ, the tongue, is directly touched by a foreign particle, in the latter case foreign particles floating in the air are ingested (see Kant 1980: 451). The sight is the most noble of all the senses because its impressions are formed farthest away from its object (ibid.: 449).[2]

Francis Coleman's (1965) defence of the beauty of wine is explicitly directed against the 'Kantian' position. Coleman comes to the conclusion that there are no sound reasons to exclude either the senses of taste or smell or the sense of touch from aesthetic experience. In the best tradition of philosophical argument, Coleman constructs a dialogue between an imaginary proponent of 'Kantian' aesthetics and an opponent who demands that taste and smell also have a right to beauty. In so doing Coleman simultaneously formulates a typical Kantian position about the conditions of beauty. These conditions were also recognized by Pierre Bourdieu (1984) as the main criteria of a 'pure' Kantian aesthetics.

As Coleman (1965: 319) admits, we do not usually call tastes or smells – like the smell of a wine or the taste of a chateaubriand – beautiful but rather good smelling or good tasting. There certainly is no reason to try to change this common usage of language – it would hardly be possible. This argument is not, however, a basic one. Instead, we have to ask whether there really are any good arguments against calling a wine beautiful. Is it a better counter-argument to say that tastes and smells are usually simple sensations which would, together with single colours or sounds, fall within the class of sensations that are merely pleasurable? There is, however, no reason whatsoever to claim that smells and tastes would in this respect radically differ from, say, the sense impressions of sight. They can be equally complex. In saying, for instance, that the touch of silk is beautiful, we can analyse our sensations in regard to the complex and many-sided relations they include (see Coleman 1965: 320).

Our imaginary Kantian opponent would not rest his case so easily: he could continue his attack by saying that even though these sensations can be complex there is no possible order within them. Even this argument can be questioned. Let us think for a moment about a delicious culinary dish. Its different flavours can form contrasts and complement each other:

> A well-prepared dish is an 'organic whole' in basically the same sense as a well-conceived painting: elements are contrasted with each other but not contrasted so sharply that they fail to cohere. We often find that a dish 'needs something', that 'there is something missing,' just as we sometimes do with a painting. This is not to say that as far as their aesthetic merit or worth are concerned a well-prepared dish and a well-conceived painting are the same, but only that both are fit subjects of an aesthetic judgement.
>
> (ibid.: 321)

Let us assume that tastes and smells can be complex and, at least in some cases, form an 'organic whole'; as such they can add to the pleasure we receive from the observation of an object. This would not, however, make any difference because, according to the proto-Kantian argument, beauty always has to do with the form of the object. Tastes and smells are formless. According to Coleman (1965: 321–2) we should, however, ask what we really mean when speaking about the form in this respect. In doing so, we are obviously talking about the relations between the elements of which the object consists. This presupposes that there must be at least two such elements and that they must somehow (spatially or chronologically) be related to each other. They can, for instance, resemble one another, or follow each other, or they can form a sequel that is repeated at definite intervals, etc. Since such relations can also be observed in other than aesthetically beautiful objects, they cannot as such act as the criteria of genuine aesthetic experience. What we can do is to observe resemblances and differences, some of which we feel are pleasant while others are not. Such resemblances and differences can be observed in tastes and smells too. It must be admitted, however, that there is no similar 'natural' scale or order in tastes and smells as there is, for instance, in tunes, but we can observe contrasts and complements in tastes and smells too.

After such a devastating argument our imaginary Kantian proponent has to take refuge in his last and, undoubtedly, strongest counter-argument. Unlike colours and tunes, smells and tastes always serve some practical purpose, like the satisfaction of hunger, and as such they cannot act as proper objects of aesthetic contemplation. Under closer scrutiny, however, this argument is no more defensible than the previous ones. Our senses of sight and hearing are equally useful and functional, and the sensations they receive often serve practical purposes too, but we do not – at least under certain conditions – hesitate to call a painting or a piece of music beautiful. The same is true of taste and smell: some observations can be made in a disinterested way and these sensations do not serve any practical purpose, even though we undoubtedly use these tastes more often in an instrumental manner, for instance, in order to distinguish a putrid fish from a fresh one. The conditions under which these senses are employed are thus decisive: according to an old saying, in order to really enjoy food, one should neither be too hungry nor too satiated when coming to the table.

One could probably defend the position of Coleman's imaginary opponent by admitting that it certainly is more difficult and less common to free the pleasures of taste from their practical purposes than it is in the case of sight, but it is enough to admit that it is not totally impossible either. The tasting of wine offers a good example of such a disinterested observation. One is not supposed to drink or ingest the wine at all, only to 'touch' it with the taste buds in the mouth. Marinetti's famous *Futurist Cookbook* (1989), which was intended as a cruel parody of gastronomy, takes this distancing to the limits of disgust by combining together foods that are not at all edible and by using 'unnatural' colours in the dishes in its menus and cooking instructions.

It is thus easy to agree with Francis Coleman that there is no *a priori* reason – in opposition to what Kant and many of his contemporaries obviously thought[3] – why tastes, smells or even touch should be excluded from the possible objects of real aesthetic judgments:

> When the data from our senses of smell, taste, and touch are attended to for their own sake, when we entertain them not to learn something on the basis of them, or merely to satisfy our wants with them, and when the data are of a certain intensity, however short-lived they may be, then they can be beautiful. . . . To take aesthetic delight in one's senses, one's needs must already be in part satisfied, though not to the point of satiety.
>
> (Coleman 1965: 324)

As a matter of fact, in emphasizing how our sensations of taste and smell can be both complex and consist of many mutually dependent, complementary or contrasted elements, Coleman actually proves that a dish or a meal can be beautiful, rather than a taste or a smell as such. It would probably therefore be safer to claim that combinations of smells and tastes can be beautiful and, thus, can figure as the objects of pure aesthetic contemplation.

## The beauty of a meal

Coleman's discussion about the aesthetic delights associated with the senses of taste, smell and touch is interesting, in particular, because in rejecting a deeply rooted prejudice about culinary delights he formulates in a compressed form the central criteria that are usually presumed in 'Kantian' aesthetics, which always deal with the form of the object and are characterized by disinterestedness.

In his essay on the sociology of the meal, published in 1910, Georg Simmel drew almost the same conclusions about the meal as Coleman did – and his conclusions are even based on similar criteria. In this essay Simmel came to the conclusion – even though he does not explicitly say so – that a meal can, at least under certain conditions, be called beautiful. But in Simmel's case this beauty has nothing to do with the taste or the smell of the dish or the foods and drinks served at a meal – not even with the visual appearance of the dish or the meal. On the contrary, the beauty of the meal is almost inversely related to the importance of the sensory-physiological aspects of eating and drinking. Even to Simmel the aesthetic aspect of the meal is associated purely with its form, but this form does not consist of the harmonious totality of tastes and smells but of the social form or interaction of the meal, which derives from sociability. It is purer and, consequently, 'more aesthetic' the more purified it becomes from its contents or the physiological aspects of eating. In other words, the less it serves the satisfaction of needs and hunger, the more its formal aspects are emphasized. The more table manners are accentuated, the more independent this social interaction and the forms of sociation at the table are from any satisfaction of needs. In order for this form to become independent from its 'contents' and, consequently, in order for the participants to be able to experience pleasure that is aesthetic, this form must be developed without serving any physiological purpose.

The 'pure' or aesthetic pleasure produced by the meal is based on two mutually dependent conditions. First, it concerns the social form of the meal, and second, it must be characterized by disinterestedness.

As is the case with so many of Simmel's essays, 'The Sociology of the Meal' was inspired by and included an implicit comment on Immanuel Kant's anthropological writing. Simmel started his discussion of eating and drinking with a paradox: namely, he stated that eating and drinking are common to all human beings but at the same time they are the most selfish and individual activities. According to Simmel's understanding, others can hear and see whatever I hear and see but no one can strictly speaking taste – or ingest – the same articles as I do. The sensual pleasure of eating is, thus, completely individual. It is this antinomy of eating as simultaneously something totally universally human and completely individual, that, to Simmel, gives the meal a social form. In a similar manner, Kant stated that taste is a particularly sociable sense, because every guest sitting at the table can choose according to his own inclination from the many 'vessels and bottles' without any need for others to be compelled to enjoy the same foods and dishes (see Kant 1980: 452). Individuality and the freedom to choose, closely connected to each other, are, according to both Kant and Simmel, the necessary preconditions of sociability: 'because the sociability with others precludes freedom, and this feeling is pleasure' (ibid.: 563).

In a manner typical of him, Simmel formulated this paradox or antinomy in another way too: the absolute selfishness of eating is connected with the regularity and frequency of being together, a state which is seldom reached in connection with the so-called higher senses and more spiritual occasions, like listening to music. Because eating combines this completely egoistical interest in an exemplary manner with social interaction and being together, it exercises an enormous importance in all communities, of which the best proof are the innumerable rules and prohibitions that regulate it everywhere. These rules can, among other things, concern the people with whom one is allowed to share a meal.

When eating becomes a 'sociological' occasion, as understood by Simmel, it is transformed into something that is both more regulated and more 'overindividual'. Insofar as the social nature of eating becomes more evident, the meal also becomes more stylized. Simmel described a kind of process of civilization or cultivation of eating which is in some respects reminiscent of the analysis of the process of civilization by Norbert Elias. As this process advances the subjective or the natural purpose of eating, the satisfaction of hunger, is gradually forgotten until it finally becomes an almost negligible quantity. In such cases, a more and more regulated and complicated etiquette regulates both the very act of eating and the social interaction taking place during a meal. In Simmel's case this 'history of the civilisatoric process' should not, however, be taken too seriously. To Simmel, eating is from the very beginning social by nature and eating alone is rather a rare exemption or almost a perverse occasion. The selfish eater who satisfies his hunger all by himself, only caring for his own purely physiological needs, and the cultivated dinner guest who is able to follow a complicated set of rules or etiquette and who does not come to the table in order primarily to satisfy his 'lower' instincts, are only conceptual abstractions in which the two significant dimensions of a meal, the satisfaction of physiological-sensual needs and social inter-action, are compressed together. Simmel, however, obviously thought that these two dimensions were in inverse relation to each other: in so far as one of them is emphasized, the importance of the other is diminished as far as both the participants of the meal and its socio-logical observer are concerned.

The historical development of the meal is described by Simmel as a kind of a civilizing process. The social form and the rules of interaction are first transformed into more complicated ones among the higher echelons of society where this can take place to such a degree that the original purpose of the meal, the satisfaction of hunger, can almost totally be forgotten.

The sociability of eating presumes social rules. The necessity of such rules, or at least of a certain regularity of action, follows directly from the chronological regularity of eating but it is greatly increased by the socialization of the meal:

With all such changes a formal norm is raised above the

changing individual needs, the socialization of the meal elevates it into aesthetic stylization, which in its turn influences back on it; because if, besides the purpose of satisfying needs, eating has to serve also the purpose of aesthetic satisfaction, an excuse is needed, and a community of several persons is not only able to take better care of such an excuse, but it also acts much better as its legitimate carrier and performer.

(Simmel 1910)

In his essay on the sociology of the meal, Simmel also explicitly argued that any step that 'elevates the meal into the higher and more synthetic social values in the immediate and allegorical expression' also lends it a higher aesthetic value. This aesthetic aspect of the meal can also totally disappear when the social 'good' form disappears, as is the case in *table d'hôte*, a form of eating which disgusted Simmel. Even if the social form of eating were only a habit that no longer has any meaning and has become a 'mere' form, in Simmel's opinion it is better than no form at all. At *table d'hôte* people are offered a meal of prearranged courses at a fixed price leaving no room for individual preferences. Under such circumstances all social interaction becomes totally instrumental. To use a conceptual distinction made by Kant, at *table d'hôte* only sensual, and not aesthetic, pleasure counts. Aesthetic pleasure must always be combined with socialized eating including some kind of social interaction and freedom of choice.

Simmel's 'The Sociology of the Meal' ends with a typical aphorism. In his opinion, the discussion has proved that as in all the other walks of life, the lowest expressions of life can form not only the starting point but the very basis of higher values:

The fact that we have to eat is in the development of our values of life so low and primitive that it is self-evidently shared by all. As such it makes possible that people gather around meals and through the socialization mediated by this the mere naturalism of eating is exceedingly overcome.

(Simmel 1910)

Simmel's sociology of the meal clearly shows that he always thought that an aesthetic dimension is combined with any social interaction – or, in fact, the very social interaction is always aesthetic by its nature. A social form that has been set apart or has become independent from its contents, like a meal as a social occasion, is according to Simmel's understanding always aesthetic by its nature and the pleasures associated with it are aesthetic pleasures. In such a case social interaction has become an end in itself – it is totally disinterested – and it does not serve any 'outer' or alien purposes. To Simmel, fashion, as analysed earlier, is both a typical and important example of such a social formation. However, Simmel warned us that under certain circumstances this form – for instance the etiquette of eating – can be transformed into a pure formality, into something that is too much an end in itself, and can thus develop into an alien scheme. In normal cases or under normal circumstances Simmel seemed to be thinking that neither stylization, 'formalization', nor the development or cultivation of an etiquette by any means restricts the freedom of the individual, which was the very starting point of sociability; on the contrary they make it possible and further develop it. A concrete example of this is offered by the utensils used by cultivated people while eating, which, Simmel thought, despite the multitude of rules and restrictions concerning their use, do not restrict the freedom and elegance of movement in the same way as the coarse mugs and cutlery of the poor.

## The aesthetic sociology of Georg Simmel

Many contemporaries recognized an aesthetic dimension in Georg Simmel's sociology.[4] According to a recent interpretation by David Frisby

> it can be argued that Simmel's emphasis upon the forms of interaction ('*Wechselwirkung*') or sociation ('*Vergesellshcaftung*') in his programme for sociology – first tentatively announced in 1890 – indicates interest in revealing an aesthetic dimension of all social interaction that we do not immediately perceive in our everyday life, composed as it is of a multiplicity of diverse and intersecting interactional frames.... The sociologist can reveal and analyse aesthetic constellations and configurations that both exist in and are originally hidden in 'the flat surface of everyday life'.
>
> (Frisby 1992:135–6)

Frisby also claimed that a change in emphasis from ethics to aesthetics took place in Simmel's sociological thinking in the 1890s when Simmel, at least to some extent, gave up his earlier Nietzschean programme of the genealogy of the morale, the attempt to analyse the social origin of moral categories (cf. Simmel 1991a).

Murray Davis (1973) analysed systematically what Simmel could have meant by treating society as a work of art. Davis referred to an earlier statement by a student of Simmel's, Alfred Salz (1959, cited in Davis 1973: 320) who once said that he had learned from his teacher Georg Simmel the following about society: '[Simmel] conceives of sociology as the study of forms of sociation. But whoever speaks of forms moves in the field of aesthetics. Society, in the last analysis, is a work of art.'

In Davis' opinion three different dimensions can be distinguished in Simmel's aesthetic sociology: the artistic modality; a particular conception of the artistic product; and an artistic method (1973: 320). The first dimension stems from Simmel's idea according to which formal sociology resembles geometry in its analysis of abstract or pure social forms. In Davis' opinion this means that its modality is visual. Social forms resemble artistic products. While they are created by life itself they can still become separated from it. All the same, they have to draw their contents from social life (ibid.: 342): 'each of these separated processes has a place outside itself, in life, from which to draw materials that it can reshape with its own forms in its own medium'. 'Harmony' and 'order' are such criteria which prove how far both aesthetic forms and social forms have, in fact, become estranged from 'real' life, which is always disorganized, spontaneous and impulsive. Simmel even claimed that the attraction which socialism exercised for his fellow men as a social formation lay in its inherent harmony and beauty (see Simmel 1986).

The third aspect mentioned and analysed by Davis, the artistic method, is the same as Frisby's sociological impressionism, the recognition of a totality in its various fragments and the interpretation of a deeper meaning from a fleeting moment. This aspect of Simmel's aesthetic sociology, emphasized both by Frisby and Davis, dates back to early modernistic art theories typical of Baudelaire and his successors, who were contemporaries of Simmel, and not to Immanuel Kant's *Critique of Judgment*. Kant, on the other hand, has given a decisive impulse to the understanding of sociology as a study of pure or 'play' forms of sociation.

While speaking about the aestheticism of Simmel's sociology, David Frisby refers to two different dimensions of aestheticism. On the one hand, the participants of social interaction experience pleasures that resemble aesthetic pleasures because they react subjectively to the form of things, 'to the mere image of things' or 'to their appearance and form' with an internally harmonious feeling. On the other hand, in observing social interaction a sociologist has an aesthetic relation to his or her object. In this sense, Frisby has aptly characterized Simmel's sociology as impressionist sociology. In so doing Frisby has in mind mainly Simmel's writing on 'Soziologische Ästhetik' from the year 1896. In this article Simmel explicitly wrote that 'the meaning of aesthetic observation and interpretation lies in the fact that one can recognise the typical in the unique, the lawlike in the occasional and the [deeper – J. G.] meaning in the superficial and the transient' (Simmel 1896: 206). In Frisby's opinion, Simmel's sociology is 'pantheistic': while every fragment can reveal the real inner meaning of a totality, no fragment as such is more important than any other (see Frisby 1985: 58).

Aestheticism is, thus, both a manner of observation and interpretation and a feature that is common to social relations and to the consciousness of the acting individual. As Frisby said, Simmel treated these two aspects inseparably as of equal importance: 'Society is an aesthetic nexus, that is experienced both by the individuals in interaction and the sociologist... by distancing themselves from the society. Simmel does not solve this tension between these two "perspectives" on behalf of the other' (Frisby 1992: 53).

By emphasizing the difference between nature and society, or between natural science and sociology (or 'human sciences' in general), Simmel explicitly claimed that the social cohesion takes place in the consciousness of the individual actors and, as such, its constitution is not dependent upon any alien observer as is the case with nature: 'it is realized immediately by its own elements, since these elements themselves are conscious and synthesizing units' (ibid.: 49). It is also interesting to notice that in emphasizing how social actors are equipped with the needed social categories, Simmel also argued that such participants' knowledge is not conceptual in the ordinary sense ('*nicht Erkennen aber Wissen*'). This could also be interpreted as referring to the aesthetic character of such knowledge: 'The subject is not related to the object gradually to form a theoretical picture of it, instead every consciousness of sociation is immediately its own carrier and inner meaning' (Simmel 1992: 47).

## Sociability and pleasure

It is certainly not difficult to recognize the aesthetic nature of Simmel's sociology or its close parallel with Kant's aesthetic writings. This connection is self-evident and it was explicitly pointed out by

Simmel, too. In this respect, Simmel presented his own ideas and the consequences to be drawn from them concerning the study of social forms, in his programmatic writing 'The Sociology of Sociability' (1949 [1910]).[5] As Arto Noro has pointed out,

> this theme was Simmel's best example of 'pure' sociology or sociology that studies the forms of sociation ('*Formen der Vergesellschaftung*'). As a matter of fact, sociability ('*Geselligkeit*') or social intercourse was exactly such a form and even a form in which the object of pure sociology was presented in the clearest manner because in it free individuals are engaged in pure interaction.
>
> (Noro 1991: 39)

Simmel's own salon, which was one of the most famous and exclusive literary salons of Berlin, can be regarded as his private experimental laboratory for the study of social interaction.

In 'The Sociology of Sociability' Simmel explicitly said that in his sociology there is a strong parallel between social forms and works of art. In this sense his sociology comes very close to aesthetics: 'Within this constellation, called society, or out of it, there develops a special sociological structure corresponding to those of art and play, which draw their form from these realities but nevertheless leave their reality behind them' (Simmel 1949: 254).

According to Simmel, it is typical of both art and play that even though they have grown from and are created by concrete reality they are estranged from it and, in a way, leave it behind them. When both play and social interaction are abstracted from all their particular contents a common element remains or is preserved. This element is the residue of satisfaction which has to do with the fact that they are all forms of art or play. The same is true of sociability; one can even speak of the impulse of sociability. Even though social interaction in general – or in most cases – has a particular purpose, for instance the satisfaction of needs or the realization of interests, there is always a feeling of satisfaction which only stems from social association; from the fact that things are done together. This, in a somewhat mystifying way, is called 'the impulse of sociability' by Simmel. In sociability, for instance in the social intercourse in a literary salon, the pure form of social interaction is realized and can be observed: 'Sociability is, then, the play-form of association and is related to the content-determined concreteness of association as art is related to reality' (Simmel 1949: 255).

More often and with more emphasis Simmel referred in this essay to the fact that sociability is a play-form of association, which can best be compared with plays, which in their turn have a lot in common with art; everything that is true of a play or of art, is also true of sociability:

> And what joins art with play now appears in the likeness of both to sociability. From the realities of life play draws its great, essential themes: the chase and cunning; the proving of physical and mental powers, the contest and reliance on chance and the favour of forces which one cannot influence. Freed of substance, through which these activities make up the seriousness of life, play gets its cheerfulness but also that symbolic significance which distinguishes it from pure pastime. And just this will show itself more and more as the essence of sociability...
> (Simmel 1949: 255)[6]

In order to be like art or play, sociability and social interaction in general have to fulfil certain conditions: something is 'abstracted' or taken away from 'real' social interaction. This means that neither the most subjective nor the most objective features or characteristics of the participants, like wealth and social position on the one hand, or love and hatred on the other, must be allowed to interfere with sociability. In addition, it is essential that sociability is always a reciprocal process in which every participant, at least in the long run, both gives something and gets something, makes a contribution to social intercourse, e.g. by telling a good story, and receives some satisfaction from it. The common denominator of all these practical instructions of abstraction which, at least half-seriously, aim at the development of a mutually satisfactory social intercourse in Simmel's salon, is that social interaction must be disinterested and impartial. Sociability must be 'fair play'. Anyone who uses wealth or power or cheats in order to benefit from the intercourse not only spoils the pleasure of everyone else, but also his or her own.

Just like art, sociability both stylizes and reveals the inner reality of life. In this respect,

> all sociability is but a symbol of life, as it shows itself in the flow of a lightly amusing play; but even so, a symbol of *life*, whose likeness it only so far alters as is required by the distance from it gained in the play...
> (Simmel 1949: 261)

That the art in question is understood in a proto-Kantian spirit is shown by Simmel's two programmatic criteria and social conditions of pure social interaction: it must be disinterested and it is only the form that matters.

Sociability just as much as table manners, or the etiquette governing them, can be transformed into a pure shell or an empty scheme, if it has totally lost touch with the reality of life, which created it and from which it draws its energy. A form turned into a scheme is a pure formalism and as such it should be strictly distinguished from Simmel's basic idea of pure forms of sociation. Art and play, as well as Simmel's sociability, are all activities and forms of intercourse that do not serve any end, but they are not totally empty either. They are transformed into empty forms only if they become petrified or solidified, only if following the rules of the game has become a pure convention or a forced habit. The development of court etiquette is presented by Simmel as a historical example. In such cases play is in danger of turning into 'empty farce, to a lifeless schematization proud of its woodenness' (Simmel 1949: 261).

Simmel's fear of the petrification of the forms of social interaction can well be seen to correspond to Immanuel Kant's critique of classicism in art: an art of judgment which relied on some universal criteria or rules of beauty would be totally independent of any subjective feeling of pleasure. In a similar way social interaction which faithfully follows rules is experienced as coercive and cannot possibly give anyone any subjective pleasure. One does not take part in it because of the pleasant feelings it can arouse but out of obligation or under constraint. In social intercourse following an etiquette is as problematic as eternal rules of beauty, i.e. harmony, are to art: they are always in danger of becoming transformed into a strait-jacket.

## PLAY AND BEAUTY

### Play, art, and social forms

According to Simmel's own interpretation, Kant had suggested that

> what we call beautiful, is something which arouses in us the subjective reflex of purposiveness without being able to say whom or what it serves. It guards in us a typical gratification of human existence in all its purity and irreality.
>
> (Simmel 1905a: 163)

In the interpretation of aesthetics presented by Simmel in his lectures on Kant, exactly the same features are emphasized as are strongly present in his formal sociology. In art as in social interaction what matters is the pure form of purposiveness which does not serve any purpose at all. According to Kant's famous definition (1987: §17) 'beauty is an object's form of *purposiveness* insofar as it is perceived in the object *without the presentation of a purpose*'. Similar definitions are familiar from Simmel's characterizations of art, play and any such pure social interaction: it is without purpose and disinterested, but still not formless; it is ordered *as if* it served some purpose.

In fact, in Simmel's writings social forms are compared with play or games more often than with art. In clarifying the principles of his sociology Simmel obviously did not feel any need to distinguish between them. Most often they are simply given as parallel examples of social interaction that has an end in itself. Play acts for Simmel as a model for experiencing beauty – and not the other way around as is the case with Kant: 'only in play, when our activity circulates only around itself, and is satisfied only with itself, we are absolutely ourselves, we are totally "men" ' (Simmel 1905a: 163–4). In this respect Simmel seemed to be following the famous dictum of Friedrich Schiller (1982: 107) according to whom 'man only plays when he is in the fullest sense of the word a human being, and he is only a fully human being when he plays'.

Kant also saw a likeness between the pleasure created by art and by play. They are both examples of disinterested and self-purposive pleasure and, as such, different from pure sensual pleasure. Nevertheless, Kant did not totally identify them as Simmel seemed to be doing. In fact, in his *Critique of Judgment* Kant analysed the differences and likenesses between these pleasures in detail. Again, many of Simmel's observations could have been made by Kant, according to whom:

> any changing free play of sensations (that are not based on an intention) gratifies us, because it furthers our feeling of health, and it does not matter whether in our rational judgment we like the object of this play, or like this gratification itself. Moreover, this gratification can increase to the level of an effect even though we are not taking an interest in the object itself, at least not one proportionate to the effect's degree.
>
> (Kant 1987: §54)

In Kant's opinion, there are three different kinds of play or games that produce a pleasure resembling the aesthetic pleasure: the play (or game) of chance, the play of tunes (in music) and the play of thought (or of wit). It is relatively easy to understand what Kant meant by games of chance. As he saw it, they require an interest either in vanity or in our own profit, as is the case with games where money is at stake. It is the explicit purpose and in the selfish interests of the players to win the game. But as Kant argued, this interest alone could not explain the great popularity and success of such games among 'high society' of which the best evidence is that no evening party could do without the entertainment provided by them. This is best explained by the fact that interest in the way the game is played far exceeds the interest in winning. Playing the game is what matters, and a person who plays only in order to win is often regarded as slightly abnormal.

According to Kant the pleasure of playing is caused by quickly changing observations, by their surprise effects and the liveliness they promote, which are totally independent of the end result of the game, of winning or losing it:

> But many effects are at play there – hope, fear, joy, anger, and scorn, alternating constantly – and are so lively that they amount to an inner motion that seems to further all the vital processes in the body, as is proved by how sprightly the mind becomes as a result, even though nothing has been won or learned.
>
> (Kant 1987: §57)

Because in his opinion games of chance are not 'beautiful', Kant does not want to discuss them in this context any further. If sporting games had been invented Kant could certainly have taken them as a more 'decent' example. Simmel could refer to the enchantment of sport which is provided by its own dynamics and by the opportunities provided by this 'even sociologically important way of acting', and not by winning or by utility alone (see Simmel 1949: 258).

Unfortunately, Kant did not have much more to say about the other two types of play, those of thought (or wit) and of tune (or music). By the former, he obviously meant riddles and jokes and other such games played at social occasions which demand wit and inventiveness. The solution of a riddle is unexpected and the end of an amusing story surprising, and their revelation produces something akin to bodily pleasure, which, like laughter, promotes health. It is more problematic to understand what Kant meant by 'play of tunes' ('*Tonspiel*'). According to Grimm's Dictionary, published in the eighteenth century, a *Tonspiel* is simply the same as music. It is, however, quite obvious that Kant wanted to emphasize that 'the play of tunes' was not the same as music. Music is a form of art, as importantly and self-evidently as painting, the pleasures of which are clearly aesthetic. The pleasure of listening to music is based on quite different features from the pleasure of *Tonspiel* which originates from the rapid and unexpected change of tunes and impressions:

> But music [in the sense of *Tonspiel* – J. G.] and something to laugh about are two kinds of play with aesthetic ideas ... it is merely the chance they involve that still enables them to gratify us in a lively way.
>
> (Kant 1987: §57)

The aesthetic pleasure promoted by 'real' music is, on the contrary, based on the recognition of a form of harmony and not on any surprise effect; in music the composition is important, in painting the drawing. However, the rapid change of observations and impressions awakens feelings that are close to genuine aesthetic ideas:

> It is not our judging of the harmony we find in tones and flashes of wit – this harmony, with its beauty, merely serves as a necessary vehicle – but the furtherance of the vital processes in the body, the effect that agitates the intestines and the diaphragm, in a word the feeling of health ...
>
> (Kant 1987: §57)

Did Kant, in his 'aesthetic theory of play', formulate the first aesthetics of popular music and culture? Or did he have in mind the kind of music found in musical boxes and other such machines that were enormously popular at the time – in other words, mechanically reproducible music? Or perhaps these 'plays of tunes' were some, now totally forgotten, form of game played at social gatherings in Kant's time. Unfortunately Kant's description on this point is meagre. The first alternative is, however, the most probable one. The main thing is that even in Kant's opinion the pleasures of such activities are reminiscent of those associated with real art in many ways but also differ from them at least in one crucial way: these pleasures are not *a priori* universally shared by all the players of the game.

Just before presenting his 'theory of the games' in *The Critique of Judgment* Kant divided arts into two groups, the fine arts or, literally, arts of beauty (*'shöne Künste'*) and agreeable arts (*'angenehme Künste'*). The delights of the dinner table, table music (*'Tafelmusik'*) and – not surprisingly – sociability all belong to the latter group:

Agreeable arts are those whose purpose is merely enjoyment. They include the art of providing all those charms that can gratify a party at table, such as telling stories entertainingly, animating the group to open and lively conversation, or using jest and laughter to induce a certain cheerful tone among them – a tone such that, as is said, there may be a lot of loose talk over the feast, and no one wants to be held responsible for what he says, because the whole point is the entertainment of the moment, not any material for future meditation or quotation. (Such art also includes the art of furnishing a table so that people will enjoy themselves, and includes, at large banquets, presumably even the table-music – a strange thing which is meant to be only an agreeable noise serving to keep the minds in a cheerful mood, and which fosters the free flow of conversation between each person and his neighbor, without anyone's paying the slightest attention to the music's composition.)

(Kant 1987: §44)

Kant ends the discussion of these agreeable arts by saying that all games which have no other purpose than that of making time pass unnoticeably belong here (ibid.). Thus, it would seem legitimate to conclude that all play and games actually belong to this category of 'agreeable arts'. Table music, mentioned in passing by Kant, is a good example of 'play with tunes'. Thus one could reasonably argue that Kant's discussion of 'play' included an aesthetic of 'light' music or popular arts. Kant's description of table music is reminiscent of the muzak played in department stores and cafés today: it contributes to a pleasant and sociable feeling without demanding that any attention is paid to its composition or performance.

The most decisive difference between fine arts and arts that are merely agreeable seems finally to be whether the pleasure can be shared with others or, rather, whether it has universal communicability and validity as its precondition.

In Kant's thinking there is also a connection between a 'purely empirical interest in beauty' and social intercourse. Robinson Crusoe apparently would not have been interested in what he or his dwelling looked like:

Only in *society* is the beautiful of empirical interest. And if we grant that the urge to society is natural to man but that his fitness and propensity for it, i.e. *sociability*, is a requirement of man as a creature with a vocation for society and hence is a property pertaining to his *humanity*, then we must also inevitably regard taste as an ability to judge whatever allows us to communicate even our *feeling* to everyone else, and hence regard taste as a means of furthering something that everyone's natural inclination demands.

(Kant 1987: §41)

Only a person living with other human beings is interested in looking good. People who are willing and ready to share their pleasure with others and who are not satisfied with pleasures they cannot share have good reason to expect others to share their gratification, as if there existed something like a 'social contract' concerning the communicability and sharing of pleasure (ibid.). The condition of the universal and *a priori* communicability of a judgment of taste demanded by Kant is, however, totally different from the empirical connection between beauty and social association, since in the first case the universal communicability is a precondition of the aesthetic pleasure. According to Kant

> we could even define taste as the ability to judge something that makes our feeling in a given presentation *universally communicable* without mediation by a concept.... Hence taste is our ability to judge a priori the communicability of the feelings that (without mediation of a concept) are connected with a given presentation.

(Kant 1987: §40)

The beautiful is that which can be imagined 'without the mediation of concepts' to be the object of general pleasure.

As has already been pointed out, Simmel did not seem to pay much attention to this demand of universal communicability in his explicit comments on Kant's critique of judgment nor in his sociological 'adaptation' of Kant's ideas (cf. for example the essay on sociability). He was mainly occupied with the criteria of disinterestedness and with the form of finality or purposiveness. This may also explain why Simmel did not seem to think it important to distinguish between fine arts and agreeable arts, or between art and play. In Kant's analysis it is this very demand of *a priori* communicability which separates them from each other: the gratification offered by a game or by a dinner table or table music is not associated with any such demand.[7]

Simmel did not need to emphasize this aspect of universal communicability included in any judgment of taste because in his

149

sociological aesthetics – or in the ideal world of play and pure social interaction – this condition is, in fact, always automatically fulfilled. The principle of reciprocity is always built into the game as well as into sociability: my enjoyment or my gratification is always dependent on the joy and gratification of all the other participants of the game or all the members of a social gathering. It only takes one to spoil the joy of all and by spoiling the joy of others, I unavoidably spoil my own. In such games and social gatherings the totally subjective and individual feeling of pleasure is not necessarily universally communicable, but every player or participant can safely make the – in a sense stronger – assumption that all the other players or participants are sharing a similar feeling of pleasure. This assumption is furthermore not based on empirical evidence alone. The presumption that all the players or participants share the feeling is built as a constitutive condition into the very logic of the play of free social interaction. This is by no means the same as the universal, *a priori* validity of a judgment of taste presumed by Kant, but neither is it only a question of an empirically observable relation between social interaction and the promotion of beauty or a question of how the communication of the experience of beauty makes it more pronounced, which is also discussed by Kant in the *Critique of Judgment*.

It is thus safe to claim that in his own aesthetic sociology Simmel is obviously after something else, something that Kant did not deal with, but in the analysis of which Kant's ideas still could be fruitfully adopted. Like Pierre Bourdieu and Terry Eagleton, Simmel turned Kant's problem into a sociological one. His intention was, however, totally antithetical to theirs. Simmel intended to show that in the world of sociability the whole antinomy of taste between the subjectivity of the feeling and its general communicability in a sense disappears or is made obsolete since we can be assured that, at least as long as the social formation exists or is preserved, as long as the game is played or the sociable gathering goes on, the feeling is shared by all. This also explains Simmel's reformulation of the categorical imperative in the world of sociability. According to this new 'imperative' everyone is entitled to as much pleasure in social interaction as is in harmony with the gratification of everyone else's impulse of sociability:

> If one stands by the sociability impulse as the source or also as the substance of sociability, the following is the principle according to which it is constituted: everyone should have as

much satisfaction of this impulse as is consonant with the
satisfaction of the impulse of all others.

(Simmel 1949: 257)

## The ideal world of play and art

The worlds of sociability and the corresponding worlds of play and art
are ideal worlds and in this sense 'artificial'. Only in them this maxim
of sociability – the gratification of all is the necessary condition of the
gratification of each – is automatically realized and only in them is,
thus, the moral imperative substitutable for the aesthetic imperative.
In all other social worlds reciprocity precludes moral maxims and
ethical principles. As Simmel explicitly stated, this kind of a pure
social interaction is possible only among equals, which is a condition
which Simmel hardly thought would reign in normal social interaction in the 'real world'.

Niklas Luhmann has criticized Simmel's analyses of sociability for
exactly this abstractness. According to Luhmann's analysis, pure social
interaction in the form of sociability and cultivated social intercourse
became ideals of social conduct among the 'high society' in early
modern times because it made it possible – in a sense in an ideal form –
to practise in a stratified society for the coming society of equals: status
which is recognized as such is at the same time marginalized. This was
made possible because the desired socialization is based on nature and
morality alone and is freed from more serious social functions like
religion, politics, and accumulation of capital (see Luhmann 1980:
87). In Luhmann's opinion, Simmel's programme of formal sociology
is, in fact, a late revival of such an attempt which is therefore doomed
to failure: '[In Simmel – J. G.] sociability ("*Geselligkeit*") is understood
as an association ("*Sozialität*") reduced to a pure form which is
practiced as an end in itself (and not because of its contents or results)'
(Luhmann 1981: 255). What is wrong with such an attempt is that the
individuality of the participating individuals is, as explicitly stressed
by Simmel, necessarily very restricted. Thus, in such interaction full
individuality cannot possibly be constituted. In other words, the very
premises negate the aimed-for conclusion (ibid.).

Luhmann is certainly justified in doubting the success of Simmel's
formal sociology as a final solution to the conflict between the
antinomy of full individuality and fully developed socialization.
What Luhmann wanted to point out is that in Simmel's ideal world
individuality is rather empty of meaning. In this respect Luhmann's

critique comes close to Terry Eagleton's critique of the whole aesthetic ideology as discussed earlier. But Luhmann's argument is not as devastating as it would seem at first glance. One can give Simmel's formal sociology another interpretation: namely, Simmel can be understood to claim something less ambitious and at the same time more interesting. Because pure social interaction in the shape of sociability or play is necessarily reciprocal, it and only it can be called beautiful without any reservations. This is true of pure social forms or pure forms of sociation alone. As the example of fashion shows there are important and general social phenomena which come close to such pure forms. What is even more important, with every other kind of social interaction – even if they are not 'pure' – an aesthetic element is associated, too – a moment or a possibility of experiencing a genuine aesthetic pleasure, in the Kantian sense of the word. This is true also of such 'normal' social interaction which is subsumed under other – 'more serious' – social purposes and interests and in which the aesthetic moment is not pronounced.

It is interesting to compare Simmel's position, in this respect, with the aesthetic theory presented by Gadamer in his study *Truth and Method* (1988). There are many parallels between their conceptions. Even in Gadamer's understanding, play is essential for understanding what the aesthetic experience is about. A subjective experience is not suited to act as the starting point of aesthetics. It leads to a relativism which Gadamer would want to avoid, with all its consequences:

> My thesis, then, is that the being of art cannot be determined as an object of an aesthetic awareness because, on the contrary, the aesthetic attitude is more than it knows of itself. It is a part of the essential process of representation and is an essential part of play as play.
>
> (Gadamer 1988: 104)

Gadamer suggested that the proper 'subject' of the experience of art is not in a normal sense the observing and experiencing subject but the work of art itself. Play is important in understanding art and the aesthetic experience, because – in the same sense as a work of art – play has its own essence, independent of the consciousness of those who play (ibid.: 92). The players of a game do not create or give birth to it, they only perform or present it. Games can be regarded as self-dynamic processes – even though Gadamer does not use the concept – in which the movement 'backward and forward' is important, a movement which does not serve any purpose or end result. One can also speak about play or games without any players at all, as is the case with the play of colours or of light. This kind of play of nature is art's model (ibid.: 97).

Play and games become art as soon as they are presented to others or performed before an audience. The difference between 'a natural game' and art is, in the end, not very great since self-presentation is a part of every game or play: 'The players play their roles as in any game, and thus the play is represented, but the play itself is the whole, comprising players and spectators' (ibid.: 98). 'The play of art' is meant to be presented to others. In Gadamer's own words, whenever art is presented to others it reveals its specific nature as play. In this sense there is a difference between a play at a theatre or a cult play, on the one hand, and children's play, on the other. Even a child presents something while playing, e.g. plays a role, but he does not play it before an audience. In contrast, both in a cult play and in a 'regular' theatre performance the 'players' or actors present a certain totality of meaning to an audience. But does this not, in fact, mean that the spectators have to interpret and construe a totality of meaning by themselves? In this case, would not the art experience once again be created in the consciousness of the spectator alone? Gadamer, however, denies such an interpretation most emphatically. The performers and the spectators are not in a different position in this respect; they both construct and interpret a meaningful totality, which is already present both in the play and the game independently of the activity of the players. In interpreting the play the spectators are privileged only in the respect that the play is presented for them:

> it becomes apparent that it bears within itself a meaning that must be understood and that can therefore be detached from the behavior of the player. Basically the difference between the player and the spectator is removed here. The requirement that the play itself be intended in its meaningfulness is the same for both.
>
> (Gadamer 1988: 99)

There is, however, one condition which must be demanded from a game before it is transformed into a work of art: it must become a separate and independent formation (*Gebilde*), which, as such, can always be repeated. To paraphrase Gadamer, one could almost claim that it must be a social formation with a certain stability – or a social institution.

The main difference between Simmel's and Gadamer's

interpretations obviously is that while Gadamer attempts to preserve the objectivity of the aesthetic experience by stressing the similarity between the social formation of a game or play and a work of art, Simmel tries to identify an aesthetic dimension in every game or play and, more generally and ambitiously, in every social formation or form of interaction. The sociability of a salon and the 'game' of sociation is not meant to be presented to anyone, although it inevitably also includes a dimension of self-presentation. Normally, in any case, there are no spectators or audience following the performance of the play of sociability. This means that the aesthetic pleasure associated with it can only be experienced by the participants of the game – unless the possible sociologist-observer is not counted. But even the observing sociologist is a member of the salon – or more generally, the social association – that he or she is observing, and not a spectator of a sports event.

## Friedrich Schiller's programme of aesthetic socialization

The social world of play and games analysed by Simmel resembles in many respects the ideas of Friedrich Schiller, presented in his famous and influential work *On the Aesthetic Education of Man* (1982 [1795]), published shortly after Kant's *Critique of Judgment*, even more than those presented by Immanuel Kant himself. To Schiller, an aesthetic dimension included in a play or a game is essential both in the process of socialization of every human individual and in the development of the whole of humanity from animal to man. The aesthetic sphere is a necessary intermediary stage between the stage of nature and the human community observing moral laws. It cultivates and moderates the human being who naturally only attempts to follow his own instincts like an animal. The aesthetic 'play' drive or instinct ('*Spieltrieb*') has the important task of moderating our instincts – or perhaps it would be better to speak of the moulding and stylizing of the wants of man without the use of violence or force. Thus one could say that for Schiller the 'play instinct' is the main socializing agent. According to Schiller, in every man, *per definitionem*, there are two basic instincts: the first instinct is sensual and has to do with the satisfaction of needs and wants. The second instinct is called the form instinct or formal drive, and one could interpret it as an instinct for order. It is essentially intellectual by its nature. The first instinct belongs to the sphere of needs, the second to the sphere of reason and morality ('*Sittlichkeit*'). Both of these instincts are equally strong and are opposed to each other; there is no means of conciliation between them. They cannot be realized at the same time or merged together. There is no possibility of reaching a compromise between them.

Schiller's main problem is that, in his opinion, the realization of such universally valid laws or norms, which our reason alone could tell us to follow, would inevitably restrict the realization of the sensual instinct and the satisfaction of individual needs and wants. The only possible solution is reached with the help of Schiller's third instinct, the play instinct. This play – or aesthetic – instinct resembles in many respects the form instinct because it too aims at a form, at an order or uniformity. It differs from the form instinct in one important respect: it does not in a similar manner violate the 'wild' or animal instincts that belong equally and naturally to everyone. The task of the play instinct is to create order or to give a form to social interaction without suppressing our sensual instincts and drives. Social interaction without at least the most elementary of forms (i.e. some simultaneity of action) would not be possible at all – it could not be called social interaction – and would end up in chaos.[8]

As was argued by Schiller, even though our needs already have a socializing effect on man and even though reason teaches us the elementary laws of social interaction, only beauty can grant us a sociable character (*'Gesellige Charakter'*, Schiller 1982: 214) . Only a message (*'Mitteilung'*) about beauty can unify mankind, because it alone refers to a factor that really is common to all as genuine members of the human species, and that still can be enjoyed individually:

> The pleasures of the senses we enjoy merely as individuals, without us having any share in them at all; hence we cannot make the pleasures of sense universal, because we are unable to universalize our own individuality. The pleasures of knowledge we enjoy merely as genus, and by carefully removing from our judgment all trace of individuality; hence we cannot make the pleasures of reason universal, because we cannot eliminate traces of individuality from the judgments of others as we can from our own. Beauty alone do we enjoy at once as individual and as genus, i.e. as *representatives* of human genus.
>
> (Schiller 1982: 215–17)

In this light it is not very difficult to see the close parallel between Simmel's sociology of social forms and Schiller's programme of aesthetic education of mankind. In arguing that sociology should study the pure forms of sociation or the play forms of sociation, like sociability, Simmel, in fact, turns Schiller's aesthetic programme into a sociological one. By doing so he also, in a way, proved that there is, after all, no need for aesthetic education. Individual action and the individual's instincts receive their form, or are cultivated, all the time, as if automatically, in every social interaction and every social association without the need of any outer force and without moral imperatives or laws of morality based on reason. These social formations do not generally repress the genuine individuality of their members. On the contrary, social interaction is based on reciprocal aesthetic pleasure which is experienced subjectively by individuals. They can, thus, be called genuinely beautiful.

While interpreting the deeper meaning of Kant's *Critique of Judgment* Simmel concluded: 'In any case it is the first and deepest attempt of reconciling in the aesthetic sphere the unique individual subjectivity of man with his equally inevitable overindividual communality' (Simmel 1905a: 168–9).

It seems as if Simmel would like to remind both Kant and Schiller that this reconciliation is not only possible in the narrow aesthetic sphere or in the 'artificial' world of play, art and games. Such reconciliation takes place in modern society daily in any possible form of interaction. The practical solution to the antinomy of taste offered by the modern fashion pattern is a good, and by no means the least important, example of this. There is a permanent tension between the individual and the social totality and their final reconciliation is not within reach; any social solution is only a temporary one. That is why social formations are in a continuous state of change. But neither are socialization and individuality eternally irreconcilable opposites.

The 'elementary' or everyday forms of sociation are, furthermore, not only pre-forms or training grounds for a 'higher' ethical community governed by moral laws. Simmel's aesthetic communities are what socialization is really about. The alternative to an ethical community governed by laws or reason is not a totally atomized and disintegrated social world but the eternally changing, but equally ordered, social reality of the multitude of social formations.

Luc Ferry (1992), in his interpretation of Kant's *Critique of Judgment*, has recently pointed out that Kant, by emphasizing in his antinomy of taste the problem of the universal communicability of subjective pleasure, transferred into the aesthetic sphere the opposition presented by Rousseau in his famous letter to d'Alambert (1948 [1758]). In this letter Rousseau stressed the difference between the indirect communication of the theatre, realized only through the scenes of a play (the symbol of monarchy), and the direct communication of a feast (the symbol of democracy). In the feast, the spectator's eye is not directed towards an alien object: the spectator is just like all the other participants who are their own actors, playing and performing only for each other. In other words, the actor and the spectator are merged together. According to Ferry:

> here a theme becomes evident which is – mutatis mutandis – adopted by Kant in his third critique, and which lays the foundation for an aesthetic conception of free communication concerning a public space which is not conceptual nor regulated by rules.
>
> (Ferry 1992: 119)

It seems as if Simmel wanted to point out that 'this space of free communication', which the aesthetes thought belonged exclusively to art, was, in fact, part of any social intercourse, not only in the exceptional situation of a feast or a revolution but – to interpret Simmel narrowly – of the sociability of cultivated people or – to interpret him more broadly – of the everyday social interaction of ordinary people. This was done by emphasizing and analysing the dimension and possibility of reciprocal and equal aesthetical pleasure and freedom inherent in almost all everyday social intercourse in general, and in fashion in particular.[9]

# 6

# CONCLUSION
## The aesthetic sociology and the aestheticization of everyday life

### Does money beautify social relations?

Simmel's sociology of social forms could easily be interpreted as including an almost utopian dimension in claiming that an element or a possibility of aesthetic pleasure is connected to every social form of interaction. In discussing Simmel's essay on the sociology of the meal, we referred to the fact that Simmel obviously thought that social formations could gradually become more and more independent from the process of 'real life' and the satisfaction of instincts and needs which originally they were meant to serve. At the same time, social formations become more complicated and differentiated, like the etiquette of eating, and the aesthetic dimension of social interaction increases. It would, however, obviously be wrong to interpret Simmel as thinking about the history of mankind as a kind of a process of civilization in terms of aestheticization. First, Simmel always thought that there was a danger with such an aestheticization or 'stylization': the etiquette is always in danger of becoming an empty formula, a schema, or a mere outer cage, which is far removed from the living forces of 'real life'. As Davis (1973: 324) pointed out, much of Simmel's analysis of different social phenomena consisted of his attempt to show that this theme of 'separation from life' runs through such diverse social forms (among many others) as 'faithfulness', 'sociability', and the 'adventure'. In Simmel's words, one should not look for the 'original source of energy' in social forms, but in the vitality of 'real individuals' (see Simmel 1949: 261).

Even this idea has an interesting parallel in Kant's thinking: since aesthetic pleasure always has to do with the free play of imagination and the world of imagination is always 'richer' than reality, one can rightly ask for what purpose are the objects of beauty, beautiful works

158

of art, needed? After all, they can only act as a limitation on the free play of imagination (see Kant 1980: 483). Simmel feared that objects of art would face the danger of becoming empty of meaning if they lost their ties with reality.

Second, Simmel's society consists of innumerable, different and simultaneous forms of sociation, of which no single one is self-evidently more important than another: every form can be taken as an object of social analysis, but it is not possible, even in principle, to make a total evaluation of the degree of complexity or purity of social forms and in Simmel's opinion it would certainly not be of interest, either.

There is, however, one social phenomenon, money, which to Simmel's mind is the symbol of modern society, and the cultural influence of which reaches most social phenomena (as analysed by Simmel in his *Philosophy of Money*). One could almost say that it permeates the whole of modern society. Money is a symbol – an empirical and narrow one – of the unity of all being. It is fixed to or grows from every style of life almost like a part of the body, and overcomes all 'one-sidedness' (Simmel 1989 [1900]: 695).

David Frisby (1985) understood aestheticization as resulting partly from the increasing cultural influence of money in modern society. According to such an interpretation, stylization would be one of the cultural side-effects of the increasing use of money (see also Böhringer 1984). Stylization can, indeed, often be interpreted as synonymous with aestheticization. The argument is not, however, as simple as that. Simmel seemed to use the concept of style and stylization in two separate ways, of which the first is connected to money, the second to art.

According to Simmel, money creates a distance both among men and between men and things. Once exchange is mediated by money, products are no longer made in order to satisfy the specific needs or wants of a particular person but in order to be sold and exchanged for money in the anonymous market. To Simmel, this meant that all personal relations and nuances become objectified (Simmel 1989: 664). Money is the 'medium of all media' or a kind of a super medium which creates a distance between us and our ends in somewhat the same way as all instruments do (ibid.: 675–6). Money makes things equal by making them commensurable.

In *The Philosophy of Money*, Simmel characterized the effects of style in very much the same way as the effects of money: 'The inner meaning of an art style lies in the series of successive distances which it creates

159

between us and things' (Simmel 1989: 659). In addition to everything else, Simmel thought that there had been a recent growing interest in stylization or in aestheticization which is achieved by creating a distance between men and objects (ibid.: 660).

Despite these similarities, there is an important difference between Simmel's concepts of style and money. Money is compared with the intellect and the law, and they are all characterized by indifference towards everything that is individually specific and original. They all try to abstract from the totality of life one feature that is common to all, which would then, on the one hand, develop according to its own rules and, on the other, penetrate the totality of interests of existence and try to determine them anew from its own standpoint. But neither the style of art nor the style of life belongs to this list of abstracting factors. Their relation to the individual and the specific is different, somehow more delicate.

In his essay 'The Problem of Style', already referred to earlier, Simmel made a distinction between two principles of generalization which both belong to style: 'style is a principle of generality which either mixes with the principle of individuality, displaces it or represents it' (Simmel 1991b: 65). Style both simplifies and generalizes, and in this respect it resembles money. In this sense, it is the opposite of a single work of art. A work of art is always unique and irreplaceable, the style of art is general, shared by many. On the other hand, according to Simmel, a shared style, characterizing works of industrial design or arts and crafts, does not suppress their individuality but can, in the best case, even promote it. In style we can once again recognize a living antinomy: it preserves the singular and specific while at the same time combining and equalizing things that in reality are different. As Simmel wrote: 'finally style is the aesthetic attempt to solve the great problem of life: an individual work or behaviour, which is closed, a whole, can simultaneously belong to something higher, a unifying encompassing context' (Simmel 1991b: 70).

In 'The Problem of Style' Simmel discussed mainly the problems of the style of art, in *The Philosophy of Money* the broader concept of the style of life. As has already been pointed out, there is a parallel between lifestyle and the style of an object of use in Simmel's thinking. It is thus possible, for instance, to speak of a personal style. Simmel did not, however, think that the whole life of a person should be stylized in order to be shared by others. On the contrary, all the individuals concerned are able to preserve their full individuality and to share a common style – or rather many different styles – each of which is shared by a different group of people. There are, thus, good grounds for claiming that the distances created by money and style are different and the relation between them – if it exists – is more empirical than conceptual by nature. The culture levelled out and made commensurable by money is not at the same time automatically an aestheticized culture in the Simmelian sense. In *The Philosophy of Money* one cannot find any general vision about the general aestheticization of modern culture followed by the increasing influence of money. If such a connection exists, it is much more indirect and complex and one should look for it in the general differentiation of modern culture, in the plurality and complexity of all those social forms in which an individual takes part, rather than in the one-dimensionality caused by money.

## The aestheticization of everyday life

Among recent German cultural theory and critique it has been almost as common to speak about the aestheticization of everyday life and culture as it has been among Anglo-Saxon cultural critics to speak about post-modernity. It has often referred to the same or similar cultural changes. For instance, Welsch interpreted rather different kinds of phenomena to be examples of such aestheticization, even though he referred, not unlike Baudrillard, mainly to the role of the sphere of signs that have recently gained in independence: 'Both these aspects, both the poietic nature of reality and the fictional nature of the means of poiesis, can be combined and summarized into the following formulation: reality is an aesthetic product' (Welsch 1991: 173). Again, according to Guggenberger (1993):

> aestheticization runs as an important imprint of the *Zeitgeist* throughout all the areas of existence. It is promoted by the fact that the borderline between culture and the world of commodities becomes more and more ephemeral. It is almost impossible to solve in any single case what is already part of culture and what is a commodity and, the other way around, what is still culture.
>
> (Guggenberger 1993: 147)

Scott Lash also shared, in an article published in 1992, the opinion that the increasing importance of an aesthetic dimension is an essential part of the process of reflexive modernization. In Lash's opinion, modern reflexivity, which is typical of modern individuals, has in general to do with self-control and self-observance. It is transformed into an aesthetic phenomenon as soon as this control becomes hermeneutic or interpretative – in other words, self-reflexive. Such a conception of self-reflexivity is essentially aesthetic. In such a case the individual does not only control and dress him or herself according to some specific picture or model of the self but also interprets anew, and continuously works upon this picture or ideal: 'Control and observance are changed into subjective interpretation of a subject who can suppress the objects only to a certain degree' (Lash 1992: 267).

Gerhard Schulze's sociological study *Die Erlebnisgesellschaft* (1992) is probably the most systematic empirical study of lifestyles that attempts to analyse processes of aestheticization explicitly and systematically. Schulze referred on many occasions to the aestheticization of lifestyles, or to their aesthetic nature. According to his interpretation, in any affluent society, like Germany in the 1980s, consumers' choices are essentially aesthetic. Like Scott Lash, Schulze emphasized the fact that the inner orientation of the actors becomes more important in interpreting the meaning of things, objects and actions and, consequently, action becomes self-reflexive. In such a 'society of inner experience', as the book's title indicates, the interpretation of inner experiences becomes important: 'The person who experiences things must first transform the objective state of affairs into his own subjective system of signs before he can react to it aesthetically' (Schulze 1992: 97). Schulze's study is, furthermore, at least implicitly inspired by the 'Kantian' problem about the universal validity and communicability of these subjective experiences. Even according to Schulze, the choices of taste are always situated in between the individual and subjective, on the one hand, and the general and objective, on the other (ibid.: 99).

Interestingly Schulze also referred to the fact that in such an aestheticized everyday life 'games and plays have become more common or, rather, a greater part of social activity resembles a play or a game' (ibid.: 99).

Schulze's interpretation is particularly interesting – from the point of view of the present argument – in claiming that the need for schematization and stylization expressed in different lifestyles stems from the very logic of these inner experiences. In Schulze's opinion, in such a situation there necessarily arises a need for schematization – or stylization – and classification of experiences. Both individuals

162

themselves and those who are observing them are apt to interpret their actions and experiences and to classify them accordingly. Schulze's argument is that this helps to minimize insecurity. It is often best to share one's experiences with others and enjoy what others seem to be enjoying. To guarantee one's satisfaction it is best to follow an example set by people who in other respects resemble oneself and who seem otherwise to like or enjoy the same things (see Schulze 1992: 122–3). Furthermore, to follow the example of one's own social milieu is now important for a different reason than it was in the nineteenth century: today people are more afraid of missing something important or particularly exciting, something that others have already experienced, than of acting foolishly and getting embarrassed because of behaving in a manner which is unsuitable under the given conditions (ibid.: 436). The schematizations and stylizations of everyday life serve the purpose of orientation in an unfamiliar social situation of which it is difficult to form a clear picture.

As the above, very sketchy presentation of some of his main ideas shows, Schulze is inclined to interpret the need for schematization and stylization functionally. In this respect his analysis of lifestyles resembles Herbert Blumer's study of fashion: both fashion and style function as necessary guidelines both for the people in question and for those who are observing or interacting with them: 'The purpose of them [different styles – J. G.] is to make orientation easier. They put together an amorphous but by no means undetermined number of signs into a syndrome of everyday aesthetics, which is normal in a certain social group' (ibid.: 123).

To Michel Maffesoli (1993) style serves a similar purpose in modern society: it guarantees the synthesis of values and therefore preserves the order and form of society. Stylization is a typical response in the most varied fields of society – from the most frivolous to the most serious ones. As Maffesoli said in a very Simmelian way, people both live their styles together with others and, in the end, create them only by themselves. Lifestyles are 'played' for others and in front of others and thus are always formed in a reciprocal relation with others. As Kant said, a man living in solitude would have no need for stylization.

One could, however, take the thesis of aestheticization even more seriously and claim that if the subjective pleasures of such a *Erlebnis-gesellschaft* are really aesthetic pleasures, as Schulze claims, then these pleasures are always both private and socially shared and communicable, both individual and general. This thesis is not the same as the empirical fact that people often increase their own pleasure by sharing it with others, nor does it refer to the dubious generalization made by Kant that only people living in a community are interested in beautifying themselves. This idea can, on the contrary, be explicated best by referring to the analogy between play and art. The shared world of lifestyles, with its shared experiences, is like a play, in which we have to deal with inner experiences which, however, are always attached to outer objects. The part played by self-reflexion and fantasy is important. One can and must 'play' with lifestyles; one does not only observe but also performs them.

Schulze's scenes of lifestyles are just like Rousseau's feasts turned into everyday life – or daily life turned into a feast. Just like a play or a game, such a shared world of meanings and experiences does not serve any purpose, it is an end in itself. Just like all plays it too has its own unwritten, more or less complicated and delicate rules, or an 'etiquette' which make it possible to say when the play is fair. These 'rules' of the game are not, however, so rigid and forced as not to allow for a lot of individual improvisation and virtuosity. Just as a good football player is not the one who follows the rules most rigidly, the virtuoso of a lifestyle is not the one who simply follows as faithfully and as closely as possible the example set by others. Despite the liberty of improvisation and the freedom of individual performance it is possible to judge who is the master of the game, who plays it best or most beautifully without referring to any explicit standards or norms of conduct.

If Schulze's and others' argumentation is taken seriously it would mean that our everyday life is becoming more aesthetic, that we could speak of something like a more or less gradual process of aestheticization, during which aesthetic pleasure becomes more important as a criteria of social action. A self-evident and unquestionable precondition of this process is general affluence and the overcoming of scarcity, which makes it possible to adopt a disinterested and non-instrumental attitude to things, to other people and to the social world in general. It can set the play-like dimension of social interaction free, but it is not enough: a great variety of social formations are also necessary.

Johan Huizinga's famous essay *Homo ludens*, or *The Playing Man* (1984), in many ways shared Simmel's interest in identifying the play forms of everyday culture. According to Huizinga

> any form of free or autonomous activity can be called a play if the player understands that it takes place outside normal life – it was not meant to be 'real'. It can still totally absorb; no part of

material interest is attached to it and from it no utility is to be expected.

(Huizinga 1984: 23)

Not surprisingly, in Huizinga's analysis play is closely associated with art. He analysed various elements of games in various cultural and social activities from war and sport to art and economy, and identified elements of play in most forms of cultural and social life. Huizinga even set it as his task to evaluate the relative importance of the play element in modern culture as compared to earlier times. In his opinion, the results of this comparison are not straightforward. At the same time that the element of play is losing ground in its former strongholds, sport in particular, some other fields, like economic competition, mass communication or trade, traditionally regarded as being more instrumental and distant from play, acquire more play elements. But what is more important to Huizinga is that no culture can exist without play. In fact, it is not that play makes an important contribution to culture; rather, culture is born through play and games. In other words, to Huizinga, a 'playing man' is a real human being.

The sociological study by Roger Caillois (1961), which deals exclusively with play and games, is more strict in separating the field of games and play from everyday social life. In Caillois' opinion, play and ordinary life always take place in domains that are incompatible (Caillois 1961: 64). His sociology of play and games is, nevertheless, as ambitious as those of Huizinga or Simmel. By categorizing and systematizing different classes of play and games Caillois aimed at understanding the differences between and even the 'destinies' of various cultures:

> it does not seem to me unreasonable to find out whether the very destiny of cultures, their chance to flourish or stagnate, is not equally determined by their preference for one or another of the basic categories into which I have tried to divide games, categories that are not equally creative.

(Caillois 1961: 67)

In other words, games are indicative of the culture in which they are embedded: tell me what games you play, and I will tell you what kind of a culture you belong to.

Simmel's intention in analysing play forms of sociation is closer to Huizinga's than to Caillois'. As has already been argued, it is doubtful whether Simmel shared the view of the increasing aestheticization of the social world – in particular, if one keeps in mind that Simmel thought that any such process of the separation of social forms from 'real life' was permanently threatened by an empty schematism.

What makes social forms beautiful and what it is in them that produces aesthetic pleasure – besides disinterestedness and the subsequent independence – is their richness of variation, as in the versatility and subtlety of the etiquette in the case of the meal analysed by Simmel. (Etiquette should be understood not as a strict collection of rules or a code, but as the 'unwritten rules' of 'good conduct', which allow a lot of variation and play and which therefore cannot be codified into a collection of laws.) What counts here is the multiplicity of the forms of non-purposive social interaction. They can consist of independent forms as such – as is the case with sport, an artistic performance, or with pure sociability, but they can equally well be present in an interaction – e.g. fashion – which realizes some other purpose or end, such as the realization of economic profit.

One can claim that Simmel followed here the footsteps of Friedrich Schiller. As Schiller claimed, only a 'playing man' is truly a man; he is interested not only in the world of solid reality but also in appearance. To play with appearances presumes affluence but, as Schiller pointed out, it is not enough that there is an abundance of material things, of 'Stoff'. There should exist a great variety of things, too. Only then can the 'form instinct' be satisfied; only then is the demanded multiformity possible:

> Not just content with what satisfies nature, and meets his instinctual needs, he demands something over and above this: to begin with, admittedly, only a superfluity *of material things* ('*Überfluss des Stoffes*'), in order to conceal from appetite the fact that it has limits, and ensure enjoyment beyond the satisfaction of immediate needs; soon, however, a superfluity *in material things* ('*Überfluss an dem Stoffe*'), an aesthetic surplus, in order to satisfy the formal impulse too, and extend enjoyment beyond satisfaction of every need.
>
> (Schiller 1982: 1205–7)

In conclusion, one could say that the importance of aesthetic pleasure in social interaction is more pronounced, first, the more different forms of association – or social worlds – there are in general in a society, with their own 'rules of beauty'; and, second, the richer and simultaneously more lenient the rules of these games are. In this sense it is probably safe to claim that modern society is characterized by an increasing aestheticization. It is also possible to understand better the great fascination that fashion exercises over modern man. The social mechanism of fashion with its rapidly changing patterns creates the 'superfluity in material things', demanded by Friedrich Schiller, and richness in life orientations. It cannot be denied that fashion can also serve the function of social differentiation and, at times, be functional to social competition. However, the pleasures of novelty associated with it are purely, or at least predominantly, aesthetic pleasures in the exact sense of the European philosophical tradition.

## The community of art and the art of a community

Hans-Georg Gadamer (1975) is probably the best example of a contemporary philosopher who explicitly followed the aesthetic-humanitarian programme of Kant and Schiller and emphasized the utopian task of art in modern society. In his opinion the function of art and aesthetic experience in general is to establish and develop a community, or at least, to act as a living example of such a community, a community which could be shared collectively without suppressing the individuality of its members. Gadamer (1975: 84) criticized, in particular, the relativistic aesthetic stance for destroying the main task of '*Bildung*': to raise man into a state of universality. As Brunkhorst (1988: 89) has pointed out, Gadamer believed that the 'hermeneutically closed anthropological basis' of art can survive over modern times and even today it is capable of creating a 'communal sense' or meaning ('*Gemeinsinn*') and of securing social integration and cohesion. In this respect, his programme is reminiscent of Herbert Marcuse's *The Aesthetic Dimension* (1978) which elevated art into the last and only stronghold of human emancipation. Such an art would act as a genuine experience of communality and make our world more genuine and more easy going.

Gadamer's programme and the task it presents to art is suspect, however, in the opinion of many contemporary critics. Modern art forms a separate sphere of reality and has lost its 'eternal value' (cf. Max Weber). Thus it could not possibly play the role of creating such strong communality. This function of art could be preserved in modern society only by sacrificing the very foundation of modern society, its differentiation.

Georg Simmel – and later sociologists who have been interested in the process of aestheticization – can be said to have solved this paradox or problem of classical humanist programmes by identifying, in everyday social intercourse and forms of sociation, a dimension of art and play. Such a position starts from the presumption that 'fine art', or art in the true meaning of the word, does not guarantee the experience of communality which could act as a real integrating force in society. (It cannot be created by 'culture' alone either, in the sense of youth culture, sub-culture or 'lower arts'.) The only chance to save Schiller's and Kant's programme is not to deny the diversity of modern culture and the genuine individuality (and the subsequent experiences of heterogeneity and contingency) and demand the return (which naturally is possible only as a thought experiment) to the pre-modern unified culture of classicist art. The cultural and social richness of modern society has, in fact, transformed the separate aesthetic sphere, which was supposed to act as an example of communality, into part of everyday social relations. *Sensus communis* is being born – and is dispersed – every day in the most multi-faceted lifestyles and in the etiquettes of the most diverse social worlds. This certainly does not make art obsolete as such, but neither has art, in this respect, any privileged position among the multiplicity and variety of different social worlds.

## The facticity of a community vs. aesthetic sociation

In his recent contribution to the book *Reflexive Modernization*, Scott Lash (1994) criticized what he called aesthetic individualism, the idea of aesthetic communities, which to his mind has been a common way of understanding the peculiar nature of modern communities in opposition to the so-called traditional communities. Lash's discussion could also be read as an attempt at self-criticism of his own earlier views (cf. Lash 1992). The target of his critique included diverse authors and thinkers extending from Nietzsche to Benjamin and Adorno, to Derrida, Rorty and Bauman, who in his opinion all are – despite their otherwise different points of view – part of 'the tradition of allegory', based on 'radical individualism – not a utilitarian but aesthetic individualism, individualism of a heterogenous desire' (Lash 1994: 144). Because of the basic individualism and subjectivity of this approach any attempt at developing the ideas of a community starting from this tradition, in order to analyse the social formations of a modern society, are doomed to failure.

In his opinion (Lash 1994: 144), to have a better access to 'community', 'it may be necessary to break with such abstract

168

aesthetic subjectivity'. The understanding of the 'we' of the unifying factors of a community is impossible under the 'star of aesthetic reflexivity, under the star of such mimetic critique of the concept' mainly because of the underlying aesthetic subjectivity. Within this aesthetic approach there is no way to come to terms with the shared meanings which, in fact, first constitute the facticity of a community.

Not surprisingly, the remedy offered by Lash to this conceptual fallacy is an old one: hermeneutics: 'This sort of interpretation will give access to ontological foundations, in *Sitten*, in habits, in background practices of cognitive and aesthetic individualism. It will at the same time give us some understanding of the shared meaning of community' (ibid.).

What Lash arrives at in his critical discussion is that without shared meanings, in the sense of *Sittlichkeit*, shared obligations and practices, there cannot be any real communities – whether modern or traditional: 'That is, cultural communities, the cultural "we", are collectivities of shared background practices, shared meanings, shared routine activities involved in the achievement of meaning' (ibid.: 147).

In the various examples taken from contemporary sociological literature and presented in his critical analysis, one can recognize three different ways of understanding the character of modern communities. First, there are so-called aesthetic communities proper, communities of taste as analysed, in otherwise very different contexts, by both Lyotard and Bourdieu, for example. Second, communities can be understood to resemble tribes, in the sense of Maffesoli's neo-tribes, united by a collective euphoria like the spectators at a sports event. Even though Maffesoli finds examples of such tribes everywhere in modern society, it is obvious that any single community of this kind is realized only occasionally and for a fleeting moment of time. These two ways of understanding modern communities are obviously evaluated by Lash to be inadequate and only the third, hermeneutic approach is the right one. Only communities based on 'shared background meanings' share the 'facticity of a community'.

It is interesting to note that, in Lash's opinion, the genuine taste community, understood in the hermeneutic meaning of the term, entails transgressing the distinction between consumer and producer (ibid.: 161). This automatically means that such communities are rare, or are on the fringes of the modern differentiated society. Lash is basically faced with the same dilemma as the early modern critics of industrial design and the enlightened propaganda aimed at cultivating consumers' tastes, which was discussed earlier: the only effective remedy suggested was to overcome the distinction between producer and consumer. But the remedy would have killed the patient it tried to save because it presupposed the dissolution of the essential conditions of modern society, thus leaving no individual tastes to be worried about. The problem disappeared, but only by wishfully thinking away what had caused it: the modern differentiated society.

The most interesting thing about Lash's argument is not whether we can think in general of any social life beyond or outside a common 'life world' ('*Lebenswelt*'), without some shared meanings in the hermeneutical sense of the word already presumed by the definition of the concept of social action in Max Weber's (1968: 22–3) system of the basic sociological categories. Neither is the real question whether or not one can really find living examples of such 'hermeneutic' communities even in a modern society, or, to formulate the question more precisely, whether there are communities of this type that are at the same time 'reflexive' and non-traditional – that is, communities into which one is not born or 'thrown' but which are freely chosen, which may be widely stretched over 'abstract' space, and which consciously pose themselves the problem of their own creation and re-invention (see Lash 1994: 161). Such communities might indeed exist in the modern world, as the – rather limited – number of examples which Lash has taken mainly from alternative milieus gives us to understand. This is basically an empirical question.

What is the most interesting question, at least from the point of view of the main argument of this study, is whether there are in a modern society other kinds of social collectivities or formations, such as the modern fashion mechanism or groups united by a common lifestyle, which might play an increasingly important role in the constitution of modern society or the sociation of the individual and which, while being of an aesthetic character, still overcome the solipsism of aesthetic subjectivity criticized by Lash.

It has been one of the main tasks of this study to show that, in the tradition of sociological thought since Georg Simmel, ways of analysing social interaction have been developed in which the opposition between the 'I' and the 'we' is overcome without sacrificing the subjectivity and reflexivity of the modern individual. As has been pointed out earlier, the explicit purpose of Simmel's sociological thinking was to overcome the duality of the individual and the social. The principle of reciprocity is always built into play, as well as sociability and other play forms of sociation: my enjoyment or my gratification is dependent on the joy and gratification of all the members of the social collectivity in question. In such games, amusements and social gatherings the totally subjective and individual feeling of pleasure is not necessarily – as was demanded from the real aesthetic judgment of taste by Immanuel Kant – universally communicable, but every 'player' or participant can still safely make the assumption that all the other 'players' or participants are sharing a similar feeling of pleasure.

Thus aesthetic sociology is not necessarily faced with the dilemma of Lazarus' (n.d.) or Gabriel Tarde's (1962) mass psychology: people who watch the same opera or read the same newspaper – or wear similar clothes – do not just happen to do so routinely or for some mysterious, inexplicable reason, the laws of which could never be discovered, each one totally independent of all the others. Instead they share a common taste and, thus, form a taste community. To be in such a taste community, 'which takes on the facticity of community', does not necessarily 'entail shared meanings, practices and obligations', at least not in the sense presumed by Lash (1994: 160–1).

As has been shown earlier, there is an in-built condition of reciprocity in such social formations, of which the modern fashion mechanism is the best example. Fashion offers a socially binding and valid standard of taste which, however, is only based on the individual 'preferences' and choices of taste of the members of such a 'community of taste'. It does not share the ideal and in a sense exemplary character of 'good taste' as demanded by the aesthetic and hermeneutic tradition, but still it is equally binding and obliging in relation to the people concerned.

What is characteristic of such 'communities of taste' is that they are in a constant state of being born and dying out. The standards of taste are in a perpetual state of change – yet they can still create order in a rapidly changing society. In this sense they do not share the 'facticity of a community', but are only a 'cloud of a community' (cf. Lyotard 1988). In order to avoid overloading this concept it would therefore be better not to call them communities at all but to use Simmel's phrase, forms of sociation.

# NOTES

## 1 INTRODUCTION: NEED, TASTE AND PLEASURE – OR UNDERSTANDING MODERN CONSUMPTION

1  See Ewen (1988) whose exposition of the history of the theme is fascinating despite the fact that even he rather uncritically adopts such a perspective of cultural critique. The worry about the unwise and detrimental habits of consumption, caused by false social pride, was widely shared by nutritionists during the first decades of the present century as evidenced by Levenstein's (1988) study (see also Levenstein 1993).

2  It was only natural that gastronomers were taking sides with the defenders of civilization and commerce. In his *Physiology of Taste* (1975 [1825]), Jean-Anthelme Brillat-Savarin joined the eminent ranks of philosophers like Voltaire, Mandeville and Adam Smith in defending the cultivation and development of taste. Luxury – or in Smithian terms, the development of needs and the increasing division of labour – was conducive to human happiness. As Schwartz (1986: 313) concluded, the great gastronomer was convinced that 'the gourmand's love of new tastes united the World in international commerce; the gourmand's good cheer at the table strengthened the bonds of society'.

3  The difference between a connoisseur and a gastronome, between one who can always decide and choose what is tasteful and good without reflecting on it and one who only follows the rules and standards of goodness, was formulated extremely well in P. de Pressac's *Considérations sur la cuisine* (1931; cited in Bourdieu 1984: 68):

> Taste must not be confused with gastronomy. Whereas taste is the natural gift of recognizing and loving perfection, gastronomy is the set of rules which govern the cultivation and education of taste. Gastronomy is to the taste as grammar and literature are to the literary sense. And this brings us to the heart of the problem: if the gourmet is a delicate connoisseur, is the gastronome a pedant? ... The gourmet is his own gastronome, just as the man of taste is his own grammarian. ... Not everyone is a gourmet; that is why we need gastronomes ... there is such a thing as bad

taste...and persons of refinement know this instinctively. For those who do not, rules are needed.

4 In the 1970s Herbert J. Gans (1974) identified empirically in the United States five different taste classes or 'taste publics', as he preferred to call them. Gans was interested in defending, against the critics of mass culture, the right of existence of an independent popular culture. Consequently, he did not acknowledge the hegemonic aspirations of the representatives of 'high culture'. To him, 'high culture' expressed only the taste of a well-educated segment of society.

5 As has already been pointed out, there was a close parallel between the gastronomic literature and aesthetic discourse in the eighteenth century. The physiological sense of taste had a priviledged position among the human senses. Among the eighteenth-century thinkers the physiological sense of taste – not eyesight or hearing – evoked the operation of judgment. The different explanations given for this affinity all amount to the fact that the sense of taste is somehow privileged to make distinctions. As Hower and Lalonde (1991) have pointed out, the sense of taste, unlike sight or hearing, is disposed to make distinctions. They argue that in the emerging modern society it was becoming both more important and more difficult unerringly to make the proper distinctions both concerning social relations (with whom to socialize) and food (what to eat). Ong (1967) and Falk (1994) have both suggested that of all the sense organs the mouth is disposed to make distinctions because whatever is introduced has to pass two gates before definitely entering the body. Immanuel Kant's (1980: 567–8) explanation, however, is still the best – if one does not take it too seriously. In his opinion, there is simply no other occasion on which one can, as regularly and in such a pleasant way, exercise one's power of judgment as at a good dinner in good company.

## 2 PHILOSOPHICAL AESTHETICS AND THE REFINEMENT OF TASTE

1 In Mennell's study there are historical details and interpretations that could be discussed (e.g. whether the modern European cuisine originated in Italy instead of France? Was it a more bourgeois phenomenon from the very beginning than Mennell gives us to understand?). In the present context Mennell's study is, however, mainly treated as a coherent and interesting example of a theoretical interpretation of the social formation and development of taste in European societies.

## 3 LUXURY, KITSCH AND FASHION

1 The same difficulty concerning the determination of the historical nature of needs was also faced by the theory of increasing misery in orthodox Marxism (see Gronow 1986).

2 This is called the trickle-down effect by marketing people. As McCracken (1988: 94) has remarked, it is, however, from the point of view of customers, a question of social ascent rather than descent – an attempt to achieve the distinctive signs of a higher social status. From the point of view of goods, on the other hand, it is a question of decline. Lloyd A. Fallers (1966: 403) has a typically functionalistic explanation for this: 'the appropriation of status symbols offers an illusion of success to those who are without any real opportunity of social ascent'. For the impression of a continuous social climb to be created, it obviously is sufficient that some – even relatively few – consumer durables such as cars, radios, televisions, outdoor barbecues, etc. – gradually 'descend' the pyramid.

3 Simmel's idea is not in itself in conflict with what Pierre Bourdieu (1984) has said. Even according to Simmel, it is the middle class and especially the so-called new middle class that constitutes the cleverest distinction strategist of all.

4 See, however, Elizabeth Wilson's study of modern dressing. According to Wilson, sartorial fashion became the means by which the bourgeoisie separated itself from aristocracy and its values during the nineteenth century. The new middle-class woman did not imitate an aristocrat at all, but represented a conservative family unit. She wanted to be both feminine and modest in her outfit, attractive but prudent (Wilson 1985, see Chapter 6 in particular).

5 In many respects, Karl Marx was a rather exceptional critic of the modern commercial – or capitalist – society. On the one hand, in his *Grundrisse* (Marx 1973 [1857–8]: 325), the first manuscript version of *Capital*, he welcomed the future rich individuality of the modern wage worker with its many-sided and unrestricted needs. He also regularly emphasized that human needs are not historically constant and in this sense universal. On the other hand, there is no doubt that in another sense Marx remained faithful to the doctrine of human nature common in the Philosophy of Enlightenment. Needs are common to all men and, in this respect, their recognition would pose no problem in the future communist society (see Gronow 1986).

6 In Kumar's own opinion the social significance of consumption has greatly increased, and has become a central area of social life which makes an appearance in many different ways. Instead of production, social conflicts are often centred around consumption. In the production process, the production of consumer goods and services has become more important, which again promotes a consumerist way of life. Social movements have also emerged which are concerned not only with consumption itself but also with leisure time, general well-being and family life (see Kumar 1983: 313).

7 Cf. Schwartz (1986: 307) for whom the fear of never being satisfied forms the other side of the fear of abundance.

# 4 TASTE AND FASHION

1 These kinds of 'stage theories' often postulated, in contrast to the modern consumer, a kind of historically preceding natural need economy in which the principle of the satisfaction of needs has reigned. For a critique of such conceptions, see Falk (1994: 113–14 and 138–41).

2 Simmel wrote three different essays on fashion (1983 [1895], 1905b and 1986 [1911]) which, however, do not differ remarkably from each other (see Noro 1991: 68–9).

3 In his *Lessons on the Analytic of the Sublime* Lyotard's (1991: 18) emphasis is slightly more 'orthodox': in criticizing or denying the possibility of all empirical interpretations of the idea of the taste community he declares that in Kant the possibility of communicability is founded upon the 'supersensible' principle of harmonious accord:

> Thus it is easy to show how the presupposition of a *sensus communis* owes nothing to experience. Consequently a 'psychological' but also a sociological interpretation of the aesthetical community is to be rejected. An interpretation of this order interferes with the critical procedure, which cannot be inductive and must begin with the given in order to establish the conditions of its possibility; the critical procedure returns to the given order to legitimate or delegitimate that for which it 'gives' itself. The demand for possible communication as it is given in the feeling of the beautiful induces a *sensus communis* as its condition of possibility, which in turn, is founded upon the supersensible principle of harmonious accord.... Communicability is a transcendental supplement, i.e. the idea of the supersensible.
>
> (Lyotard 1991: 218)

In Lyotard's words,

> taste is a sensation that immediately demands to be communicable. It demands this immediately. This exigency or expectation is inscribed in the sensation, without any extrinsic mediation. One could say that taste immediately demands to be communicated immediately. This does not mean in the same instant, but, rather, without the mediation of any argument, as if by a direct transitiveness.
>
> (ibid.: 191)

4 To Bourdieu (1984: 59–60; see also Rahkonen 1995: 15) taste is always primarily determined through negation, more through disgust than liking. This would also mean that the 'push' exercised by the lower classes is stronger than the positive 'pull' of the upper strata.

5 The most vulnerable groups would be those with the greatest investment in self-identity achieved through adornment or consumption in general. Similarly, those groups which have a tendency to high stylization (youth, cultural intermediaries, conformists) are likely to feel

anxiety (see Warde 1994: 892). These would also be the groups that pay a lot of attention to fashion.

6 As Lohmann (1992: 355) has pointed out, Simmel, in fact, presumed that there is some unifying principle which determines or first creates the uniqueness and totality of an individual's life span. It makes it possible also to recognize even the most superficial expressions of his life as expressions of *his* life. It is an individual principle, unique to the individual and not shared by others. In Simmel's words, it is an individual law. To Simmel, this individual law obviously was a central principle of his philosophy of life ('*Lebensphilosophie*') and as such it cannot be determined in any more concrete terms. It can best be understood as a parallel to the harmonic unity of a painting in which every detail serves as an expression of a totality (see Lohmann 1992: 361–2).

7 The record industry offers a good example of this mechanism. It has been estimated in the music industry that only 10 to 20 per cent of all the records produced for the market make a profit (see Burnett 1990: 77 and ESEK 1994). In this sense the industry is characterized by permanent and heavy overproduction. It is in most cases extremely difficult to foresee which of the future products of a recording company will become 'hits'.

8 The study was conducted by Aino Sinnemäki, Arto Noro and the author of this book (see also Sinnemäki 1994). Among the 18 fashion designers who were interviewed with open-ended questionnaires there were two men. All the respondents had received their professional schooling between the 1950s and 1980s. Two had completed their schooling abroad, one in the School of Industrial Design in the city of Lahti, and all the rest at the Helsinki University of Art and Design. The main criterion in selecting the interviewed designers was that they had been professionally active in the fashion industry for at least five years. A great part of all the important Finnish fashion firms and factories were represented among the employers of the people interviewed. At the time these designers were occupied either with industry or with trade. Taken together they had experience in various fields from ribbons and buttons to furs, from underwear to shoes, from uniforms and work clothes to evening dresses.

9 The difficulties in understanding the role of vitamins in nutrition and in argumentation concerning their 'need' are aptly illustrated by the attempt to come to terms with their importance with the help of a new concept: 'hidden hunger'. According to this theory, people overeat and become fat because they have a hidden hunger for something which they could not possibly feel or recognize themselves. Something invisible was missing from their food. By adding the correct amount of vitamins to their diets, they could be satisfied and could stop eating too much (see Schwartz 1986: 229).

10 On the role of patent medicines in the development of early advertising, see Richards 1990: 196–203.

11 Päivi Lehto (1993), who has analysed television advertisements of margarine since the 1960s in Finland, came to the conclusion that the

standard margarine spread (FLORA) still concentrates its efforts on convincing the public that it is as good as butter. Mika Pantzar (1992) has, on the contrary, claimed that the 'fight' was already over in the 1960s when margarine 'came of age' and started an independent life with a good character of its own, which butter now tries to imitate.

## 5 THE BEAUTY OF SOCIAL FORMS

1 As Zammito (1992: 119–20) has pointed out, the real problem with Kant's conception is not the fact that smells and tastes do not really fit into the sphere of aesthetic pleasure. Not even colours or tunes are beautiful without certain reservations. Even though Kant obviously thought that the colours of a painting or the typical sound of an instrument can add to the enchantment of the painting or the composition, only the drawing and the composition are the proper objects of the real judgment of taste (Kant 1987: §14).

   As has been pointed out by Zammito, such a position is very suspect. In addition, it is in contradiction with Kant's other principle according to which judgments of taste cannot be based on any universal standards or general criteria, in opposition to the classicist conception criticized by him. In the case of a smell or a taste Kant does not even believe it necessary to try to argue that they belong to the sphere of aesthetic pleasures.

2 Friedrich Schiller was even more polemical, claiming that when touched an object executes an act of violent force against us whereas in the case of sight and sound our role is both more active and more distanced:

   What we actually see with the eye is something different from the sensation we receive; for the mind leaps out across light to objects. The object of touch is a force to which we are subjected; the object of eye and ear a form we engender.

   (Schiller 1982 [1795]: 195)

3 Despite the fact that culinary delights were obviously the only kind of aesthetic pleasures that Kant expressed any strong personal feelings about – he obviously loved to drink and dine well with friends – his philosophical aesthetic was strongly prejudiced against them (see Onfray 1990: 67–83).

4 In a recension of Simmel's *Philosophie des Geldes* Rudolf Goldscheid (1904: 411) wrote: 'Simmel's whole work is characterized by an aesthetic ideal. And it is this very aesthetic ideal that determines his interpretation about the whole life and, consequently, all his scientific activity.'

5 As has been pointed out by Noro (1991: 29–31), even the context in which this essay was first presented at the First German Conference of Sociology in 1910 gives support to the thesis that it should be taken seriously as Simmel's programme of sociology.

6 One of Simmel's teachers in Berlin, the philosopher and *Völkerpsycholog* Moritz Lazarus, argued in his lecture *Über Gespräche* in 1876 how

> the most important effect of discussion or social intercourse is the fulfillment of life, the concession of life, what is totally opposite to silence characterized by the stupid state of the flow of all internity, a motion. In this respect our discussions remind us of plays; besides, reading plays and discussion fill our pastime. During our pastime we do not want to be totally idle, instead we have something to do, to strengthen our own being.
>
> (Lazarus n.d.: 36)

7 Like Simmel, Schiller does not make such an explicit difference between play and art, but he, on the other hand, separates two different forms of play, the first of which is based on a mere variety of impressions and the gratification of totally random change. The second is different from this

> play of *freely associated ideas*, which is still of a wholly material kind, and to be explained by purely natural laws, the imagination, in its attempt at a *free form*, finally makes the leap to aesthetic play.
>
> (Schiller 1982: 209)

8 Kurt (1991) has attempted to show that there is an interesting parallel between Talcott Parsons' voluntaristic theory of action and Schiller's aesthetic programme. In Kurt's opinion they both share a conception according to which it is not enough for an individual to be adopted into a society by performing a norm-conforming action or by following 'beautiful norms'. Kurt's interpretation of Schiller's play instinct as designating only an empty social form – or an etiquette – can, however, be questioned. According to such a conception the aesthetic freedom would be best realized whenever the individual's inclinations and the demands of society would fit together. Such conduct would deserve to be called beautiful which would, as if by nature, follow 'the good form' and to conform to the demands of the society. Schiller does speak about the joy of appearance ('*Freude am Schein*') which together with the play instinct is a universal human inclination which differentiates man from animal (see Schiller 1982:191–3). This interest in the appearance ('*Schein*') and the following negligence of the demands of reality is something which is typical of culture and its development. On the other hand, as was emphasized many times by Schiller himself, this interest in the appearance has nothing to do with fraud, deception or counterfeit (see Schiller 1982: 197–9).

9 Cf. Schiller's answer to his own question whether the state – or the society – of the beautiful appearance exists anywhere at all:

> As a need it exists in every finely attuned soul; as a realized fact, we are likely to find it, like the pure Church and the pure Republic, only in some few chosen circles, where conduct is governed, not by some soulless imitation of the manners and morals of others, but by the aesthetic nature we have made our own; where men make their

ways, with undismayed simplicity and tranquil innocence, through even the most involved and complex situations, free alike of the compulsion to infringe the freedom of others in order to assert their own, as of the necessity to shed their Dignity in order to manifest Grace.

(Schiller 1982: 219)

# BIBLIOGRAPHY

Adorno, T. W. (1941) 'Veblen's Attack on Culture', *Zeitschrift für Sozialforschung* 9, 3: 389–413.

Amerine, M. A. and Roessler, E. B. (1976) *Wines. Their Sensory Evaluation*, San Francisco, Cal.: W. H. Freeman & Company.

Appadurai, A. (1986) *The Social Life of Things*, Cambridge: Cambridge University Press

Aronson, N. (1982) 'Social Definitions of Entitlement. Food Needs 1885–1920', *Media, Culture and Society* 4, 2: 57–61.

—— (1984) 'Comment on Bryan Turner's "The Government of the Body: Medical Regimens and the Rationalization of the Diet" ', *The British Journal of Sociology* 35, 1: 62–5.

Barber, J. (1990) 'The Working-Class Culture and Political Culture in the 1930s', in H. Günther (ed.) *The Culture of the Stalin Period*, London: Macmillan.

Barthes, R. (1983) *The Fashion System*, New York: Hill & Wang.

Bauman, Z. (1990–1) 'Communism: a post mortem', *Praxis International* 10, 3–4: 185–92.

—— (1991) *Modernity and Ambivalence*, London: Cornell University Press.

Becker, H. (1982) *The Art Worlds*, Berkeley, Cal.: University of California Press.

Bell, D. (1974) *The Coming of Post-industrial Society*, London: Heinemann.

—— (1976) *The Cultural Contradictions of Capitalism*, New York: Basic Books.

Bell, Q. (1992) *On Human Finery*, London: Allison & Busby.

Bellah, R. N., Madsen, R., Sullivan, W. M., Swidler, A. and Tipton, S. M. (1986) *Habits of the Heart*, New York: Harper & Row.

Beriya, S. (1995) *Moi otets – Lavrenti Beriya*, Moskva: Sovremennik.

Blaxter, M. (1990) *Health and Lifestyles*, London: Tavistock and Routledge.

Blumer, H. (1969) 'Fashion: From Class Differentiation to Collective Selection', *The Sociological Quarterly* 10, 1: 275–91.

Böhringer, H. (1984) 'Die "Philosophie des Geldes" als Ästhetische Theorie', in H-J. Dahme and O. Rammstedt (eds) *Georg Simmel und der Moderne*, Frankfurt am Main: Suhrkamp.

180

Bourdieu, P. (1983) 'The Field of Cultural Production, or: the Economic World Reversed', *Poetics* 12, 4/5: 311–56.
—— (1984) *Distinction. A Social Critique of the Judgement of Taste*, London: Routledge & Kegan Paul.
—— (1986) 'Modeskaparen och hans märke. Bidrag till en teori om magin', in P. Bourdieu (ed.) *Kultursociologiska texter*, Lidingö, Sweden: Salamander.
Boym, S. (1994) *Common Places. Mythologies of Everyday Life in Russia*, Cambridge, Mass.: Harvard University Press.
Brillat-Savarin, J-A. (1975) *Physiologie du goût*, Paris: Heiman.
Brunkhorst, H. (1988) 'Die Ästhetische Konstruktion der Moderne', *Leviathan* 16, 1: 77–96.
Burke, E. (1987 [1757]) *A Philosophical Enquiry into the Origin of Our Ideas of the Sublime and Beautiful*, Oxford: Basil Blackwell.
Burnett, J. (1966) *Plenty and Want: A Social History of Diet in England from 1815 to the Present Day*, London: Scolar Press.
Burnett, R. (1990) *Concentration and Diversity in the International Record Business*, Gothenburg: Kompendiet.
Caillois, R. (1961) *Man, Play and Games*, New York: The Free Press.
Campbell, C. (1987) *The Romantic Ethic and the Spirit of Modern Consumerism*, Oxford and New York: Basil Blackwell.
—— (1991) 'Conspicuous Confusion? A Critique of Veblen's Theory of Conspicuous Consumption', *Sociological Theory* 13, 1: 37–47.
Carlsen, J., Schanz, H-J., Schmidt, L-H. and Thomsen, H-J. (1980) *Kapitalisme, behov og civilisation*, Århus, Denmark: Modtryk.
Caygill, H. (1989) *The Art of Judgment*, Oxford: Basil Blackwell.
Cheyne, G. (1991) *The English Malady*, London: Tavistock and Routledge.
Coleman, F. (1965) 'Can a Smell or a Taste or a Touch be Beautiful?', *American Philosophical Quarterly* 2, 4: 319–24.
Counihan, C. M. (1992) 'Food Rules in the United States: Individualism, Control, and Hierarchy', *Anthropological Quarterly* 65, 1: 55–65.
Craik, J. (1994) *The Face of Fashion*, London: Routledge.
Davis, F. (1992) *Fashion, Culture and Identity*, Chicago and London: University of Chicago Press.
Davis, M. S. (1973) 'Georg Simmel and the Aesthetics of Social Reality', *Social Forces* 51, 1: 320–9.
Dawson, S. and Cavell, J. (1986) 'Status Recognition in the 1980s: Invidious Distinction Revisited', *Advances in Consumer Research* 14: 487–91.
Dunham, V. (1976) *In Stalin's Time*, Cambridge: Cambridge University Press.
Eagleton, T. (1990) *The Ideology of the Aesthetic*, Oxford: Basil Blackwell.
Ehrenreich, B. (1983) *The Hearts of Men: American Dreams and the Flight from Commitment*, London: Pluto Press.
Ekström, M. (1990) *Kost, klass och kön* (Food, Class and Gender), Umeå, Sweden: University of Umeå.
Elias, N. (1978) *Über der Prozess der Zivilisation*, Frankfurt am Main: Suhrkamp.
—— (1983) *The Court Society*, Oxford: Basil Blackwell.
ESEK (1994) *ESEKin tuotantotukijärjestelmän seurantatutkimus* (A Follow-up

Study of the System of Production Support by ESEK), Helsinki: Esittävän säveltaiteen edistämiskeskus.

Etzioni-Halevy, E. (1981) *Social Change. The Advent and Maturation of Modern Society*, London: Routledge & Kegan Paul.

Ewen, S. (1988) *All Consuming Images*, New York: Basic Books.

Falk, P. (1990) ' "Oikean" elämän ongelma' (The Problem of 'Real' Life), *Sosiaalilääketieteellinen aikakauslehti* 27, 4: 314–18.

—— (1991) 'Miten "hyvää" myydään' (How to Sell the 'Good'), in V. Salin (ed.) *Maailman merkkejä*, Helsinki: MV.

—— (1994) *The Consuming Body*, London: Sage.

Falk, P. and Gronow, J. (1985) 'Ravintotiede ja ruokahalun disiplinointi' (Nutrition Science and the Disciplining of Appetite), *Tiede & Edistys* 10, 1: 47–53.

Fallers, L. A. (1966) 'A Note on the "Trickle Effect" ', in R. Bendix and S. Lipset (eds) *Class, Status, and Power. Social Stratification in Comparative Perspective*, New York: The Free Press.

Featherstone, M. (1990) 'Perspectives on Consumer Culture', *Sociology* 24, 1: 5–22.

—— (1991) *Consumer Culture and Postmodernism*, London: Sage.

Ferry, L. (1992) *Der Mensch als Ästhet. Die Erfindung des Geschmacks im Zeitalter der Demokratie*, Stuttgart: J. B. Metzler.

Firat, F. A. (1991) 'The Consumer in Postmodernity', *Advances in Consumer Research* 18: 70–6.

Fischler, C. (1980) 'Food Habits, Social Change and the Nature/Culture Dilemma', *Social Science Information* 19, 6: 937–53.

—— (1986) 'Learned versus "Spontaneous" Dietetics: French Mothers' Views of What Children Should Eat', *Social Science Information* 25, 4: 945–65.

—— (1990) *L'homnivore. Le Goût, la cuisine et le corps*, Paris: Odile Jacob.

Fisher, J. E. (1986) 'Social Class and Consumer Behavior: The Relevance of Class and Status', *Advances in Consumer Research* 14: 492–6.

Fitzpatrick, S. (1979) *Education and Social Mobility in the Soviet Union 1921–1934*, Cambridge: Cambridge University Press.

Foucault, M. (1987) *The Use of Pleasure. The History of Sexuality*, Vol. 2, Harmondsworth: Penguin.

Fretter, W. B. (1971) 'Is Wine an Art Object?', *Journal of Aesthetics and Art Criticism* 30, 1: 97–100.

Frisby, D. (1981) *Sociological Impressionism. A Reassessment of Georg Simmel's Social Theory*, London: Heinemann.

—— (1985) *Fragments of Modernity. Theory of Modernity in the Works of Simmel, Kracauer and Benjamin*, Cambridge: Polity Press.

—— (1992) *Simmel and Since. Essays on Georg Simmel's Social Theory*, London: Routledge.

Gadamer, H-G. (1975) *Wahrheit und Methode*, Tübingen, Germany: J. C. B. Mohr (Paul Siebeck).

—— (1988) *Truth and Method*, London: Sheed & Ward.

Gans, H. J. (1974) *Popular Culture and High Culture*, New York: Basic Books.

Goffman, E. (1951) 'Symbols of Class Status', *The British Journal of Sociology* 2, 4: 294–304.

Goldscheid, R. (1904) 'Jahresbericht über Erscheinungen der Soziologie in den Jahren 1899–1904', *Archiv für Systematische Philosophie* 10: 397–413.

Gordon, L. A. and Klopov, E. V. (1989) *Shto eto bylo?* Moscow: Izd. Polititseskoi literatury.

Gramsci, A. (1975) *Letters from Prison*, London: Jonathan Cape.

Grean, S. (1965) *Shaftesbury's Philosophy of Religious Ethics*, s.l.: Ohio University Press.

Gronow, J. (1986) *On the Formation of Marxism*, Commentationes Scientiarum Socialium 33, Helsinki: Societas Scientiarum Fennica.

Guggenberger, B. (1993) 'Die Politische Aktualität des Ästhetischen', *Leviathan* 21, 1: 146–61.

Gusfield, J. R. (1992) 'Nature's Body and the Metaphors of Food', in M. Lamont and M. Fournier (eds) *Cultivating Differences. Symbolic Boundaries and the Making of Inequality*, Chicago: University of Chicago Press.

Hebdige, D. (1983) *Subculture. The Meaning of Style*, London and New York: Methuen.

Heller, A. (1976) *The Theory of Need in Marx*, London: Allison & Busby.

Hirdman, Y. (1983) *Magfrågan. Mat som mål och medel*, Kristianstad, Sweden: Raben & Sjögren.

Hooker, E. N. (1934) 'The Discussion of Taste from 1750 to 1770. Trends in Literary Criticism', *PMLA* 49: 577–92.

Horowitz, T. (1975a) 'From Elite Fashion to Mass Fashion', *Archives Européennes Sociologie* 16, 2: 283–95.

—— (1975b) 'The Man in the Middle', *Journal of Market Research Society* 17, 1: 26–40.

Hower, D. and Lalonde, M. (1991) 'The History of Sensibilities: of the Standard of Taste in Mid-Eighteenth Century England and the Circulation of Smells in Post-revolutionary France', *Dialectical Anthropology* 16, 2: 125–35.

Huizinga, J. (1984) *Leikkivä Ihminen (Homo ludens)*, Juva, Finland: WSOY.

Jones, P. L. (1991) *Taste Today. The Role of Appreciation in Consumerism and Design*, Oxford: Pergamon Press.

Kahn, H. and Wiener, A. J. (1967) *The Year 2000*, London: Macmillan.

Kant, I. (1980) 'Anthropologie in Pragmatischer Hinsicht', in I. Kant *Werkausgabe Bd. XII*, Frankfurt am Main: Suhrkamp.

—— (1987) *Critique of Judgment*, trans. W. S. Pluhar, Indianapolis: Hackett.

Karisto, A., Prättälä, R. and Berg, M-A. (1993) 'The Good, the Bad, and the Ugly? Differences and Changes in Health Related Lifestyles', in U. Kjearnes, L. Holm, M. Ekström, E. Fürst and R. Prättälä (eds) *Regulating Markets, Regulating People*, Oslo: Novus Forlag.

King, C. W. and King, L. J. (1980) 'The Dynamics of Style and Taste Adoption and Diffusion: Contributions from Fashion Theory', *Advances in Consumer Research* 7: 13–16.

Kornai, J. (1982) *Growth, Shortage and Efficiency*, Oxford: Basil Blackwell.

Kumar, K. (1983) *Prophecy and Progress. The Sociology of Industrial and Post-industrial Society*, Harmondsworth: Penguin.

Kurt, R. (1991) 'Die Ästhetische Dimension des Parsonschen Voluntarismus', *Zeitschrift für Soziologie 20, 1*: 64–76.

Lasch, C. (1978) *The Culture of Narcissism*, New York: Norton.

Lash, S. (1992) 'Ästhetische Dimension Reflexiver Modernisierung', *Soziale Welt 42, 3* : 261–77.

—— (1994) 'Reflexivity and its Doubles', in U. Beck, A. Giddens and S. Lash (eds) *Reflexive Modernization*, Cambridge: Polity Press.

Lazarus, M. (n.d.) *Über Gespräche*, s. l.: Henssel.

Lefebvre, H. (1991) *Critique of Everyday Life*, Vol. 1, London: Verso.

Lehto, P. (1993) 'Nautinnon ja itsekurin kamppailu. Margariinimainokset maalailevat mielikuvia' (The Struggle between Pleasure and Self Control), *Kulttuuritutkimus* 10, 1: 21–8.

Lenin, V. I. (1980) *The State and Revolution*, in V. I. Lenin *Collected Works*, Vol. 25, Moscow: Progress Publishers.

Levenstein, H. (1988) *Revolution at the Table. The Transformation of the American Diet*, New York and Oxford: Oxford University Press.

—— (1993) *The Paradox of Plenty*, New York and Oxford: Oxford University Press.

Levine, L.W. (1988) *Highbrow/lowbrow: The Emergence of Cultural Hierarchy in America*, Cambridge, Mass.: Harvard University Press.

Lieberson, S. and Bell, E. (1992) 'Children's First Names. An Empirical Study of Social Taste', *American Journal of Sociology* 98, 3: 511–54.

Link-Heer, U. (1986) 'Überlegungen zur Manier und Stil', in H-U. Gumbrecht and K. L. Pfeiffer (eds) *Stil. Geschichte und Funktionen eines Wissenschaftlichen Diskurselementes*, Frankfurt am Main: Suhrkamp.

Lipovetsky, G. (1994) *The Empire of Fashion*, Princeton, NJ: Princeton University Press.

Lohmann, G. (1987) 'Georg Simmel yhteiskunnallista indifferensiä purkamassa' (Dismantling Georg Simmel's Social Indifference), *Sosiologia* 24, 2: 83–96.

—— (1992) 'Fragmentierung, Oberflächlichkeit und Ganzheit Individueller Existenz. Negativismus bei Georg Simmel', in E. Angehrn *et al.* (eds) *Dialektischer Negativismus. Michael Theunissen zum 60. Geburtstag*, Frankfurt am Main: Suhrkamp.

Luhmann, N. (1980) 'Interaktion in Oberschichten: Zur Transformation ihrer Semantik im 17. und 18. Jahrhundert', in N. Luhmann *Gesellschaftsstruktur und Semantik*, Bd. 1, Frankfurt am Main: Suhrkamp.

—— (1981) 'Wie ist Soziale Ordnung Möglich', in N. Luhmann *Gesellschaftsstruktur und Semantik*, Bd. 2, Frankfurt am Main: Suhrkamp.

—— (1986) 'Das Kunstwerk und die Selbstreproduktion der Kunst', in H-U. Gumbrecht and K.L. Pfeiffer (eds) *Stil. Geschichte und Funktionen eines Wissenschaftlichen Diskurselementes*, Frankfurt am Main: Suhrkamp.

Lyotard, J-F. (1988) *Peregrinations. Law, Form, Event*, New York: Columbia University Press.

—— (1991) *Lessons on the Analytic of the Sublime*, Stanford, Cal.: Stanford University Press.

Maag, G. (1986) *Kunst und Industrie im Zeitalter der ersten Weltausstellungen. Synchronische Analyse einer Epochenwelle*, Munich: Wilhelm Fink Verlag.

McCracken, G. (1988) *Culture and Consumption*, Bloomington, Ind.: Indiana University Press.

McKendrick, W. J., Brewer, J. and Plumb, J. H. (1982) *The Birth of a Consumer Society*, London: Europa Publications.

Maffesoli, M. (1993) *La Contemplation du Monde*, Paris: Bernard Grasset.

Mäkelä, J. (1994) 'Kunnon ateria: naisten käsityksiä ruoasta' (The Proper Meal: Women's Ideas about Food), unpublished licentiate thesis, University of Helsinki.

Marchand, R. (1985) *Advertising the American Dream: Making Way for Modernity 1920–1940*, Berkeley, Cal.: University of California Press.

Marcuse, H. (1978) *The Aesthetic Dimension: Toward a Critique of Marxist Aesthetics*, Boston: Beacon Press.

Marinetti, F. (1989) *The Futurist Cookbook*, London: Trefoil Publications.

Marx, K. (1973) *Grundrisse*, Harmondsworth: Penguin.

Matthiesen, U. (1988) 'Outfit & Ichfinish. Zur Beschleunigten Wandlung-Stypik der gegenwertigen Bekleidungsmoden', *Soziale Welt* Sonderband 6: 413–48.

Mayntz, R. and Nedelmann, B. (1987) 'Eigendynamische Soziale Prozesse. Anmerkungen zu einem analytischen Paradigma', *Kölner Zeitschrift für Soziologie und Sozialpsychologie* 39, 4: 648–68.

Mennell, S. (1985) *All Manners of Food. Eating and Taste in England and France from the Middle Ages to the Present*, Oxford and New York: Basil Blackwell.

—— (1987) 'On the Civilizing of Appetite', *Theory, Culture and Society*, 4, 3: 373–403.

Mennell, S., Murcott, A. and van Otterloo, A. (1992) 'The Sociology of Food: Eating, Diet and Culture', *Current Sociology* 40, 2 (special issue).

Michl, J. (1989) 'Industrial Design and Social Inequality', in S. Parko (ed.) *Den stoda nordiska utställningen i Köpenhamn 1898*, Helsingfors: Nordisk forum för formgivningshistoria.

Miller, D. (1987) *Material Culture and Mass Consumption*, Oxford: Basil Blackwell.

Mills, C. W. (1963) 'The Man in the Middle', in L. Horowitz (ed.) *Power, Politics and People*, Oxford: Oxford University Press.

Nietzsche, F. (1990) 'Zur Genealogie der Moral', in F. Nietzsche *Das Hauptwerk IV*, Munich: Nymphenburger.

Noro, A. (1986) 'Simmel, muoti ja moderni' (Simmel, Fashion and the Modern), introduction to G. Simmel *Muodin filosofia*, Helsinki: Odessa.

—— (1991) *Muoto, moderniteetti ja 'kolmas'. Tutkielma Georg Simmelin sosiologiasta* (Form, Modernity and the 'Third'. A Study of Georg Simmel's Sociology), Jyväskylä, Finland: Tutkijaliitto.

—— (1993) 'Simmelin salonki: ideaalinen sosiaalinen maailma' (Simmel's Salon: the Ideal Social World), in A. Noro *Postfranzenia*, Helsinki: Tutkijaliitto.

Onfray, M. (1990) *Der Bauch der Philosophen*, Frankfurt am Main: Campus.

Ong, W. (1967) *The Presence of the Word*, New Haven, Conn.: Yale University Press.

Packard, V. (1960) *The Status Seekers. An Exploration of Class Behaviour in America*, London: Longmans.

Pantzar, M. (1992) 'Voin ja margariinin julkinen dialogi Suomessa

1923–1987' (The Public Dialogue between Butter and Margarine in Finland 1923–1987), *Sosiaalilääketieteellinen aikakauslehti* 29, 3: 146–55.

Pastuhov, V. (1991) *Obshtchestvennoye dvizheniye Rossii v epohu Perestroiki*, Moscow: Institut mezhdunaradnogo rabotchego dvizheniya.

Peterson, S. T. (1994) *Acquired Taste*, Ithaca, NY: Cornell University Press.

Pope, D. (1983) *The Making of Modern Advertising*, New York: Basic Books.

Prättälä, R., Berg, M-A. and Puska, P. (1992) 'Diminishing or Increasing Contrasts? Social Class Variation in Finnish Food Consumption', *European Journal of Clinical Nutrition* 46: 279–87.

—— (1993) 'Työntekijä-ja toimihenkilömiesten elintavat 1978–1990' (The Living Conditions of Male Blue Collar and White Collar Workers 1978–1990), *Sosiaalilääketieteellinen Aikakauslehti* 30, 2: 122–33.

Prättälä, R., Rahkonen, O. and Rimpelä, M. (1986) 'Consumption Patterns of Critical Fat Sources among Adolescents in 1977–1986', *Nutrition Research* 6: 485–98.

Rahkonen, K. (1995) 'Maku taisteluna: Bourdieu ja Nietzsche' (Taste as Struggle: Bourdieu and Nietzsche), *Sosiologia* 32, 1: 12–25.

Rahkonen, O. (1992) 'Tupakoiva suomalainen' (The Smoking Finn), in A. Karisto *et al.* (eds) *Terveyssosiologia*, Juva, Finland: WSOY.

*Recommended Dietary Allowances* (1989), Washington, DC: National Academy Press.

Revel, J-F. (1979) *Erlesene Mahlzeiten*, Frankfurt am Main: Propyläen.

Richards, T. (1990) *The Commodity Culture of Victorian England. Advertising and Spectacle 1851–1914*, Stanford, Cal.: Stanford University Press.

Richardson, D. P. (1990) 'The Acceptance of Novel Foods in the Market', in J. C. Somogyi and E. H. Koskinen (eds) Nutritional Adaptation to New Life-Styles, *Bibliotheca Nutr. Dieta* Vol. 45, Basel: Karger.

Rimpelä, M., Rimpelä, A. and Paronen, O. (1983) 'Maidon ja voileipärasvojen laatu' (The Quality of Milk and Vegetable Fats), in M. Rimpelä *et al.* (eds) *Nuorten terveystavat Suomessa. Nuorten terveystapatutkimus 1977–79. Lääkintöhallituksen julkaisuja. Sarja Tutkimukset 1983: 4*, Helsinki: Lääkintöhallitus.

Riukulehto, S. (1995) 'Luxury and Waste in American Discourse at the Turn of the Century', unpublished licentiate manuscript, University of Jyväskylä.

Rousseau, J.-J. (1948) *Lettre à M. d'Alambert sur les Spectacles*, Ed. Critique par M.Fuchs, Textes Litteraires Français 22, Lille: Librairie Giard.

—— (1994) *Discourse on Political Economy and the Social Contract*, Oxford and New York: Oxford University Press.

Rozin, P., Fallon, A. E. and Pelchat, M. L. (1986) 'Psychological Factors Influencing Food Choice', in C. Ritson *et al.* (eds) *The Food Consumer*, Chichester: John Wiley.

Salz, A. (1959) 'A Note from a Student of Simmel's', in K. Wolff (ed.) *Georg Simmel 1958–1918*, Columbus, Ohio: Ohio State University Press.

Santanen, S. (1991) 'Kritiikin lapsu(u)s. Huomioita Kantin Arvostelukyvyn kritiikistä', in A. Haapala (ed.) *Taiteen kritiikistä*, Porvoo, Finland: WSOY.

Sartorti, R. (1990) 'Stalinism and Carnival: Organisation and Aesthetics of

Political Holidays', in H. Günther (ed.) *The Culture of the Stalin Period*, London: Macmillan.

Schiller, F. (1982) *On the Aesthetic Education of Man*, Oxford: Clarendon Press.

Schmidt, L-H. (1987) *Den Sociale eksorsisme*, Århus, Denmark: Modtryk.

Schulze, G. (1992) *Die Erlebnisgesellschaft. Kultursoziologie der Gegenwart*, Frankfurt am Main: Campus.

Schümmer, Fr. (1955) *Die Entwicklung des Geschmacksbegriffs in der Philosophie des 17. und 18. Jahrhunderts*, Archiv für Begriffsgeschichte. Bd. 1.: 120–99. Göttingen: H. Bouvier & Co.

Schwartz, H. (1986) *Never Satisfied. A Cultural History of Diets, Fantasies and Fats*, New York: The Free Press.

Sekora, J. (1977) *Luxury: The Concept in Western Thought, Eden to Smollett*, Baltimore and London: Johns Hopkins University Press.

Sellerberg, A-M. (1991) 'In Food We Trust: Vitally Necessary Confidence and Unfamiliar Ways of Attaining It', in E. Fürst *et al.* (eds) *Palatable Worlds. Sociocultural Food Studies*, Oslo: Solum.

—— (1994) *The Blend of Contradictions*, New Brunswick, NJ: Transaction Publishers.

Siegelbaum, L. H. (1988) *Stakhanovism and the Politics of Productivity in the USSR, 1935–1941*, Cambridge: Cambridge University Press.

Simmel, G. (1896) 'Soziologische Ästhetik', *Die Zukunft*, 17: 204–216.

—— (1905a) *Kant. 16. Vorlesungen*, Leipzig: Duncker & Humblott.

—— (1905b) *Philosophie der Mode*, Berlin: Pan.

—— (1908) 'Problem des Stiles', *Dekorative Kunst* 16: 307–16.

—— (1910) 'Soziologie der Mahlzeit', *Berliner Tageblatt*, 10 October.

—— (1920) *Grundfragen der Soziologie: Individuum und Gesellschaft*, Berlin and Leipzig: de Gruyter.

—— (1949) 'The Sociology of Sociability', *American Journal of Sociology* 55, November: 254–61.

—— (1950) 'The Metropolis and Mental Life', in K. Wolf (ed.) *The Sociology of Georg Simmel*, Chicago, Ill.: Free Press.

—— (1981) 'Fashion', in G. B. Sproles (ed.) *Perspective on Fashion*, Minneapolis, Minn.: Burgess (originally published in *International Quarterly* (1904) 10: 130–55).

—— (1983) 'Zur Psychologie der Mode. Soziologische Studie', in H-J. Dahme and O. Rammstedt (eds) *Georg Simmel. Schriften zur Soziologie. Eine Auswahl*, Frankfurt am Main: Suhrkamp.

—— (1984): 'Die Grossstädte und das Geistesleben', in G. Simmel *Das Individuum und die Freiheit*, Berlin: Klaus Wagenbach.

—— (1985) *Rembrandt: ein Kunstphilosophischer Versuch*, Munich: Matthes & Seitz.

—— (1986) 'Die Mode', in G. Simmel *Philosophische Kultur*, Berlin: Klaus Wagenbach.

—— (1989) *Philosophie des Geldes*, Frankfurt am Main: Suhrkamp.

—— (1991a) *Einleitung in die Moralwissenschaft. Eine Kritik der ethischen Grundbegriffe* 1–2 Bd, Frankfurt am Main: Suhrkamp.

—— (1991b) 'The Problem of Style', *Theory, Culture and Society* 8, 3: 63–71.

—— (1992) *Soziologie. Untersuchungen über die Formen der Vergesellschaftung*, Frankfurt am Main: Suhrkamp.

Sinnemäki, A. (1994) 'Muodin luojien muoti' (The Fashion of Fashion Designers), *Muoto* 14, 3: 56–7.

Sombart, W. (1986) *Liebe, Luxus und Kapitalismus*, Berlin: Klaus Wagenbach.

Somogyi, J. C. (1990) 'Convenience Foods and the Consumer – Current Questions and Controversies', in J. C. Somogyi and E. H. Koskinen (eds) Nutritional Adaptation to New Life-Styles, *Bibliotheca Nutr. Dieta* Vol. 45, Basel: Karger.

Springborg, P. (1981) *The Problem of Human Needs and the Theory of Civilization*, London: George Allen & Unwin.

Srubar, I. (1991) 'War der Reale Sozialismus Modern? Versuch einer Strukturellen Bestimmung', *Kölner Zeitschrift für Soziologie und Sozialpsychologie* 43, 3: 415–32.

Stare, F. J. and Behan, E. (1986) 'Food Fallacies and Food Faddism', *Bibliotheca Nutr. Dieta* Vol 36, Basel: Karger.

Stites, R. (1992) *Russian Popular Culture. Entertainment and Society since 1900*, Cambridge: Cambridge University Press.

Sulkunen, P. (1992) *The European New Middle Class*, Aldershot: Avebury.

Sussman, W. I. (1984) *Culture as History. The Transformation of American Society in the Twentieth Century*, New York: Pantheon Books.

Tarde, G. (1962) *Laws of Imitation*, Gloucester: Peter Smith.

Timasheff, N. S. (1946) *The Great Retreat. The Growth and Decline of Communism in Russia*, New York: E. P. Dutton.

Turner, B. S. (1982) 'The Government of the Body: Medical Regimens and the Rationalization of the Diet', *The British Journal of Sociology* 33, 2: 254–69.

Veblen, T. (1961) *The Theory of the Leisure Class*, New York: Random House.

Vinnikov, A. (1994): 'The End of Soviet Power in St Petersburg: An Insider's View', *Europe–Asia Studies* 46, 7: 1215–30.

Volkogonov, D. (1989) *J. V. Stalin. Polititsesky portret* Vol. 1: 2, Moscow: Novosty.

Volkov, V. (forthcoming, 1997) 'The Concept of Kul'turnost': Notes on Stalinist Civilizing Process', in D. Shepherd and C. Kelly (eds) *Introduction to Russian Cultural Studies*, Oxford: Oxford University Press.

Warde, A. (1991) 'Notes on the Relationship between Production and Consumption', in R. Burrows and C. Marsh (eds) *Consumption and Class: Divisions and Change*, London: Macmillan.

—— (1994) 'Consumption, Identity-Formation and Uncertainty', *Sociology* 28, 4: 877–98.

Wark, M. (1991) 'Fashioning the Future: Fashion, Clothing, and the Manufacturing of Post-Fordist Culture', *Cultural Studies* 5, 1: 61–6.

Weber, M. (1968) *Economy and Society*, New York: Bedminster Press.

Weber, S. (1987) *Institution and Interpretation*, St Paul, Minn.: University of Minnesota Press.

Welsch, W. (1991) 'Esteettisen Ajattelun Ajankohtaisuudesta' (On the Actuality of Aesthetic Thinking), *Tiede & Edistys* 16, 3: 164–77.

Wheaton, B. (1985) *Savouring the Past. The French Kitchen and Table from 1300 to 1789*, London: Chatto & Windus.

Williams, R. (1982) *Dream Worlds. Mass Consumption in Late Nineteenth-Century France*, Berkeley, Cal.: University of California Press.

Wilson, E. (1985) *Adorned in Dreams: Fashion and Modernity*, London: Virago.

Wilson, G. (1989) 'Family Food Systems, Preventive Health and Dietary Change: A Policy to Increase the Health Divide', *Journal of Social Policy* 18, 2: 167–85.

Zaleski, E. (1980) *Stalinist Planning for Economic Growth 1933–1952*, London: Macmillan.

Zammito, J. H. (1992) *The Genesis of Kant's Critique of Judgment*, Chicago: University of Chicago Press.

Zhukov, N. (1954) 'Vospitanye vkusa', *Novy Mir*, 30, 10: 159–78.

# NAME INDEX

# SUBJECT INDEX

aesthetic form 140
aesthetic sociology *see* sociology,
    aesthetic
Aestheticism 140, 141
aestheticization 15, 44, 45, 46, 160
aesthetics ix–x, 10, 14, 85,
    139–42, 144, 147, 152;
    empiricist 85; Kantian x, 85,
    132, 135; of everyday life 12,
    163; of popular culture 147; of
    taste 2, 3, 10, 11, 84, 90; of the
    'lower' arts 12; of wine 131;
    philosophical ix, 17; pure x, 10;
    sociological ix, 150
aesthetization 17, 158, 159, 161,
    162, 163, 164, 166, 167
anomie 91
anomy 45, 117, 129
architecture 34, 56; contemporary
    34, 45
aristocracy 174; old 39; rural 19
art xii, 36, 39, 44, 56, 95, 98, 107,
    108, 142–8, 151–3, 156, 157,
    159, 164, 165, 167; agreeable
    art 147, 148, 149; applied 96,
    98; classical 61; classicism in
    144; commercial 26; empirical
    interest in 148; fine 12, 102,
    147, 148, 149, 168; its relation
    to play 142–9, 151–4, 156,
    164–5, 168, 178; objects of 43,
    45, 95, 99, 108, 152, 159; of
    beauty 147; reform of 43, 45,
    73; style of 95, 159, 160;

theories of 140; work of 14, 16,
    95, 96, 98, 140, 142, 152–4,
    159, 160
art education 45
art industriel 43, 44, 73
art social 44, 73
arts and crafts 43, 96, 160
asceticism 2, 24, 124

beauty; classical criteria of 92;
    conditions of 132; feeling of 11,
    87; genuine 35, 39; objects of
    34, 93, 158; pecuniary 35, 39,
    40, 41; rules of 144, 166; sense
    of x, 9, 12, 35, 39, 41, 45
bourgeoisie 18, 19, 21, 25, 44, 46,
    174; *see also* petite bourgeoisie;
    avant-garde of 22; classical 22;
    declining petite 22; English 19;
    higher 19; new 22, 23, 24; new
    petite 22, 23; petite 22, 24

capital; cultural 21, 33; economic
    71; social 68
carnival 58
categorical imperative 150
cigarette 50, 60, 67, 126
civilization 172; critic of 6, 121;
    process of 120, 137, 158; theory
    of 18, 137
collective selection; process of 101,
    102, 103, 110
commodity; culture 67;
    production 4

194